Green Supply Chains

Green Supply Chains

An Action Manifesto

Stuart Emmett and Vivek Sood

A John Wiley & Sons, Ltd., Publication

Registered office
John Wiley & Sons Ltd, The Atrium, Southern Gate, Chichester, West Sussex, PO19 8SQ,
United Kingdom

For details of our global editorial offices, for customer services and for information about how to apply
for permission to reuse the copyright material in this book please see our website at www.wiley.com

A catalogue record for this book is available from the British Library.

IBSN 978-0-470-68941-7

Typeset in 11/15pt Goudy by Toppan Best-set Premedia Limited
Printed in Great Britain by TJ International Ltd, Padstow, Cornwall, UK

Contents

Foreword   ix
Preface   xi
About this book   xvii
About the authors   xix

Part I: INTRODUCTION   I

Chapter 1: Introduction to Green Supply Chains   3

  1.1 Benefits of Green Supply Chains   6
  1.2 Traditional and Green Supply Chains   9
  1.3 Green Supply Chains and Corporate
      Social Responsibility (CSR)   10
  1.4 Drivers of Green Supply Chain   12
  1.5 Green Supply Chain Framework   13

Chapter 2: Impact on Bottom Line through Green
Supply Chains   17

  2.1 Key Contributors to the Profitability of
      Green Supply Chains   17
  2.2 Construction Industry   19
  2.3 Logistics Industry   20
  2.4 Automobile Industry   21
  2.5 FMCG Industry   21
  2.6 Chemical Industry   22

2.7   Electronics Industry   22
2.8   Conclusion   22
Appendix: Analytical Methodology and Details for
            Cost-Benefit Analysis from Green Supply Chains   25

Part 2:   GREEN SUPPLY CHAIN PLANNING   27

Chapter 3:   Green Supply Chain Planning   29
3.1   Life Cycle Management   30
3.2   Benefits of Life Cycle Management   30
3.3   Goals of Life Cycle Management   32
3.4   Green Sales and Operations Planning (S&OP)   38

Part 3:   GREEN PROCUREMENT AND SOURCING   57

Chapter 4:   Green Procurement   59
4.1   Procurement Definitions, Aims, and Scope   59
4.2   Benefits of Green Procurement   63
4.3   Drivers of Green Procurement   67
4.4   Challenges   69
4.5   Factors Affecting Green Procurement   73
4.6   Moving towards Green Procurement   87
4.7   Reflections on Green Procurement:
      Joined-up Thinking   88

Part 4:   GREEN SUPPLY CHAIN EXECUTION   93

Chapter 5:   Green Production   95
5.1   Benefits of Green Production   96
5.2   Drivers of Green Production   98
5.3   Challenges of Green Production   99
5.4   Key Components of Green Production   102

Chapter 6:   Green Logistics   123
6.1   Drivers of Green Logistics   124
6.2   Benefits of Green Logistics   126

6.3   Challenges in Green Logistics   126
6.4   Moving towards Green Logistics   132

Chapter 7:   Green Packaging   139
7.1   Benefits of Green Packaging   142
7.2   Drivers of Green Packaging   143
7.3   Getting Started with Green Packaging   145

Chapter 8:   Green Marketing   151
8.1   Importance of Green Marketing   152
8.2   Drivers of Green Marketing   153
8.3   Challenges in Green Marketing   157
8.4   Elements of Green Marketing   158

Chapter 9:   Supply Loops   165
9.1   Examples of Supply Loops   166
9.2   Components of Supply Loops   168
9.3   Drivers of Supply Loops   175
9.4   Benefits of Supply Loops   178
9.5   Moving towards Supply Loops   179

Part 5:   CARBON MANAGEMENT   181

Chapter 10:   Carbon Footprint Minimization across
the Supply Chain   183
10.1   Carbon Measurement   186
10.2   Carbon Minimization   192
10.3   Carbon Monitoring   196
10.4   Carbon Reporting   196

Part 6:   MIGRATION STRATEGY   199

Chapter 11:   Green Supply Chain Migration Strategy   201
11.1   Phase I, Detailed Analysis   205
11.2   Phase II, Design and Implementation   208
11.3   Phase III, Organizational Change Management   211

**Part 7:   CONTINUOUS IMPROVEMENT AND
PERFORMANCE EVALUATION**   215

Chapter 12:   Green Supply Chain Continuous Improvement   217

12.1   Benefits of Continuous Improvement in Green
       Supply Chains   218
12.2   Prerequisites of Continuous Improvement   219
12.3   Methodology of Continuous Improvement   219
12.4   Green Supply Chain Benchmarking   221
12.5   Pareto Analysis   222
12.6   Example of Green Supply Chain Continuous
       Improvement   223

Chapter 13:   Green Supply Chain Performance Evaluation   225

13.1   Benefits of Performance Evaluation   225
13.2   Performance Evaluation Methodology   227
13.3   Presenting Finding of Performance Evaluation   230
13.4   Using Information from Performance Evaluation
       for Making Decisions   232
13.5   Measurement Toolkit   233

Part 8:   APPENDIX – CASE STUDIES   235

Case Study 1:   Making an End-to-end Supply
                Chain Green: the GFTN/WWF Initiative   235
Case Study 2:   Collaboration in Supply Chains   254
Case Study 3:   Green Reverse Supply Chain Waste and Kodak   263
Case Study 4:   Green Packaging and Reverse Logistics –
                The Free Pack Net SRL Case Study   264
Case Study 5:   Chicago Climate Exchange   269
Case Study 6:   Green Grocery Stores in the Retail Sector   272
Case Study 7:   Product Design and Recycling and Sony   273
Case Study 8:   Renewable Energy and Geothermal
                Power Usage   274

References and Bibliography   277
Index   279

Foreword

The time for action on greening supply chains has come. Daily headlines report food shortages and concerns about energy security and dangerous climate change. Current forecasts suggest that by 2050 the human population will grow to around 9 billion, and that per capita consumption of hard and soft commodities is set to increase. An incredible challenge lies ahead of us: already the production, extraction, and consumption of basic commodities are contributing to humanity's unsustainable ecological footprint.

But it's not just the challenge of meeting rising global demand for food, fibre, fuel, and hard commodities in a resource constrained world. It is also the impact of how global industries obtain these commodities: for example, biodiversity is being lost, illegal logging continues to plague the forest sector, and three-quarters of all global fisheries are fished at, or beyond, capacity.

Effective national regulation provides a basis for managing the impacts of these changes, but increasingly important are voluntary approaches that use market dynamics to reward producers for moving ahead of regulation and enable buyers to manage supply chain risks associated with the extraction or use of natural resources.

The Forest Stewardship Council (FSC) is the prime example of such a voluntary approach which is now being emulated across a range of commodities that span marine fish, agriculture, aquaculture, and minerals. The FSC is a certification scheme for forest products backed by major global companies, NGOs, and governments.

Yet our experience has shown that a certification scheme is not enough by itself. Companies throughout the supply chain need a comprehensive methodology, and a toolkit, to guide them on implementation. That is why over 10 years ago WWF created the Global Forest and Trade Network (GFTN). Over time the GFTN has evolved such that it now provides structured support, and a framework that provides confidence and encouragement for both suppliers and buyers to take the necessary steps to green their operations and the supply chain that connects them.

The GFTN today works with over 350 companies across the world, linking together sawmilling companies in places as far apart as Peru, Malaysia, and Sweden, with furniture manufacturers, construction companies, and retailers in the major global markets such as the US, China, and the EU.

It is clear that access to resources will be a major strategic corporate issue in the coming decades. WWF is now using the experience gained with GFTN to work on similar initiatives with other commodities.

We are convinced that the winners will be those companies that are able to demonstrate that their supply chains are clean and Green.

Duncan Pollard
Director, Conservation Practice & Policy
WWF International

Preface

Five fundamental questions that every environmentally aware CEO needs to ask about their supply chains.

It is generally accepted that environmental consciousness is now changing to environmental proactiveness as organizations are discovering that it makes good commercial sense. Boards are asking the management to review their policies related to environmental norms, not only to bolster their corporate social responsibility aims, but also because consumers are asking for this. It is widely agreed that consumers will increasingly prefer to buy more – and even pay more for – products or services provided in an environmentally sound manner.

Our recent analysis has, however, revealed four key additional points:

- Companies are still primarily focused on environmentally conscious internal production. Any company can become totally carbon neutral by outsourcing all its production. Shifting the carbon producing activity up or down the supply chains does nothing more than hide the dirt under someone else's carpet. A holistic approach to carbon management is required, and this is provided by adoption of Green Supply Chain methodology.
- Environmental proactivism is generally assumed to come at an additional cost to the corporations. It is widely thought that going Green is expensive. On the contrary, our modelling indicates that adoption of Green Supply Chain methodology should result in overall cost reduction providing this is done in a thorough and logical manner.

- Most business models are focused on growing the volume of their current offerings of goods or services to increase profits. A change in this focus towards providing customer end outcomes will not only reduce the impact on the environment, but also secure and/or increase market share whilst improving profitability.
- Well beyond mainstream business thinking on the environmental impact of technology, our discussions with Professor Ernst von Weizsacker (co-author of the book *Factor Four; Doubling Wealth, Halving Resource Use* (1998) with Amory and Hunter Lovins) highlight a radical concept aimed at doubling wealth, whilst concurrently halving resource consumption through innovative technological push. The implications for Green Supply Chains, and for business performance more generally, are staggering. However, in the rest of this book, our conclusions are based on current technological limitations whilst noting that the "Factor 4" thinking and its associated technological push would actually multiply the benefits significantly, if brought into practice.

So it is clear that a move to Green Supply Chains is not only necessary for sound environmental management, but it is also profitable and provides sound financial management.

How can companies start making the move? From our research and practical work in this area, we believe the following five fundamental questions really help to focus the discussion and crystallize action plans:

1. **What are the tangible and intangible benefits of moving towards a Green Supply Chain?** In our experience these benefits are frequently neither fully explored, nor adequately quantified. Even where a robust analysis is carried out, analysts tend to either ignore some of the potential benefits, or find it hard to analyse their full impact on the business. As a result, the overall benefits do not get adequate attention at the board level and therefore do not generate enough interest to release the necessary finance to create the transformation.

   In one company we know (a large global industrial and building products company with revenues in excess of $5 billion) the task of exploring opportunities in Green Supply Chains was handed over to a senior executive as an additional job over and above his regular job, without any funding, clear direction, or expectations. In a situation like this (which is very common), all the potential benefits cannot be fully understood and agreed by the key stakeholders, resulting in understaffed projects and poor implementation.

Our analysis has also found that without any new technologies being utilized, just a move to a Green Supply Chain can reduce costs by 5–20%. The adoption of new technologies, however, can take cost reductions to a whole new level.

In addition, by raising their Green credentials amongst customers, employees, government authorities, and other stakeholders, companies also move rapidly towards ensuring a sustainable and successful future.

2. **What are the costs, both direct and indirect?** This is the flip side of the question above. For the same reasons, while companies have vague ideas of the costs, these are rarely fully explored and analysed. In our experience, these are also frequently exaggerated because of uncertainty surrounding many of the costs. While all future costs have a certain amount of uncertainty, and there is a general tendency to allow a buffer, our analysis finds that the costs of going Green are generally more uncertain, but the buffers allowed are disproportionately higher.

The indirect costs are generally the source of most complications. It is really hard to estimate costs of process changes, disassembly lines planning and set up, waste collection and recycling modelling, additional research and development, inventory reduction, and Green Supply Chain modelling etc. Once each one of these systems is fully functional, the costs will follow a predictable experience or learning curve pattern, but it is difficult to predict the transitional costs, and these make the analysis complicated and perhaps insurmountable for many project teams.

Our research indicates that direct and indirect costs associated with Green Supply Chains are substantial but can be fully funded and more than offset by the benefits they generate.

3. **What influence do we have over our suppliers, their suppliers, and our customers (especially the party with the most power in the supply chain) that would allow us to jointly work together and move the supply chain towards a Green Supply Chain?** This question is easier to answer as most pragmatic managers have a good idea of the relative power balance in their customer–supplier relationships. While occasionally the influence is underestimated or overestimated, in general we

found that just asking this question helps to focus action in the right direction. Some organizations have broken the intra-organizational silos and started thinking in terms of end-to-end supply chains. However there are still many more organizations that need to do this. Thinking holistically outside the boundaries of the organization, when applied to Green Supply Chain methodology, can yield some outstanding results. Under this primary question, a few additional secondary questions will help sharpen the focus even further to create the clarity, impetus, and momentum towards positive plan and action.

Clearly, the organization which has the most influence over an end-to-end supply chain is best positioned to create the clarity and impetus towards the Green Supply Chains. For example, in the retail supply chains, most retailers such as Tesco (UK) or Wal-Mart (USA) are best positioned to exercise this type of influence. However with the automobile supply chains, retailers have far less influence than the manufacturers.

In each supply chain, the entity which has the most influence needs to be encouraged to think holistically, in the interest of all parties that form part of that supply chain. It is perhaps also clear why this crucial third question can only be answered after we answer the first two questions. Once the benefits, costs, and influences are clearly expressed, defined, and analysed, then it is much easier to have an informed discussion with the party that "controls" the supply chain.

A corollary to this discussion is then going to be just how to distribute the costs and benefits of movements towards Green Supply Chains. Unless all the incentives are properly aligned, some parts of the supply chain may well end up sabotaging the overall Green Supply Chain project.

4. **How will we communicate and measure our progress towards the Green Supply Chain to the key stakeholders? How will we engage them?** A new road needs new milestones. Traditional supply chain or financial measurements will not suffice in this case. We found several organizations which have started to make some progress towards vague environmental goals and have defined this in terms of carbon impact reduction but without any clear definition of the four or five key measurements that relate to supply chains at all levels. Not only were the measurements not clearly defined, but even the traditional key performance

indicators (KPIs) adapted for the purpose could not be uniformly and easily accessed by the key personnel who needed the information.

A typical Green Supply Chain project has far more stakeholders than any other transformational projects inside an organization. Besides internal staff, key suppliers, customers, and even the public, media, regulators, and government are also stakeholders in a Green Supply Chain transformation. Therefore, a well thought out stakeholder engagement strategy, diligently executed, that includes clear and regular communication, is essential to success.

5. **What barriers to Green Supply Chains can be expected and how can these be overcome?** There are several categories of barriers to Green Supply Chains and these include legislation conflicts, inadequate or misaligned stakeholder incentives, lack of environmental norms and tools, lack of resources, and high costs of implementation and technology.

Within each of these categories are several specific components, making the total number of potential barriers quite formidable and daunting.

Like in any other change initiative, barriers can be overcome through a properly structured, comprehensive, and phased migration strategy. A "Big-Bang" approach is not to be recommended.

Rather, each major project stream is dealt with by a series of phases that cover detailed analysis, design and implementation, and organization change management. Time and care should be taken on the first phase to ensure its success and the ability to leverage subsequent phases.

In summary, all of the leading organizations that have started Green Supply Chain projects ask some fundamental questions.

The answers are then found to be illuminating their way towards innovation, profitability, and sustainability. As is the case in all groundbreaking endeavours, the first mover advantage is enormous, as are the challenges.

About this Book

In writing this book, we have made best-efforts endeavours not to include anything that, if used, would be injurious or cause financial loss to the user. The user is, however, strongly recommended before applying or using any of the contents to check and verify their own company policy/requirements.

No liability will be accepted by the authors for the use of any of the contents.

It can also happen in a lifetime of learning and meeting people that the original source of an idea or information has been forgotten. If we have actually omitted in this book to give anyone credit they are due, we apologize and hope they will make contact so we can correct the omission in future editions.

About the Authors

Stuart Emmett

My own journey to "today", whilst an individual one, does not happen, thankfully, without other people's involvement. I smile when I remember so many helpful people. So to anyone who has ever had contact with me, please be assured you will have contributed to my own learning, growing, and developing.

After spending over 30 years in commercial private sector service industries, working in the UK and in Nigeria, I then moved into Training. This was associated with the, then, Institute of Logistics and Distribution Management (now the Chartered Institute of Logistics and Transport).

After being a Director of Training for nine years, I then chose to become a freelance independent mentor/coach, trainer, and consultant. This built on my past operational and strategic experience and my particular interest in the "people issues" of management processes.

Trading under the name of Learn and Change Limited, I now enjoy working all over the UK and on five other continents, principally in Africa and the Middle East, but also in the Far East and North and South America.

Additionally to undertaking training, I also am involved with one-to-one coaching/mentoring, consulting, writing, assessing, and examining for professional institutes' qualifications. This has included being Chief Examiner on the Graduate Diploma of the Chartered Institute of Procurement and

Supply and as an external university examiner for a Masters Degree in Procurement and Logistics.

My previous publications include, as co-author with Barry Crocker, *The Relationship Driven Supply Chain* (2006), *Excellence in Procurement* (2008), and *Excellence in Supplier Management* (2009). Other titles include, *Improving Learning & for Individuals & Organizations* (2002), *Supply Chain in 90 Minutes* (2005), *Excellence in Warehouse Management* (2005), *Logistics Freight Transport—national and international* (2006), *Excellence in Inventory Management* (2007, co-written with David Granville), *Excellence in Supply Chain Management* (2008), *Excellence in Freight Transport* (2009), and a series of seven *Business Improvement Toolkits* (2008) with individual titles on motivation, learning, personal development, customer service, communications, systems thinking, and teams. Whilst these toolkits are written for a general audience, the case studies and examples have many supply chain applications.

I can be contacted at stuart@learnandchange.com or by visiting www.learnandchange.com. I welcome any comments.

Vivek Sood

My life's journey has neither been straightforward, nor easy. However, one thing which has made it immensely enjoyable so far has been my passion for all things that move. That is what has led me to specialize in Supply Chains, and further into Green Supply Chains.

I started my career as a deck cadet on a merchant ship and sailed around the world many times till I became a master mariner. Deciding that I needed some shore legs, I did an MBA with full intentions of returning to general management in the shipping field after that. However, post my MBA, I was advised to join a reputed strategy consulting company for a few years to complete my 'education' and for 'branding'. This started my passion for Supply Chains and led me to co-found in January 2000 Global Supply Chain Group, a boutique strategy consulting group specializing in supply chain strategies.

Now I provide strategic operations and supply chain advice to boards and senior management of global corporations, private equity groups, and other stakeholders in a range of industries including FMCG, food, shipping, logistics, manufacturing, chemicals, mining, agribusiness, construction materials, explosives, airlines, and electricity utilities.

I have served dozens of worldwide corporations in nearly 80 small and large projects on all continents with a variety of clients in many different industries. Most of these projects have involved diagnostics, conceptualization, and transformation of supply chains – releasing a significant amount of value for the business. I estimate that my project work in supply chain management has added cumulative value in excess of $500 m incorporating projects in major supply chain infrastructure investment decisions, profitable growth driven by global supply chain realignment, supply chain systems, negotiations, and all other aspects of global supply chains.

I continue to write articles and commentaries that are published in several respected journals and magazines. I also speak at numerous supply chain conferences, forums, and workshops in various parts of the world and lecture at reputed MBA schools occasionally. In addition, I also conduct strategic workshops on various aspects of supply chain management with a passion for Green Supply Chains.

I can be contacted at v.sood@globalscgroup.com or by visiting www.globalscgroup.com. I look forward to hearing from you.

PART 1
Introduction

1

Introduction to Green Supply Chains

Arguably, since the wide recognition of Supply Chain Management (SCM) in the late seventies, nothing in SCM has captured the imagination of the public, corporate management, and policy makers as much as the recent concept of Green Supply Chains. This is driven by a multitude of reasons which appeal to all these constituencies in different ways.

Green Supply Chain Management (GSCM) has emerged as a key approach for enterprises seeking to make their businesses environmentally sustainable. The notion of GSCM implies the insertion of environmental criteria within the decision-making context of the traditional supply chain management.

At our current place in history, Green Supply Chain Management has become a key strategic issue for organizations of all sizes and types rather than just a talking point for idealists and hobbyist do-gooders. For example, the idea of Corporate Social Responsibility (CSR) is now fully incorporated in many legal and ethical frameworks governing how organizations function within society. Society now fully expects organizations to be responsible for all direct and indirect impacts of their actions, and those of their suppliers, employees, directors, and even customers.

For the CEOs, the boards, and the senior executive teams, Green Supply Chain Management offers a systematic way to comprehensively manage their entire business in a manner that meets their CSR obligations and profitability targets.

Demographics, information explosion, and past environmental degradation are creating organizational pressures and market opportunities for more and more Green products and services. Public activism is forcing policy makers and organizations to accept that sustainability is more than just a buzzword. Key decision makers in organizations are now expected to consider the social and environmental impacts of their current activities. Indeed, the more strategic the view of environment-related CSR activities is within a supply chain, the more benefit to the organization. Environmental considerations are now key centre points of the decision-making process rather than an unpalatable afterthought to the decision.

Our Green Supply Chain Planning framework also introduces a systematic way to win in this new game of putting environmental considerations in the centre of decision making, whilst still being the most profitable.

Green Supply Chain Management will therefore fully integrate environmental considerations into traditional supply chain management. This covers all aspects of supply chain management including product design, procurement, sourcing and supplier selection, manufacturing and production processes, logistics and the delivery of the final product to the consumers, along with the end-of-life management of the product. Therefore the total or the end-to-end supply chain can be covered (for example see Part 8, Case Study 1 that shows how this has been tackled by one organization).

Green Supply Chains therefore address four interrelated areas of the supply chains: upstream, downstream, within the organization, and the connecting logistics process:

- Upstream activities of a manufacturing product organization include the Green Design, Green Procurement, and evaluation of suppliers' environmental performance.
- Downstream activities usually comprise those activities related to the usage of the products till it is finally consumed. This includes any recovery and recycling opportunities after it has provided its utility and also the disposal and sale of excess stocks.
- Within the organization, Green Supply Chain Management includes those activities related to Green Design, Green Packaging, and Green Production.

- In logistics, activities such as just-in-time, fulfillment, lot size management, and quality management all have clear connections to environmental criteria.

As consumers have become more aware of environmental issues, such as global warming, they have now started asking questions about the products they are purchasing. Nowadays, organizations routinely face queries about how Green their manufacturing processes and supply chain are, how wide the carbon footprint is, how wasteful their packaging is, and how they will recycle.

Some organizations have been able to convert the public's interest in Green issues into increased profits. A number of projects within organizations have shown that there is a clear link between improved environmental performance and financial gains. Organizations that have looked to their supply chain have discovered areas where operational and environmental improvements can produce profits.

For example, General Motors was reported to reduce disposal costs by $12 million by establishing a reusable container programme with their suppliers. While the motivation for this project may have been a desire to reduce costs, GM found that the environmental cleanup that resulted was actually a very marketable message for the public and policy makers.

Numerous such projects remain deeply buried in many organizations despite their best intentions and attempts to flush them to the surface. A systematic approach is therefore very clearly required.

Similarly, cost savings can also result from reducing the environmental impact of the organization's processes. By re-evaluating the organization's supply chain, from purchasing, planning, and managing the flow of materials through the entire supply chain, savings are often additionally identified as a benefit of implementing Green policies.

Despite the public's focus on the environment, benefits attributed to reducing an organization's environmental impact are not in the forefront of many supply chain executives' minds. It appears that many executives are still unaware that improved environmental performance means lower waste disposal, lower training costs, and often, reduced materials costs. For this reason Green Supply Chain Management is a cause for the boards and the CEOs, as well as the senior executive teams of organizations.

1.1 Benefits of Green Supply Chains

Organizations can enjoy several benefits by greening their supply chain and the following are some of the key benefits.

1.1.1 Positive Impact on Financial Performance

Despite ample evidence to the contrary, there persists a myth that going Green involves additional expense. Some of the factors responsible for persistence of this myth are inertia, the lack of a systematic approach, and an unwillingness to engage in sustained and changed thinking that is necessary to create a Green Supply Chain.

However, the most fundamental benefit of Green Supply Chains is a positive long-term net impact on the financial performance of the organization. This has been proven by both analysis and empirical evidence.

1.1.2 Sustainability of Resources

Green Supply Chains sponsor the effective utilization of all of the available productive resources of organizations. By incorporating Green Supply Chain Management thinking through their entire business decision-making process, organizations may now purchase Green input resources that will flow through an environmentally friendly production process to produce the desired Green outputs.

1.1.3 Lowered Costs/Increased Efficiency

At the core of Green Supply Chain Management is the principle of reducing waste by increasing efficiencies. Effective management of resources and suppliers can reduce production costs, promote recycling and also the reuse of raw materials. Also, the production of hazardous substances can be reduced, thereby preventing organizations from being fined as a result of violating environmental regulations.

Consequently, the relevant operational costs are reduced whilst the efficiency of using resources is improved.

1.1.4 Product Differentiation and Competitive Advantage

It helps an organization to position itself and its products as environmentally friendly in the customers' perception. Besides attracting new profitable customers for organizations, it will give a competitive edge in the market place. It will also strengthen the brand image and reputation in the market place.

1.1.5 Adapting to Regulation and Reducing Risk

Organizations adopting Green Supply Chain practices can reduce the risk of being prosecuted for anti-environmental and unethical practices. A demonstrated effort towards creating an effective Green Supply Chain through the sustained dedication of resources, activity, measurement, and management protocol will be highly regarded in the event that any questions arise.

1.1.6 Improved Quality and Products

Organizations that produce products which are technologically advanced and environmentally friendly will find that this will enhance the brand image and brand reputation in customers' minds.

Besides the above six benefits, there are additional advantages that can be generated by GSCM:

- effective management of suppliers;
- dissemination of technology, advanced techniques, capital, and knowledge among the supply chain partners;
- transparency of the supply chain;
- large investments and risks are shared among partners in the supply chain;
- better control of product safety and quality;
- increased sales and revenue;
- beneficial uses for waste.

Benefits of Green Supply Chain are further described in Table 1.1.

Table 1.1: *Benefits of Green Supply Chains*

	Benefits
Environmental	Integrated environmental considerations and supply chain management process reduces emission of greenhouse gases by recognizing that supply chains consist of discrete decisions, each of which has environmental impacts Reduction in waste, pollution, and environmental degradation
Technological	Creates a platform for further technological advancement by identifying areas where they would have maximum impact on reducing environmental degradation Provides a systematic process whereby greening opportunities can be identified throughout a supply chain Dedicated technologies can be developed for the processes having greening opportunity Enables more efficient use of resources Increased visibility of the financial and operational benefits
Economical	Increased organizational profitability due to positive net financial impact of Green Supply Chain projects Reduced procurement costs from more efficient energy and materials use Reduced compliance and disposal costs from decreased waste generation and use of hazardous materials Significant new organization because of customer-related environmental initiatives Increased benefits by merging supply chain optimization efforts and environmental management efforts
Regulatory	Keeps the organization well ahead of the regulatory wave, creating an impetus for innovation, organizational learning, and change Addresses the issue of global warming which is one of the most important concerns of environment experts and policy makers across the world Addresses public and regulatory hostility towards environmentally harmful organizations
Social	Positive word-of-mouth, viral marketing opportunities, and recognition as one of the leaders Increased sales for environmentally preferable products result in clean neighbourhood Safer workplace and clean working environment Better health, reduced occupational health and safety costs, and manpower costs

1.2 Traditional and Green Supply Chains

In a traditional supply chain, the flow of materials and information is linear and from one end to the other. There is a limited collaboration and visibility. Each supply chain partner has limited information regarding, for example, the carbon footprint and greenhouse gas emission of the other partners. Hence, each player may be concerned about his own footprint and may try to reduce this, irrespective of the impact on upstream and downstream supply chain. There may be some focus on end-to-end supply chain costs but due to limitations of information sharing, the costs are far from optimized in most cases.

An example follows in Figure 1.1.

In contrast, Green Supply Chains consider the environmental effects of all processes of supply chain from the extraction of raw materials to the final disposal of goods. Within the Green Supply Chain (see Figure 1.2), each player motivates other players to go Green and provides the necessary information, support, and guidance, for example, through suppliers' development programmes or customer support. Environment objectives and performance measurement are then integrated with financial and operational objectives.

With this integration, the Green Supply Chains then will strive to achieve what any individual organization on its own could not possibly achieve: minimized waste, minimized environmental impact while assuring maximized consumer satisfaction, and healthy profits.

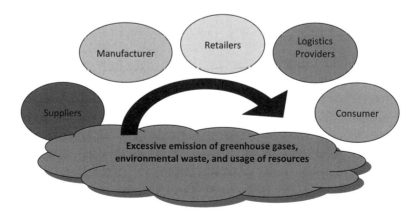

Figure 1.1: *Traditional supply chain*

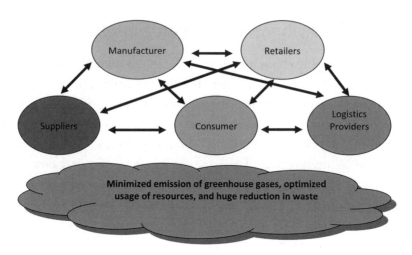

Figure 1.2: *Green Supply Chains*

Some of the key differentiators of Green Supply Chains are:

- The top management commitment to a culture of continuous improve-ment and the ongoing collaborative innovation towards "Greener" supply chains.
- Allowing all of the supply chain partners a role in creating specifications, options, and examining alternatives during the product design phase itself.
- The efficient use of technology to capture data, run scenarios, communi-cate information, and to make decisions.
- The removing and getting out of a traditional strategic "stage gate" sourc-ing mentality that creates rigid parameters on information dissemination, collection, and analysis.
- Making sustainability a cost issue, as well as a CSR issue.

1.3 Green Supply Chains and Corporate Social Responsibility (CSR)

One of the best definitions of Corporate Social Responsibility is perhaps provided by Archbishop Desmond Tutu's *The Benchmark Foundation*. It states:

"Corporate Social Responsibility (CSR) is the decision-making and implementation process that guides all company activities in the protection and promotion of international human rights, labor and environmental standards and compliance with legal requirements within its operations and in its relations to the societies and communities where it operates. CSR involves a commitment to contribute to the economic, environmental and social sustainability of communities through the on-going engagement of stakeholders, the active participation of communities impacted by company activities and the public reporting of company policies and performance in the economic, environmental and social arenas."

There is a strong connection between Corporate Social Responsibility and Green Supply Chains. One of the most effective tools to achieve Green transformations in the corporate world is Green Supply Chain Management. It focuses on sustainable design that increases environmental and social awareness across the supply chain. Sustainable design involves re-engineering of design processes to meet current and future human needs without compromising the environment. The basic objectives of sustainability are to reduce consumption of non-renewable resources, minimize waste and create healthy, productive environments through:

- using fewer materials;
- avoiding toxic substances and choosing renewable or recyclable substances;
- designing for disassembly;
- minimizing energy use, moving to the use of renewable energy, and extracting energy from waste in some cases;
- keeping a product or its parts or materials in productive use for their optimal lifespan, so slowing or preventing the linear flow of materials from extraction and processing to disposal.

Despite an area of significant overlap, GSCM is however not a subset of CSR. While CSR focuses on areas under the direct control of a particular organization, Green Supply Chain thinking goes beyond that to recognize that in today's corporate world, the area of influence of an organization persists far beyond its boundaries. Hence GSCM calls on all partners of a particular supply chain to collaborate to create an end-to-end Green Supply Chain to assure a sustainable and prosperous future.

1.4 Drivers of Green Supply Chain

There are five types of environmental stakeholder group who drive Green initiatives within an organization (see Figure 1.3):

1. Regulatory stakeholders, who either set regulations or have the ability to convince governments to set standards.
2. Consumers, who seek emotional resonance alongside the cost and convenience factors of where and when they buy a particular product.
3. Organizational stakeholders, who are directly related to an organization and can have a direct financial impact on the organization.
4. Community groups, environmental organizations, and all those other potential lobbies, who can mobilize public opinion in favour of, or against, an organization's environmental policies.
5. Media, who have the ability to influence society's perceptions.

Based on the roles of each player in the supply chain there are different incentives to migrate towards Green Supply Chains and briefly these are as follows:

- Factors that drive manufacturers towards Green Design and Green Production include:
  - Legislation
  - Corporate customer requirements

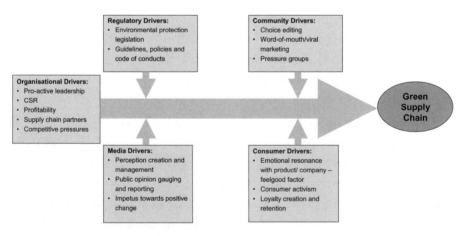

Figure 1.3: *Drivers of Green Supply Chain*

- Competitor standards
- Voluntary agreements
- Maximizing product understandings
- Environmental drivers of suppliers include:
  - Customers requirements
  - Consumers
  - Legislation
  - Consumer organizations and NGOs
- Logistics providers are implementing Green practices due to government regulations and customer expectations and agreements.

1.5 Green Supply Chain Framework

At this stage, we introduce our Green Supply Chain Framework which forms the foundation of our action manifesto towards Green Supply Chains and will be used throughout this book

This framework broadly divides the movement towards Green Supply Chains into the following seven key areas of interest:

- Green Supply Chain Planning
- Green Procurement and Sourcing
- Green Supply Chain Execution
- Carbon Management
- Green Supply Chain Migration Strategy
- Green Supply Chain Continual Improvement
- Green Supply Chain Performance Evaluation.

This book will be organized around these key areas:

- Green Supply Chain Planning is covered in Chapter 3.
- Green Procurement and Sourcing are covered in Chapter 4.
- Green Supply Chain Execution is covered in Chapters 5 to 9.
- Chapter 10 covers Carbon Management.
- Chapter 11 covers Migration Strategy and our implementation blueprint.
- Chapter 12 covers Continuous Improvement.
- Finally, Chapter 13 covers Green Performance Evaluation.

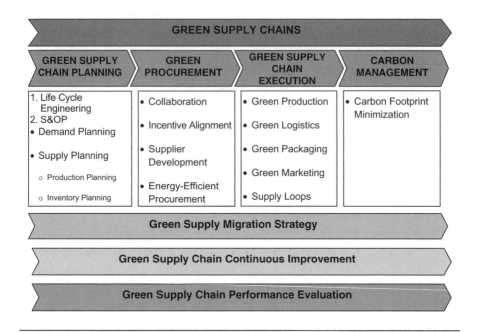

Figure 1.4: *Green Supply Chain Framework*

The simplified framework in Figure 1.4 is based on the detailed framework explaining each of the parameters and processes of Green Supply Chains which is reproduced above. This detailed framework summarizes various processes of Green Supply Chains and provides an overview of the migration strategy and continuous improvement. This can serve as a roadmap and a guide in readers' journey towards Green Supply Chains (see Figure 1.5).

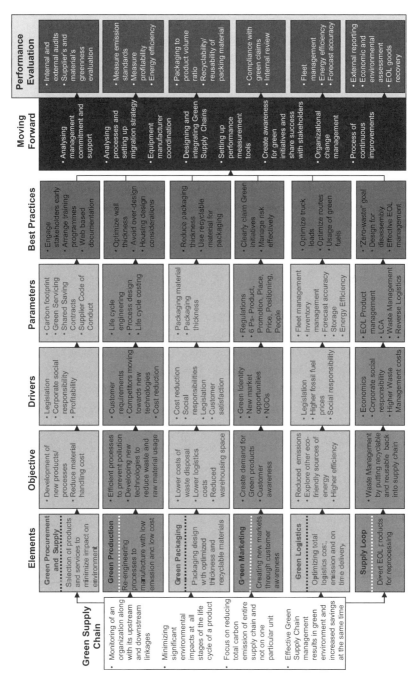

Figure 1.5: *Green Supply Chain – Detailed Roadmap*

2

Impact on Bottom Line through Green Supply Chains

It's a common belief among many organizations that moving towards environmentally friendly practices can have a negative impact on an organization's bottom line. Commonly, in forums, workshops, and conferences we are asked the question 'Would customers pay the extra costs associated with going Green?' However, the analysis we have conducted shows that efficient and effective implementation of Green practices can have a significant positive impact on the bottom line profits. This applies to most organizations, in most industries, irrespective of size or location. (For our methodology on this analysis please see the Appendix at the end of this chapter.)

It often surprises people to consider the possibility of there being a positive increase in profits. However, as enumerated in several case studies in this book, many have found profitability gains. This has also been revealed when we have worked with many organizations that had taken steps towards having Green Supply Chains. Our modelling across a wide cross-section of industries and countries gives consistent estimates of an overall net positive impact on the bottom line (see Figure 2.1).

2.1 Key Contributors to the Profitability of Green Supply Chains

Industry-wise profitability assessments show a much clearer picture of the factors that contribute to increased profitability when going Green.

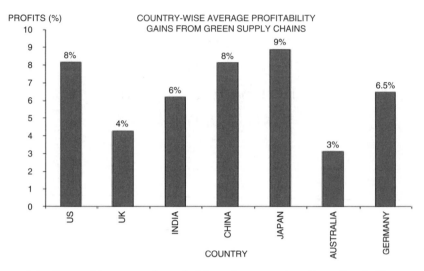

Figure 2.1: *Estimated by country the profitability enhancement from Green Supply Chains*

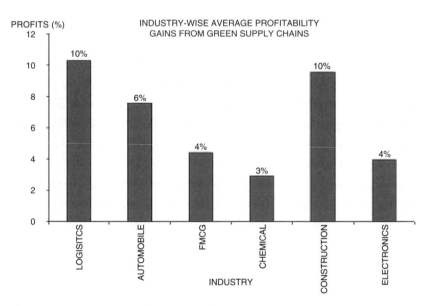

Figure 2.2: *Estimated by industry the profitability enhancement from Green Supply Chains*

Different industries were analysed on the basis of the profitability of various parameters from the procurement of raw materials to the recycling of end-of-life products. Contribution of various parameters to the bottom line of organizations is tabulated in Figure 2.2 and Table 2.1.

We now will briefly examine what can be done in these industries so that they can gain from proven Green Supply Chain Management applications.

Table 2.1: *Factors responsible for Green Supply Chain profitability*

		Logistics	Automobile	FMCG	Chemical	Construction	Electronics
	● Cost / ○ Profit						
Green Procurement	Substitute for Hazardous Material			●	●	●	●
	Minimal Usage of Raw Material		●	●	●	●	
	Supplier Development		●	●	●	●	●
	Reduced Resource Consumption	○	○	○	○	○	○
	Improved Quality of Raw Material		○	○	○	○	○
Green Production	Process Design		●	●	●		
	Product Design		●		●		●
	Higher Efficiency	○	○	○	○	○	○
	Employee Satisfaction	○	○	○	○	○	○
Green Logistics	Alternative Fuels	●	●				
	Logistics Optimization	●		●		●	
	Vehicle Maintenance	●	●			●	
	Optimized Truck Load	○				○	
	Fewer Trips	○				○	
	Longer Life of Vehicles	○	○				
Green Packaging	Packaging Material	●		●			●
	Packaging Thickness	●		●			●
	Lesser Packaging Material	○	○	○			○
Green Marketing	Market Estimation	●	●	●	●	●	●
	Increased Market Share	○	○	○	○	○	○
	Corporate Image	○	○	○	○	○	○
Supply Loops	Waste Collection	●	●	●	●	●	●
	Waste Reprocessing	●	●	●	●	●	●
	Reduced Cost of Disposal	○	○	○	○	○	○
Carbon Management	Carbon Credits	○	○	○	○	○	○

2.2 Construction Industry

Nowhere in the business world is the cost-benefit ratio of going Green virtually totally underestimated as it is in the construction industries. For some time now the world has been focusing on the concept of Green Buildings.

As per one recent estimate, the total greenhouse gases emitted by all the buildings in the world were a startling 40% of the world's total greenhouse gas emissions (World Business Council for Sustainable Development Report, 2007). In a survey of key members in the industry, the average surveyed estimate of this number was 19%.

While one may not expect construction professionals to necessarily know the actual greenhouse gas savings from Green Buildings, one would, however, expect the majority of them to know the additional costs incurred for Green Buildings. But their estimates were more than triple the actual additional costs at an estimate of 17% against an actual of 5%.

Meanwhile, savings from Green Buildings over their lifetime from Green Design and the increased energy efficiency can reduce heating costs by up to 80% in an average building.

It is estimated that by adopting Green Supply Chain principles for their end-to-end supply chains, the construction industry can increase its profitability by up to 10%. The additional costs of Green Design, substitution of inputs, and Green Processes would be more than offset by cost savings and additional revenues from Green Procurement and energy efficiencies.

2.3 Logistics Industry

Going Green can bring a gain in profits by as much as 10% when compared to a traditional supply chain in logistics industries. Some key logistics activities that have potential to reduce greenhouse gas emissions are:

- newer fuel-efficient vehicles against older end-of-life vehicles;
- truckload and vehicle fill optimization;
- fleet management;
- route optimization;
- waste recollection and reverse logistics;
- waste treatment;
- change management and continuous improvement.

Of the above factors, many will require new and additional investments, like new vehicles, waste recollection, and change management; however, these are offset by the reduced number of vehicle trips with more fuel-efficient vehicles and by enhanced recycling. Investment on R&D activities for optimizing truckloads and the usage of alternate fuels is similarly compensated through reduction in the number of vehicle trips. Meanwhile, any additional trips made to recollect waste is compensated through the increase in recycling and reduced procurement.

2.4 Automobile Industry

Green Supply Chains in the automobile industry can increase profitability by up to 6%. Key contributing factors towards profits are:

- design for disassembly;
- reduced procurement costs and increased recycling of material;
- reduced costs of disposal of unrecyclable waste due to minimal or no use of hazardous material;
- effective maintenance of vehicles requires lower maintenance costs.

Additional investment in activities to enhance fuel efficiency and design for disassembly is offset by increased recycling and lesser maintenance cost. Higher fuel efficiency will also result in increased acceptance of the vehicle, potentially at a higher price.

2.5 FMCG Industry

Profitability can be improved up to 4% by implementing Green Supply Chains in the consumer goods industry. This change can be an important factor considering the lower margins and excessive competition in this industry. Key additional investments required while going Green are:

- retooling plants and change in packaging material;
- supplement for hazardous material;
- analysis and change management.

These factors are primarily offset through an increased consumer base as eco-friendly consumer goods can be targeted to specific market segments as such consumers are willing to pay more for environmentally friendly products. Additionally, effective packaging can reduce packaging costs which also contributes significantly to overall cost reduction of the product. Increased recycling and waste minimization will reduce the cost further and result in increased profitability.

2.6 Chemical Industry

Green practices can result in overall profitability enhancement of up to 3% in chemical industries. Key factors that increase costs when compared with traditional supply chains are as follows:

- risk management for efficient product handling;
- substitution of hazardous materials;
- treatment of hazardous waste;
- retooling plants and new manufacturing techniques.

Increased plant yields, enhanced plant uptime, lower disposal cost of hazardous materials, and reduced accidents offset the costs for the above factors. Additionally, clean and safe working environments increase productivity and employee satisfaction.

2.7 Electronics Industry

Profitability can be improved up to 4% by implementing Green Supply Chains in the electronics industry. Reduced packaging, design for disassembly and recycling, and raw material procurement are all key Green Supply Chain Planning parameters that will reduce the overall cost of the product. While there are additional costs in the short run, these are more than offset by the ongoing financial benefits accruing from going Green.

2.8. Conclusion

The above examples are just some analytically derived cost-benefit results for various industries. Later in this book we will also examine real life case studies that corroborate these findings. This preliminary analysis was done at a macro level by industry by country. The reason for carrying out this analysis was to reconcile the myth of the additional costs of going Green with actual experience of increased profitability reported by several industrial organizations. The model did not reveal a single instance of net additional lifetime costs of going Green and this is across seven countries and six industry sectors. It appears that most of the barriers are perceived as they exist in people's minds or, the barriers are actually being erected and driven by the narrow self-interest of special interest groups.

We can see that the rapid industrialization and urbanization in China and India tend to follow the over a century old development path and pseudo fixed track from the western world. However, there is an opportunity to leapfrog ahead with newer technologies, methodologies, and thinking. This will ensure an enhanced standard of living for the public while ensuring environmental sustainability. Political and industrial leadership in these countries can do their people no bigger disservice than locking themselves into outdated industrial or supply chain models which have been copied blindly from the west.

Unfortunately we have also found that underestimating benefits, apathy, and inertia prevail in industry after industry.

While senior executives may have started to acknowledge the need for a Green change, most still remain committed to their existing business models and supply chains, largely we believe for want of a clear methodology and impetus. It is for the business leaders in the developed world to show the way, not only to safeguard the environment for future generations, but also to unleash a new wave and burst of innovation that will ensure continued economic growth.

In the developing world that is undergoing rapid twin transformations, urbanization and industrialization, the "blind" adopting of such archaic developmental models from the largely western industrialized world has created massive global issues. All western political, industrial, and thought leaders have an obligation to create awareness, understanding, and action towards more sustainable developmental models before it is too late.

Surely a new thinking style is now very much needed?

Continuing the idea of new thinking, as this book was being written, the global economic crisis of 2008/2009 was in full swing and prompted the following personal blog from one of the authors (Stuart Emmett) in May 2009:

The UK's current economic recession and management problems

Many hope that our current problems will be a "wake up call" but, so far, most organizations seems to be in the "curl up and hide in the shell" mode.

No surprise perhaps, after a sharp hard shock to the system brought about by the current way we have been doing things.

"Live now, pay later", was a 1960s mantra; forty years on, it now seems to be "pay back time".

However, if we continue to carry on in this hideaway mode for too long, then we will go nowhere fast.

Therefore, I say, let us try to change the thinking that has got us to here; then we might have a better chance as we move forward.

For example, what was the thinking that said it was right to spend money that you cannot repay?

Is this thinking really being challenged effectively at our national and all organizational levels?

Is it also being questioned at an individual personal level?

It is now clearly the time for everyone to face up to the realities and also it is time for many of us to take on board some personal responsibility.

We must challenge our past thinking and our resultant behaviour and ways of doing things. In doing this let us also please stop looking for that "knee jerk" quick instant fix, for example "if we do this, then we get that", and with a belief that then, "it will all be over and better tomorrow".

History always writes very clear lessons on the potential dangers of going for quick fixes.

UK organizations, for example, can bear witness to the general failure of TQM initiatives in the late 1980s/early 1990s (apart from a few notable exceptions like Unipart).

When many organizations tried to only use the superficial TQM tools, they often found they would not work as they wanted to. Then they effectively said that, *"TQM does not work"*.

This was plainly total nonsense, but many had been using a quick fix ignorance approach that ignores the reality that TQM is full of many good ideas that can revolutionize and revitalize both management and organizations, but to do this, it needs, first, a fundamental foundational change to the thinking and to the beliefs.

Our current problems are, plain and simple, due to wrong thinking; thinking that has said, for example, it was right to loan and spend money that cannot be easily repaid.

Recently there is some very clear evidence of changes in consumer buying, with the turning away from more expensive brands and a return to value for money spending; a change in thinking, and then behaviour, has happened here.

Let us hope this change in thinking from the consumer continues and goes right through to organizations, leaders, and government.

Appendix: Analytical Methodology and Details for Cost-Benefit Analysis from Green Supply Chains

Purpose

1. To create a high level estimate of the additional costs of Green Supply Chains.
2. To compare these with estimates of the tangible financial benefits of Green Supply Chains.
3. To prove or disprove the generally held view that "going Green" is costly.

Scope

Six key industrial segments were chosen in seven key countries and the net financial impact was calculated for each of them and then reported in aggregate.

Methodology

Traditional supply chain costs were modelled for each industry and country based on the commonly used supply chain benchmarks. These estimates were next checked for reality by using available company level data.

Green Supply Chain costs were estimated from the net impact of each of key changes needed to turn the traditional supply chains into Green Supply Chains. Additional costs of going Green were then offset against the additional savings resulting from Green Supply Chains.

Most of the changes modelled incorporated using the existing technologies and any impact of new or as yet untested technological breakthroughs were not taken into account.

There may therefore be scope for further cost savings/reductions by incorporating this impact, which is however more difficult to model unless the technology curve – for example, Moore's Law in computers – is already well developed in the industry; however this is beyond our current technical understanding of most industries.

Results

These have been reported above in a summary form; however for more details please do contact the authors.

PART 2

Green Supply Chain Planning

GREEN SUPPLY CHAINS			
GREEN SUPPLY CHAIN PLANNING	**GREEN PROCUREMENT**	**GREEN SUPPLY CHAIN EXECUTION**	**CARBON MANAGEMENT**

1. Life Cycle Engineering
 	
2. S&OP
• Demand Planning
• Supply Planning
  o Production Planning
  o Inventory Planning
	• Collaboration
	• Incentive Alignment
	• Supplier Development
	• Energy-Efficient Procurement
	• Sustainable Sourcing
		• Green Production
		• Green Logistics
		• Green Packaging
		• Green Marketing
		• Supply Loops
			• Carbon Footprint Minimization

Green Supply Migration Strategy			
Green Supply Chain Continuous Improvement			
Green Supply Chain Performance Evaluation			

3

Green Supply Chain Planning

Green Supply Chain Planning introduces a revolutionary new mindset to the traditional Supply Chain Planning (see Figure 3.1). All activities across the entire supply chains are planned with a viewpoint of minimizing the environmental impact of the overall endeavour while still achieving the same results. How? Let us consider its constituent parts below.

Figure 3.1: *Green Supply Chain Planning processes*

3.1 Life Cycle Management

Life Cycle Management (LCM) is an integrated approach to managing the total life cycle of products and services for sustainable consumption and production. Life cycle management takes the concept of life cycle engineering (LCE) further as the focus is not only on a particular product, but uses the activities of all those partners in the supply chain who actually manufacture and service the products.

Life cycle management need not be expensive or complex to implement and also helps companies to ensure that their choices are ecologically sound. In addition, it helps to identify opportunities to design better products, make cost reductions, gain a stronger competitive advantage, have superior strategic decision making, identify new business opportunities and markets, improve relationships with key stakeholders, and can even manage any inherent risks in the end-to-end supply chain. We will examine these aspects below.

3.2 Benefits of Life Cycle Management

Competitive advantage

Improved and holistic information is available to all decision makers and therefore by capitalizing on this information, companies can improve revenues, strengthen their market position, and increase shareholder returns.

Cost reduction

Life cycle management instils innovative thinking that can lead to reduced energy and raw material consumption, and reduced waste and emissions. Since life cycle management triggers improved communication and collaboration between partners in the entire supply chain, as supply chain partners get involved early in the product/service life cycle, therefore even better cost efficiencies can be made in the overall supply chain functions, for example in procurement, design, manufacture, distribution, sale, use, and disposal.

Having lower quantities and reduced toxicity of emissions and wastes will also mean less risk of fines and penalties for any non-compliance with health and environmental regulations and will give a better image of the organization.

Superior strategic decision making

Now that the implications of capital investments, operating expenses, and future liabilities can be assessed all together and earlier, life cycle management leads to superior decision making across the whole organization and even the supply chains. More investment options can also become available as a more complete financial assessment is now feasible.

Improved product/service design and value

Life cycle management can trigger innovative product and service design that helps to produce improved products with more value to the consumer. Holistic product designs often do result in eco-friendly products and services that will consume less energy, water, or resources and produce less waste during service.

Life cycle management therefore encourages designers and suppliers to think outside of the box to discover opportunities for improvements and to identify new ways of doing things that will provide both economic and environmental gains.

New business opportunities and markets

These improvements on product and service design can also lead to new ideas for providing the same products or services, but with reduced environmental impacts. Companies can offer the existing products and services to new markets and therefore expand and differentiate on the basis of reduced environmental impacts. The result is new business opportunities and new markets for existing products and services.

In addition, life cycle management assists in the development of new or improved services, techniques, or technology that will decrease or eliminate environmental impacts. Indeed, life cycle information is becoming a requirement to do business in some markets.

Improved workplace culture

A commitment to life cycle management helps organizations to attract and retain their quality workforce. It presents them as a socially and environmentally responsible progressive entity working for the betterment of future generations. Businesses can secure productive employees in an increasingly competitive labour market, and reduce their costs associated with recruitment, training, and discontinuity.

Better risk management

Life cycle management can help businesses reduce their risk of future liabilities by helping to minimize the environmental, safety, and health problems associated with the production, consumption, maintenance, and disposal of products. It also helps in future scenario analysis and assists businesses to adapt in advance, manage the risks, and capitalize on the opportunities that it presents.

3.3 Goals of Life Cycle Management

The main goals of life cycle management that lead to sustainable development are:

- minimize toxic waste;
- minimize raw material used in producing goods and services;
- promote recycling and reuse;
- increase process efficiency;
- minimize energy intake;
- increase the use of renewable resources;
- increase the durability or lifetime of the product;
- reduce obsolescence.

We will now look at these goals in detail using the Life Cycle Engineering (LCE) approach, life cycle engineering being directly related to the product, whereas life cycle management is focused not just on a particular product, but on the activities of all the partners in the supply chain.

3.3.1 Life Cycle Engineering

Advancement in technology and the abundance of raw material has resulted in the increased consumption of products and services leading to increased production and, eventually, increased waste products. All these activities take a toll on the environment. Organizations are producing more and users are consuming more than ever before in history; the world population is ever increasing and, consequently, more waste is being produced and will continue to be produced if it is not checked. Organizations underestimate the real cost of waste, both the economic and the ecological costs. In addition to this waste production, the excessive consumption results in increased consumption of energy, water, and machine utilization that leads to increased global warming.

The concept of sustainable production is emerging to counter these impending environmental, economic, and social crises. An LCE approach therefore aims to reduce the waste by reusing it and thus readily assists in promoting sustainable development.

Since life cycle engineering promotes systems thinking and is proactive, it leads to collaboration and integration between various groups such as marketing, engineering, production etc. This helps organizations to get up-to-date data and possibly run in parallel activities which otherwise would be left to a later date.

Organizations, and the leaders and managers in them, will however need to change their mindsets to make room for life cycle engineering. For example, currently packaging development is not considered by many to be an integral part of product development but rather is considered to be an external activity performed by third party suppliers. It is also generally considered as a production task and is therefore not started until the production phase.

With life cycle engineering, however, the packaging development can now become an integral part of product development. Life cycle engineering will allow companies to make sourcing, reuse, and recycling decisions for packaging while they are still in the product development phase. As a result, this provides space in decision making, gives bargaining power to suppliers, and assists organizations in making time to market reductions.

This also means that organizations need to make changes to their current working at all of the following three levels:

- Strategic: to define integrated product development policy.
- Tactical: to integrate the full life cycle into the product development planning process.
- Operational: to integrate the full life cycle thinking right through production, logistics and procurement.

Life cycle engineering forms a basis of the Green Supply Chain Planning process in contrast to traditional supply chain strategic planning where supply chain strategy aligns to business strategy. With life cycle engineering the potential economic, environmental, and technical impacts of products, services, or processing methods are analysed for the entire life cycle at conceptualization and design phases. Life cycle engineering will therefore allow organizations to:

- save cost by reusing/recycling within a stage and therefore avoid shifting the burden along different phases of the life cycle;
- reduce potential costs relating to environmental issues;
- focus on preventing pollution and avoiding producing unnecessary products;
- instil systems thinking at each stage of the product life cycle and become more responsible ecologically;
- make holistic decisions;
- increase attractiveness of the organization both internally to employees and to external parties;
- be better at collaboration and cooperation along the supply chain and increase their attractiveness as a supply chain partner.

When doing this, organizations will then have Greener and cleaner sustainable products and will be using methods that are innovative, improved, competitive, and growth orientated.

Figure 3.2 shows that Reuse, Reduce, and Recycle are very important elements of sustainable product development.

Reuse: this is an operation through which the function and value of products or parts can continue to be used once they have been discarded by users and taken back to collection points by recyclers, distributors, or manufacturers.

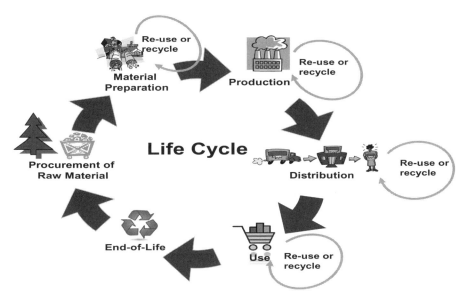

Figure 3.2: *Life cycle engineering*

Reduce: decreases the consumption of material, energy, and other natural resources and reduces emission of pollutants while producing or using products.

Recycle: recycles energy or material from end-of-life products.

The impacts of all the above on life cycle engineering are shown below.

Life cycle engineering and procurement

In contrast to traditional procurement, LCE procurement focuses on the reuse and recycling of material either from the same process, or from another process within or outside the company. The goal is to make sure that a significant percentage of the raw material procured comes from sources that would have otherwise wasted that material by putting it out in the environment. As a result of their holistic systems thinking, typical LCE thinking procurement managers are always asking three additional questions:

1. For the material I want to procure right now, which process could be producing it as a by-product or a waste product?

2. How to reconfigure our internal processes in order to accept that by-product and turn that into reusable material for our purpose?
3. How to make it acceptable to our internal team by highlighting cost and environmental savings achieved?

Life cycle engineering and material preparation

LCE materials preparation is an important stage at which both the procurement and production are equally involved. Very few by-products or waste products from other processes will be available in such a form that they can readily substitute an existing raw material. For this reason additional processing and perhaps even capital investments will be required in order to carry out materials preparation. This will partially erode the potential savings from reuse and recycling. However, the environmental and cost savings are still overwhelmingly positive in most instances.

Life cycle engineering and production

LCE production will involve usage of these recycled and reused materials that have gone through an extensive materials preparation phase to make them suitable for the production process. Despite this materials preparation phase, frequently further changes to production processes will be required for two reasons:

• In order to make use of materials as a result of substitution
• In order to make sure all the by-products and waste products of the production process itself are captured, recycled, and reused properly, either within the company, or outside it.

Both of the above are equally important points. The first point is important because not only do engineering and process need to be changed, but also the management of this change is extremely important. The second point is important because setting up a positive reinforcement loop of capture, recycle, and reuse at each production point is crucial in order to minimize the net environmental impact while assuring economic well-being.

It must be pointed out that many industries have carried out these practices in an ad hoc manner for many decades so they will find nothing new in reuse of their by-products by another industry. However, taking a systematic LCE approach to every by-product and every waste product at every production point in order to capture, recycle, and reuse these will result in far greater cost and environmental impact.

Life cycle engineering and distribution

LCE distribution is an integral part of the overall LCM-related systems thinking. In order to reuse or recycle the material by-products or waste products, these will need to be transported and distributed in an efficient and effective manner. This means making sure that the distribution process is as environmentally sound as all the other processes within the Green Supply Chain. In Chapter 6 on Green Logistics, we will discuss a number of these in great detail.

Life cycle engineering and use

Holistic systems thinking of LCE places some obligations on the users as well, whether they are end consumers or industrial customers. As part of consumption processes, waste and by-products are generated, whether in packaging or in materials. Users therefore have the same obligation as the other participants in the LCE, i.e. to make sure that all by-products and waste products are captured, recycled, and reused properly. To assist end consumers to play their part effectively, the manufacturers, local and regional governments, and industry bodies have an obligation to provide information and facilities necessary to carry out the recycling and reuse.

Life cycle engineering and end of life

At the end of the product life, once it has provided all the utility to the consumer, it becomes all the more important to make sure that the product is recycled into the next generation of products. It is paramount that this phase of its life is fully taken into account when planning the entire product life cycle. It can be generally argued that most manufacturers think about this phase only when pushed to do so by regulators. However, there is growing awareness and action towards planning for the entire life cycle and making sure a greater and greater percentage of the end-of-life cycle product is recycled.

3.3.2 Life Cycle Costing

Life Cycle Cost (LCC) plays an important part in sustainable procurement and production process. It is the total cost of ownership (TCO) of a product, equipment, or machinery throughout its entire life. It includes various costs such as procurement, operations, maintenance, and decommission or disposal costs. All significant costs which are likely to arise are identified as future costs and are referred back to present day costs using standard accounting techniques such as Present Value.

The costs examined are as follows:

1. Procurement costs incurred when the product is initially acquired.
2. Operational costs incurred during its operational life.
3. Maintenance costs (or service charges) are the costs of maintaining the product in working state during its useful life.
4. Disposal costs are the cost of recycling it at the end of its life.

LCC therefore helps management to make an informed decision when different options are being considered.

3.4 Green Sales and Operations Planning (S&OP)

Sales and Operations Planning (S&OP) as a supply chain management concept is traditionally seen as an organization process aimed at harmonizing plans across different functional departments within an organization. When first proposed, the scope of sales and operations planning included the harmonization of strategic plans through to operational plans, as well as the harmonization across disparate operational planning environments. However, to the detriment of the overall S&OP process to deliver value to the organization, this strategic alignment aspect of sales and operations planning has been increasingly de-emphasized during recent years.

Traditional sales and operations planning, as it is practised today, reminds us of people from two different planets trying to communicate with each other. In the parable John Gray weaves around the battle of the sexes, men and women frequently have problems communicating with each other because their brains' anatomies are hardwired in very different ways. Similar to the Martians and Venusians of John Gray's creation, the two predominant groups in the room essentially approach the communication from mindsets that might have been hardwired on two different planets.

In many companies the traditional S&OP process, including the agenda, key steps, preparatory work, and documentation, are unwittingly set up for failure. How so? Let us first describe a typical traditional S&OP process that we see played out month after month at countless organizations around the world.

The sales department, the operations department, the logistics department, and statistical forecasting analysts get together in a room. The meeting starts with a review of what happened last month. The forecast accuracy is reviewed and found inadequate. The blame game now starts. Operations and logistics blame the sales department for getting the forecasts wrong again. Sales people blame the customers, the weather, the economy, the government, the statistical analysts, and any other thing they can lay the blame on. And from here the meeting just keeps getting worse and worse. All the participants are generally good political game players with lots of experience, and therefore they come well prepared with the necessary ammunition; genuine collaboration is therefore right out of the window from the start.

Ultimately, there is a vague conclusion on what is going to be achieved over the next month or so, and hopefully some actions assigned. Rushed and reluctant agreement comes about due to shortage of time at the end of the meeting rather than from any sudden bursts of inspiration or teamwork. Everyone now leaves the room dissatisfied and with rancour towards most of the other participants. Depressingly the whole cycle then repeats itself the next month.

However, it need not be this way. There are better ways to structure, support, and run the S&OP process that will encourage internal collaboration, support Green Supply Chain Planning, genuinely enhance communication, and create much more positive and effective outcomes. Let us highlight, in Table 3.1 overleaf, the key differences between traditional sales and operations planning and Green Sales and Operations Planning.

Let us therefore examine the key failings of traditional sales and operations planning in a bit more detail.

Table 3.1: *Sales and operations planning*

Attribute	Traditional S&OP	Green S&OP
Measure of success	Each departmental silo has its own measure of success for the outcomes from the S&OP process	The whole group has the same measures of success: profit and environmental impact
Attitude	Defensive/Offensive	Collaborative
Focus	Blame others	Teamwork
Orientation	Reactive	Proactive
Communication	Stilted, stale, formulistic	Open, honest, guided, and not controlled by a toolkit
Tools	Strict process charts and checklists	Dynamic balancing tradeoff approaches
Leadership	Battle hardened corporate warriors	Pragmatic, positive, results-oriented business people

Attitude

People in many organizations can start to develop a silo mentality in the first few months they join the organization. If they dare to think of the greater good or company as a whole, they are frequently rapped on their knuckles for not being corporate savvy. The organizations' objectives and reward process and structures will often only reinforce this attitude.

Over time this silo mentality becomes ingrained as normal behaviour and is now "the way we do things around here" that leads to each person defending the position of their own silo and attacking the other silos, so that they can now score points in the game.

By its very nature, sales and operations planning is a collaborative exercise, and it cannot be carried out properly with a defensive or offensive attitude. An open, trusting attitude is a must for success. Every participant has to believe that they all share a common goal, and that everyone else is doing their best for the common success of the team. Every participant who has this belief will then do their best. It is always what we choose to believe in that will ultimately guide what we do; additionally, as Henry Ford noted, "If you think you can, or think you can't, you are right."

The way most S&OP meetings begin, however, sets the scene for exactly the opposite. There are few positive stories of shared victories or of meeting some difficult-to-achieve outcomes during the past month. On the contrary, the meetings start with failures of the past month. Any rational discussion is soon highjacked by self-interest and whilst learning from past failures is often most useful, the timing and manner in which this is done could be vastly improved.

Focus

In traditional sales and operations planning the focus of participants is on blaming others for the bad outcomes and taking credit for the fortuitous good ones (of which there are a few). With this focus, no wonder that few people can think outside the box to find creative, lateral solutions to the end-to-end supply chain and the real operational problems that beset their organization.

Sales and operations planning is a collaborative exercise that requires a great deal of teamwork. Most companies do pay some respect to teamwork, but the definition of teamwork is generally restricted to those functional teams within a silo. Cross-functional teams have a mixed track record where hidden agendas, inadequate training, lack of understanding of shared goals, and a history of dysfunctional behaviour towards each other will frequently sabotage the required teamwork.

Orientation

Most S&OP meetings are oriented towards the past. This is a surprise, because by definition planning is for future. The only reason one needs to refer to the past is for some guidance for the future. However, the way most S&OP processes are structured, even those certified by the best process certification consultants, result in a majority of the time being spent rationalizing what happened and making sure it does not happen again.

This time would be best spent on planning for the future (obviously while taking into consideration what happened in the past). This reactive orientation of most S&OP processes is perhaps its most visible weakness.

Communication

In the absence of collaborative attitude and a focus of teamwork, the communication during an S&OP meeting becomes formulaic, stale, and stilted.

People are saying things for the sake of saying them and to be seen to be saying them. There is no commitment to joint problem solving and instead, it is just a chore to be over with as soon as possible. Whilst there may be an occasional breakthrough of open, honest communication when a large, threatening problem confronts the whole group, these occasional bouts of collaboration are soon forgotten when people later settle back into the comforts of their own departments.

Tools

Guiding the communication of traditional S&OP process and setting the tone of the whole event is a set of archaic check lists and formulaic process charts, designed by the process consultants that certify these processes. While in the 70s and 80s they were a huge step forward when none of these things existed, the newer versions of the 90s and 00s are barely adequate to guide modern global organizations with their since advanced supply chain process and to assist them with some of the most important decisions they make every month.

The newer collaborative tools are still being forged; however the danger here is that none of the old guard, who are well set in their ways, will have the motivation or the capacity to provide them. Dynamic, light, open, collaborative, balancing tools are the way forward and we expect to see a few more of these in the future, but probably not from those existing suppliers of standard S&OP supply chain processes.

Leadership

In a traditional S&OP meeting, each silo sends its most battle hardened corporate warrior to fight it out with the competing interests in the other silos to maximize its chances of getting the glory and resources that it needs to flourish. And they play this role with relish. However, in the process the shared goals of the organization are frequently forgotten.

Collaborative, forward looking teamwork requires positive, pragmatic business leaders to jointly sit down together and solve problems by building on each other's ideas. We find this is frequently missing in the traditional S&OP processes.

Measure of success

Each silo measures the success of S&OP process differently. Sales might believe it is successful if it manages to "hoodwink" the production to produce so much that there is no likelihood of stock-outs. On the other hand, production might believe that making sure that sales acknowledge the past forecast inaccuracies was its biggest success in sales and operations planning. In turn, logistics may believe it is successful if its representative walks out of the meeting without too much blame for missed deliveries or stock-outs.

Common measures of success, linked to overall performance of the business – profit and carbon impact for example – are frequently given only superficial consideration by team members. It is no wonder that under the circumstances profits are frequently suboptimized, though each department will ensure it manages to look good using its own measures.

If these ring true in your organization, then there are ways to ensure a better outcome by using Green Sales and Operations Planning.

Green Sales and Operations Planning

Green Sales and Operations Planning only partly uses tools, formulas and check lists to make it a success. The key to its success lies really in its collaborative approach, both internally and externally, that is built into the process from the beginning. As indicated above, the leadership and participants are selected and trained for a positive, results-oriented attitude to joint problem solving using lateral thinking. Open and honest communication is guided by the instruments and tools created especially for this purpose. Finally, common measures of success are used for all participants in the process.

In a quotation, famously and perhaps apocryphally, attributed to Intel Corporation's founder Andy Grove, he said, "For one brief moment the demand will equal supply and we will have the perfect union. The rest of the time we struggle with either too much supply or too much demand."

Understanding the acceptance of the fundamental truth in the above quotation is perhaps the start of Green Sales and Operations Planning. No demand forecast is perfect and no supply system is capable of meeting all the demand perfectly all the time. The result we are seeking is to work collaboratively to create an organization that is capable of maximizing profitability and minimizing environmental impact under every demand and supply condition it could possibly encounter. That, in itself, is a lofty goal when we don't even know the whole range of demand and supply conditions that could possibly be encountered.

The goals we are therefore seeking from a Green S&OP process are profit maximization and environmental impact minimization. Green S&OP brings together two disparate but essential mechanisms to look at an even bigger picture.

On one hand, demand management is about maximizing revenue achieved out of a pool of customers and products in a given period. The key questions asked are: which customers to serve; where; with which products; at what price; to be charged in which way?

All these questions are extremely important, and are generally thought to be the exclusive domain of sales departments. Some industries such as telecommunications and airlines are renowned for being extremely good at what is euphemistically called 'yield management' which is essentially a revenue maximization exercise from managing demand in different ways.

On the other hand, supply management is about minimizing the total cost of fulfilment while meeting all the demands placed on the supply systems. The key questions are: where to buy, produce and store; for how long; when and how to move, and to where, in order to keep the customers happy?

These questions are thought to be the exclusive domain of production, procurement, and logistics departments. The ability to simultaneously focus on maximizing end results for the customers and minimizing the costs, while making sure that the environmental impact is minimal, is the foundation of the emerging supply ecosystems that are based on Green S&OP-based thinking.

Starting with these clear goals, it is much easier to create a collaborative process for sales and operations planning. Technically, every supply chain professional knows that the objective function of profit maximization embodies inventory minimization, cost minimization, revenue maximization, and stock-out minimization at the same time. The technical problem is relatively easy enough to define using the operations theory. However, in reality, it is much harder to create and infuse a collaborative process that

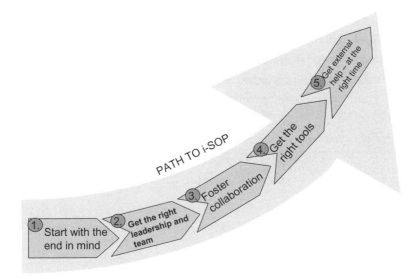

Figure 3.3: *The road to Green Sales and Operations Planning*

achieves that purpose, while at the same time making sure that the environmental impact is minimized, into an organization's DNA. That is the aim of Green Sales and Operations Planning.

As Einstein pointed out, no problem can be solved at the same level of thinking at which it was experienced. The following key principles (shown in Figure 3.3) underlying Green Sales and Operations Planning rely on raising the level of thinking to that required for the purpose of achieving its fundamental goals outlined above.

Start with the end in mind

The end goals defined above should be paramount in everyone's mind from the beginning to the end of the process. The S&OP leader should make it a priority that the end goals are clearly articulated and how each of the subgoals, in areas such as delivery performance and inventory, will all contribute to and support the end goal. Success in this step will go a long way to ensure the total success of this process.

Get the right leadership and right team

The next most important principle in creating a Green Sales and Operations Planning is to get the right leadership and team on board. This is easier said than done. In the current job market place, the demand for top level supply chain professionals outstrips the supply with pragmatic thought leaders writing their own terms and conditions. Therefore finding the right people is difficult and, yet still more difficult, is to retrain the current staff. However, it is important and necessary to believe that it is possible and necessary to do both.

Generally, a few charismatically strong and effective leaders in the team will be enough to create the momentum and give the critical mass that is needed to firstly lead, and then to develop the right culture.

Foster collaborative teamwork through an open, proactive attitude

With the right team and leadership in place, it is important to create a collaborative team environment. The team should share the responsibility of maximizing profit through dynamic decision making to balance supply with demand. There should be no bigger agenda than the end goal and there are many ways of achieving collaborative teamwork.

Get the right tools

All the above steps are necessary preconditions before discussing the dynamic, light, open, collaborative, balancing tools that are required to support the above steps.

Green Sales and Operations Planning incorporates some of the most effective, yet easiest to use tools that will dynamically match demand and supply to highlight the excess or deficit in facilitating collaborative decision making. These tools are not resource or data hungry but most importantly they do not take over the whole process, as they act as an aid to collaborative decision making.

Get external help at the right time

This advice will sound slightly self-serving coming from authors who are external consultants! However, after decades of significant strategic experience in operations, supply chains, and their effectiveness, we do have the strong belief that the right external help at the right time can save a lot of pain, heartache, and time.

Just like the top golfer who regularly gets coaching from a swing coach (who might be a much more ordinary player than the player himself), it really does help to get, on a periodic basis, an objective and an external viewpoint.

Additionally, most internal consultants find it hard to make effective change as they are too entrenched in the organization's culture and processes to be able to effectively make the needed breakaway.

We believe that the above five steps, if carried out in the proper order and spirit, will go a long way to ensure success of the Green S&OP process. This process is at the core of every production and manufacturing organization, and is therefore at the heart of all product supply chains; it needs to move with time.

Now let us look at the basic components of the Green S&OP Process.

3.4.1 Green Demand Planning

Traditional demand planning has a fundamental flaw. Most participants in the traditional sales and operations planning see it as nothing more than statistical forecasts with a small bit of market intelligence thrown in. This thinking is encouraged by many of the suppliers of demand planning (forecasting) systems, and in training of most demand planners. Effective demand planning should be all about the manipulation of historical demand that is tweaked into the future using statistics, coupled with the future educated but "blue sky views" from the expectations of marketing and sales personnel. Put in another way, demand planning must be the combination of objective rationality and subjective opinions.

Most of the fundamental questions, however, in traditional demand planning are completely ignored, some of these being:

- What customer segment are we serving with which product groups?
- How Green do our customers perceive our offering to be?
- How can we manage the demand in order to maximize the revenues?
- How is the Green Demand Planning related to Green Marketing?
- How can we shape the demand in order to reduce the environmental footprint?
- What business risks and contingencies are inherent in our current demand model?

It is indeed ironic that demand planning is an activity carried out vicariously by demand planners in almost total isolation from the customers and usually with only some marginal inputs from the sales team. In Chapter 8 on Green Marketing, we discuss why customers are the centre point of Green Supply Chains and should also be kept in the forefront of Green Demand Planning activity as well.

Green Demand Planning recognizes that because operational decisions can have an impact on different parts of an organization, it is often necessary to involve the various stakeholders both inside and outside an organization. Discussions of the fundamental questions given above must occur both inside and outside the organization, so that multiple perspectives are considered collaboratively and simultaneously. The key to making decisions quickly is to have a common modelling framework for evaluating different perspectives.

Collaborative decision making provides concrete savings and studies show that:

- Collaboration can provide up to a 40% contribution to supply chain improvement.
- Collaborative scheduling alone may provide up to 15% reduction in inventory.
- Forecast accuracy can be increased by as much as 15%.
- Transport costs can be reduced by 3 to 5%.

There can be a 20 to 30% reduction in the time spent on expediting (conducting large-scale expediting shows there is no planned and negotiated supply lead time and reliability, an admission of defeat that reveals non-effective supply chains)

Collaborative decision making also routinely increases the ownership for process changes, it transfers key organization knowledge from one function to another, it focuses the internal organization on external goals. and it decreases the lost information between handoffs by as much as 30%.

Impact of forecasting on Green Processes

Forecasts are an essential feature of the Green Demand Planning and Supply Chain stakeholder's decision-making processes. Almost all decisions utilize forecasts and these can be enhanced through collaborative forecasting among supply chain stakeholders.

Green Procurement

Demand forecasting can be used to estimate the quantity of raw materials required for production. Inaccurate prediction might result in buying too much or too little. Buying too much wastes time, money, and space and can result in potential losses from liquidating overstocks. Underestimating demand leads to back orders, cancellations, and unsatisfied customers (who may turn to competitors). Accurate forecasting therefore can help achieving Green objectives through:

- minimizing raw material inventory waste;
- minimizing need for raw material procurement.

Green Production

Once production managers have accurate demand levels for a specific time period, they can schedule orders in a much more efficient manner and work out an efficient and productive assembly line schedule for finished products.

This can also help inventory managers in managing optimum levels of inventories and takes the entire supply chain one step closer to Greenness by:

- Reductions in defective products and the minimizing of semi-finished products due to the optimized scheduling.
- Optimized inventory carrying cost and the minimization of waste.

Green Marketing

Accurate production schedules assist in creating Green Marketing campaigns for new products and optimized sales force allocation.

Green Logistics

Accurate prediction eliminates occurrences of non-availability of product and hence avoids any unplanned logistics activities. The planning of resources such as logistics to service the demand is often not regarded as being part of the forecasting process. However, for supply chain planning to function effectively, it must be well integrated with the forecasting process.

Green Demand Planning process

Collaborative forecasting is the process for collecting and reconciling the information from diverse sources across the supply chain, so that there is one single unified statement of demand. It consists of four key elements (see Figure 3.4):

- Applying statistics and other algorithms to past data to recover relevant information.
- Processes and systems that collect customer level input from the markets routinely. These also incorporate economic, market, and competitor information. In some organizations, this may be referred to as geographic information.
- Processes that merge management decision overrides with the data collected at the customer level.
- Processes that merge Green Marketing input, which is usually product focused, with the sales view, which is usually customer focused.

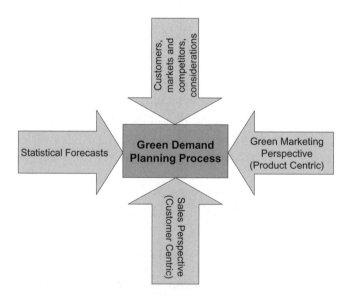

Figure 3.4: *Green Demand Planning process*

Some of the key mainstays of Green Demand Planning process are given below.

Forecast at the right level

It is possible to carry out forecasting at multiple levels of detail; however we have seen very few people carrying out the process at the right level of detail. Sales people forecast intuitively at a customer level. They might add another layer, say product family by customers' level. In most cases their forecasts are neither rigorous, nor deep enough to be useful for proper demand planning.

On the other hand, most statistics-oriented people may go down too deep, perhaps at SKU level, and they then tend to get lost in the detail. The consequence is that they lose focus on the big picture and fail to take a balanced perspective.

Recognize variability for your advantage

Knowing the causes of both supply and demand variability, understanding the reasons, and using the variability data for inventory planning are all part of a good demand planning exercise. Most people do not fully understand or challenge the reasons for variability and discard valuable information incorporated in the variability itself, to their organization's detriment.

Focus on stakeholders

One of the key mainstays of Green Demand Planning is to incorporate multiple perspectives, including non-traditional stakeholders such as environmental groups and non-governmental organizations (NGOs).

Ask "What if"

At the most basic level, demand planning is an exercise in taking a guess at the unknown. With all the science built into the process, some people start believing that the process is infallible or somehow based on laws of statistics.

However, the reality almost always has some surprise in store.

There is a lot of room for contingency planning, scenario planning, and even simulations to try and uncover the possibilities and allow for them in the demand planning process.

Ownership at the right place

Frequently the process ownership is neither at the right level, nor in the right place. An inventory analyst, a statistician, or a junior supply chain person does not have enough seniority to take in, appropriately, all of the various stakeholders' perspectives.

Manage demand and go beyond demand planning

Most organizations are still stuck at demand planning level; whereas the more proactive organizations are clearly moving beyond that stage into demand management. This means using all the tools at their disposal including pricing, channels, communications, bundling etc. in order to manage the demand to suit their overall business model.

3.4.2 Green Supply Planning

Supply needs to come essentially from production or from inventory. Hence Green Supply Planning has two main components:

1. Green Production Planning
2. Green Inventory Planning.

Many of the key decisions of Green Supply Planning will form part of the LCE exercise carried out at the strategic stage. For Green Production Planning these will include key product attributes, production processes deployed, raw materials used, and customer order penetration in the supply chain.

An overarching and fundamentally important consideration is in what stage of production do we store the material to achieve maximum profitability and 'Greenness'. The following stylized diagram (Figure 3.5) highlights forecast driven and order driven possibilities.

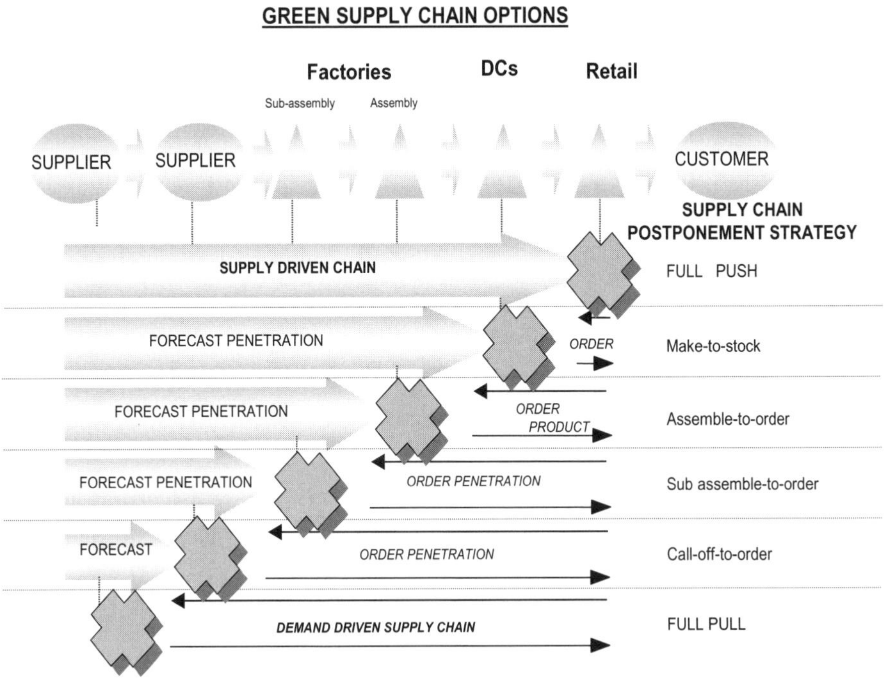

Figure 3.5: *Green Supply Planning options*

This postponement of production to an appropriate time/place in the supply chain in order to maximize profitability and minimize waste, rework, and environmental impact is also known as production postponement. As can be seen above, modelling involves a combination of production planning and inventory planning, at both strategic and tactical levels, in order to facilitate this decision. It must be pointed out that an appropriate model will vary from company to company, industry to industry, place to place, and time to time.

Green Production Planning

Green Production Planning incorporates Green principles within traditional production planning. Traditional production planning includes the planning of all activities related to production of goods within the organization. Traditionally, the three key variables that are managed are variable costs, throughput, and inventories. The variable costs are minimized, throughput is maximized, and the inventories are minimized as part of the traditional production planning process.

Green Production Planning adds variables related to the environmental impact in the decision-making process, such as the carbon footprint and waste. Both of these need to be minimized at the same time. While most of the time there will be little conflict between these two categories of objectives, occasionally the Green Production Planner will have to be satisfied with a zone of optimality where these two categories will be near optimal without either being fully optimal. In real life these tradeoffs are much easier to make than when used in a modelling exercise because of the nature of, and the interrelationship between, the various constraints that exist around the objective functions.

As shown in the conceptual framework below (Figure 3.6) there will be a zone of optimality for the various possible production plans in any given situation that will resolve the perceived tradeoff between profit considerations and environmental considerations. The easiest or most apparent option might be one of options 6, 7, or 8 as all of them have a very high profitability impact. However close to them are other options, such as options 4 or 5, which would give a much better environmental result at nearly the same profitability.

It is therefore for the Green Production Planner to explore various options in any given situation, understand the tradeoff, and choose the right option.

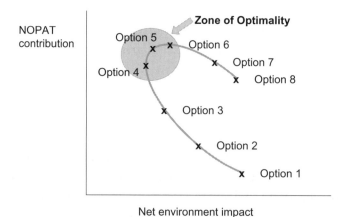

Figure 3.6: *Green Production Planning – options and zone of optimality*

In general where conflicts between 'Green' and profitability are highlighted, a closer understanding reveals other options that were previously unexplored or discarded without sufficient analysis.

Green Inventory Planning

In an ideal world, supply would be just enough to meet the demand at each point of the supply chain. However this is in reality only a dream. The rest of the time we need inventory to allow for the variability of demand; assuming also of course that the variability in supply has already been controlled by having fixed and known supply lead times (a false expectation, however, for many organizations where the supply lead times are often badly managed. This is well covered in Emmett and Granville, *Excellence in Inventory Management* (2007)).

However, in the last few decades there has been awareness and campaigning on inventory minimization because of the detrimental impact of inventories on the bottom line. Besides all the cash tied up in the inventories, there are costs from obsolescence and wastage, inventory theft, storage, and multiple handling, such costs being why inventories have grown out of favour.

However, inventory minimization campaigns may result in unintended consequences such as increased cost of fulfilment due to more frequent and part shipments. In addition, the optimal network footprint can keep changing based on relevant variables such as the demand footprint and cost of key inputs such as gas, labour and capital equipment, supply chain real estate etc.

In this scenario, introducing environmental considerations into the decision making appears to make the problem far too complex for practical solution within an appropriate timeframe.

There is some truth in this difficulty and the solution lies in resolving the problem at a higher level by taking a comprehensive supply chain approach to the decision making. Here, as a result of asking questions about where to keep the stock, in what quantities and how frequently to replenish, then there should be consideration of the overall supply and demand position.

In essence, this will involve an analysis similar to that shown in the conceptual framework accompanying Figure 3.6 where the key focus is to still find the zone of optimality that maximizes the profitability while minimizing the environmental impact. However, now we take into consideration all of the supply chain considerations of demand, supply, production, inventory, logistics (transportation, warehousing), and procurement. By making inventory planning a key part of the overall framework we can now aim to make sure that nothing slips through the net and results in unintended environmental impact.

PART 3

Green Procurement and Sourcing

GREEN SUPPLY CHAINS			
GREEN SUPPLY CHAIN PLANNING	**GREEN PROCUREMENT**	**GREEN SUPPLY CHAIN EXECUTION**	**CARBON MANAGEMENT**

1. Life Cycle Engineering
2. S&OP
• Demand Planning
• Supply Planning
  ○ Production Planning
  ○ Inventory Planning
	• Collaboration
	• Incentive Alignment
	• Supplier Development
	• Energy-Efficient Procurement
	• Sustainable Sourcing
		• Green Production
		• Green Logistics
		• Green Packaging
		• Green Marketing
		• Supply Loops
			• Carbon Footprint Minimization

Green Supply Migration Strategy

Green Supply Chain Continuous Improvement

Green Supply Chain Performance Evaluation

4

Green Procurement

4.1 Procurement Definitions, Aims, and Scope

Procurement, also known as buying, sourcing, or purchasing, is the organizational process through which all products, materials, labour, and services enter the supply chain from the following economic sectors:

- **Primary sector:** Raw materials from farming/fishing (food, beverages, and forestry); quarrying/mining (minerals, coals, metals); or drilling (oil, gas, water), such materials originating in the ground or the sea.
- **Secondary sector:** Conversion of raw materials into products: milling, smelting, extracting, refining into oils/chemicals/products and then maybe machining, fabricating, moulding, assembly, mixing, processing, constructing into components, sub-assemblies, building construction/structures and furniture/electronic/food/paper/metal/chemicals and plastic products. These materials involve manufacturing, production, or the assembly from parts.
- **Service or tertiary sector:** Business, personal, and entertainment services, which involve the channels of distribution from suppliers to customers, via direct, wholesale, or retail channels. Services include packaging, physical distribution/logistics, hotels, catering, banking, insurance, finance, education, public sector, post, telecoms, retail, repairs etc.

The so-called five rights of procurement give us one definition of procurement:

"Securing supplies, materials, and services of the right quality in the right quantity at the right time from the right place (source) at the right cost price."

Other aims for procurement being:

"To obtain bought in goods/services at the lowest acquisition cost."

"To provide the interface between customer and supplier in order to plan, obtain, store and distribute as necessary, supplies of materials, goods and services to enable the organization to satisfy its external and internal customers."

How far procurement involves the lowest acquisition cost whilst accounting for Green issues is debatable, and will be discussed further below; however the required interface aspect for Green Procurement will require collaboration between suppliers, manufacturers, and producers and requires suppliers to implement, and possibly certify, Environmental Management Systems (EMS).

In turn, therefore, Green Procurement provides education to suppliers about the use of efficient materials for pollution prevention. This also helps manufacturers to design for disassembly and develop with their own suppliers new materials, parts, or processes to address environmental concerns. Therefore Green Procurement represents an important aspect in the total end-to-end Green Supply Chain.

The role of Green Procurement in Green Supply Chains will require the creation of a healthy relationship with the buyer's first level of suppliers and of a platform to build a model to align incentives for suppliers, manufacturers, and other service providers; who in turn, will need to engage with their own supply chain through the second level of suppliers and so on up the supply chain back to the primary sector suppliers.

Green Procurement aims to reduce overall expenditure on organizations, products, and services by removing or minimizing the usage of "hazardous to Green initiatives" in the entire supply chain. This also reduces expenditure on waste treatment of end-of-life products and other by-products.

A conventional procurement process can be divided into four important segments or categories (Figure 4.1).

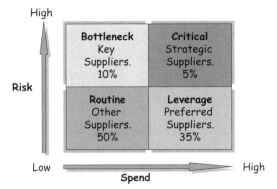

Figure 4.1: *Kraljic product/service categorization by spend/cost and criticality/risk (the percentages are an indication of a typical ranking of supplier numbers)*

A conventional procurement process is therefore evaluated through the above two parameters of spend/cost and criticality/risk, where the former covers analysing the following criteria:

- Value of spend (high to low);
- Market structure (many to monopoly);
- Supply/demand balance (spare to no capacity);
- Efficiency of buying process (identical for all to tailored buying);
- Development of buying process in the company (e.g. users agree specifications to cross-functional reviews);
- Knowledge of suppliers' pricing (e.g. cost plus to market based).

The risk analysis will cover the following criteria:

- Financial aspects of disruption (high to negligible);
- Safety consequences of disruption (high to low);
- Experience with product/service (new to repeats);
- Supply/demand balance (short supply/excess capacity);
- Supply chain complexity (many parties to "direct");
- Design maturity (new to established);
- Manufacturing complexity.

After undertaking such an analysis the following procurement strategies could then be followed:

Leverage items are low risk, high spend items, therefore there is a need to create competition in the market place for these items to drive down price. There are many suppliers for such standard commodity type of products, therefore buyers have the power with large spends and can continually look to save item costs, i.e. to leverage spend with preferred (but only in the short term) suppliers.

Routine items are low risk, low spend items, for example stationery, that have many suppliers available and minimal effort is needed for sourcing these items due to the relatively little impact purchasing can make on reducing item costs. Therefore acquisition costs are targeted, for example by the use of credit cards, EDI, internet ordering, and call offs by users who are directed to place orders direct with the selected supplier, who then reports on usage.

Critical items are high risk, high spend items that are often difficult to source due to there being a relatively low number of suppliers who can provide the specialist products and services, for example a global third party logistics service provider. Such critical item suppliers being strategically important for the buying organization, close supplier relations are therefore needed with possible use of joint working and multifunctional teams.

Bottleneck items are those high risk, low spend items that have difficulties with sourcing as there are few suppliers. Indeed suppliers may have a monopoly, such as with OEM spare parts, meaning, effectively, that the supplier has the power. However as these are key suppliers, bottleneck items will require a concentrated effort to secure continual supply.

Whilst the above is a brief summary, it will be seen that "one size does not fit all" and the following diagram (Figure 4.2) provides a summary of

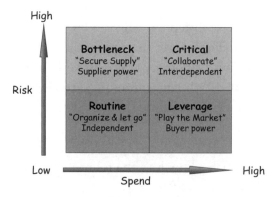

Figure 4.2: *Variable procurement aims and power distribution*

the variable procurement aims and the variable power distribution that is found between buyers and suppliers.

(More on procurement and dealing with suppliers is found in the books *Excellence in Procurement* (2008) and *Excellence in Supplier Management* (2009) both by Emmett and Crocker).

4.2 Benefits of Green Procurement

Meanwhile, Green Procurement approaches will also emphasize a few additional important factors:

- How procured material will affect the carbon footprint in the upstream and downstream chain, including, for example, the location from where the raw material is being sourced.
- Asking if there are any recycled material substitutes.
- The supplier's Green record.

Green Procurement emphasizes waste reduction at source and sets up the procedure to consider this before procuring any goods.

Figure 4.3 summarizes the Green Procurement approach.

There are a number of quantifiable benefits measured from Green Procurement. Cost savings, performance improvement, and risk reduction are perhaps the most universal across all types of industries and organizations; additionally working more closely with suppliers facilitates innovation, and product development; after all, the supplier more than likely knows more than the buyers about a specific product/service as this is the supplier core business.

Qualitative benefits such as an improved image, brand, or ability to meet policy commitments are other key benefits. In the retail sector, for example, end consumer demand and requirements can sponsor Green initiatives and indeed increasingly do so.

The public sector is also increasingly influenced by public opinion, so that non-governmental organizations and employees are often well informed and educated about the environmental and social issues related to products and services.

However, the measurement of these by public and private sector organizations varies. In general, organizations will see the benefits of Green Procurement practices as outlined in Figure 4.3 overleaf.

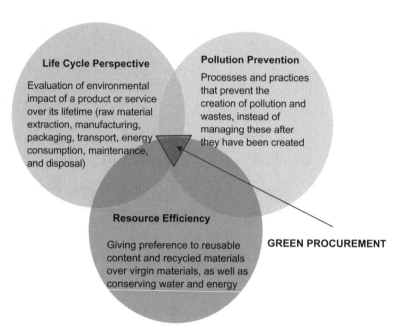

Figure 4.3: *Green Procurement framework*

4.2.1 Cost Avoidance

The procurement of environmentally preferable products can lower waste management fees, lower hazardous material management fees and reduce spending on pollution prevention.

Green Procurement approaches can offer cost savings by focusing on minimizing the consumptions and use of basic raw materials such as energy in the initial manufacture of products. For example, energy-efficient appliances are cheaper to run and water-efficient products offer ongoing cost savings on water bills. Liquefied petroleum gas (LPG) fuel is cheaper than petrol or diesel, and electric or dual-fuel vehicles offer direct tax benefits in some parts of the world.

Examples of Green Procurement are the conservation of energy and water by buying Green products such as energy- and water-efficient equipment.

Alternatively, the inefficient use of energy and water results in increased energy tariffs, water bills, and fuel prices.

4.2.2 Savings from Conserving Energy, Water, Fuel, and Other Resources

Energy-, water-, and resource-efficient products, buildings, and vehicles can significantly reduce utility bills and operating costs.

For example, making paper from recycled waste consumes up to 50% less energy than using the raw virgin materials and, additionally, halves carbon dioxide emissions. Using biodiesel made from used cooking oil in vehicles also conserves natural resources.

4.2.3 Create Markets for Recycled Materials

Buying recycled products ensures the materials we recycle are used as an economically valuable resource. Recycling becomes a redundant exercise if the markets for recycled products do not exist. By encouraging organizations to purchase recycled products and manufacturers to incorporate recycled materials into the production process, a market for recyclable materials is created.

4.2.4 Easier Compliance with Environmental Regulations

Environmentally preferable products, processes, or services that utilize less toxic and hazardous materials or reduce harmful emissions can help organizations avoid expensive local permit applications, or any environmental approvals from local/regional governments. This is of particular relevance to organizations with process, manufacturing, or service facilities.

4.2.5 Contribute to Government Legislation

Waste production is too often seen as an inevitable part of organization processes and waste management as a necessary cost. Organizations that continue to take this approach will find their waste costs rising as their dependence on landfill will certainly attract an increasing financial penalty. Additionally, the costs of regulation and waste disposal are being passed on to waste producers.

Organizations should therefore invest now in systems, processes, and infrastructure to save on these higher costs coming, certainly in the medium term.

4.2.6 Reduced Risk of Accidents, Reduced Liability and Lower Health and Safety Costs

Organizations who use environmentally preferable products, materials, or substances can improve worker health and safety, while also reducing health risks and liability. Organizations can also reduce costs by avoiding listed (e.g. toxic) substances, thus eliminating all of the reporting, training, handling, storing, and disposal requirements.

4.2.7 Keep up with Your Competitors

An organization that anticipates the need to shift to more sustainable resource use patterns is making an investment in its future. Other organizations will then follow the same path in order not to get left behind.

4.2.8 Help Combat Climate Change

Climate change is regarded as the single biggest threat to the future development of human civilization.

We must become more efficient and move from high energy use to conserving energy and minimizing waste.

Purchasing Green products and appliances can help achieve this.

4.2.9 Support of Environmental/Sustainability Strategy and Vision

Governments have used Green Procurement to promote environmentally responsible products and services.

Private organizations have seen Green Procurement as a means of improving both environmental and social performance.

4.2.10 Improvement in Corporate Profile

Consumers are increasingly demanding products to be manufactured and delivered in an environmentally responsible way. Consumer support lies with organizations promoting a Green agenda. Implementing environmental measures such as Green Purchasing can raise corporate profile and help win new organizational support.

Organizations that have eliminated listed toxic substances from their products and production may both benefit from positive coverage in the media and strengthen cooperative relations with suppliers in developing alternatives.

4.2.11 Improve Staff Morale

Green Procurement can result in improved employee and community health through cleaner air and water, less demand for landfill, and less demand for resources. Adopting an environmental stance can encourage staff loyalty and increase morale. Several surveys have shown that certain employees think that organizations should address environmental issues in their policies, therefore organizations need to recognize this if they wish to attract the highest calibre of staff. Such employees are typically the so-called "Generation Y", the offspring of the baby boomer generation, who were born between the mid 1970s and the early 1990s, and who are said to want to "work to live", rather than having the "live to work" attitude of their parents.

Measuring and communicating these benefits can provide significant incentives for organizations to adopt Green Procurement practices.

4.3 Drivers of Green Procurement

There are a number of reasons why Green Procurement should continue to be promoted within organizations and across the value chain. These are commented upon below.

4.3.1 Stimulating New Product and Service Innovation for the Markets of the Twenty-first Century

There is growing activity in organizations to identify and address the environmental impacts of their products and processes. Leading organizations are seeking out opportunities for innovation, product improvement, and process efficiency to increase customer satisfaction, shareholder value, and open new markets. Efforts to create new, innovative products and services with reduced environmental impacts generate markets for environmentally responsible products and services. This can be stimulated by using widespread Green Procurement activities.

4.3.2 The Number of Environmentally Preferable Products and Services Are Increasing

Ecolabels, national-level standards, multi-country initiatives (such as the Nordic Swan and the Euro-Flower), and global initiatives (such as the Forestry Stewardship covered more fully later and the Marine Stewardship Councils) have made it easier to start Green Procurement initiatives. Ecolabelled products simplify purchasing decisions for consumers and organizations who want to purchase products of a verified environmental performance standard.

4.3.3 Opportunities for Collaboration

Many private sector organizations are working to improve the environmental performance of their products and services and are defining environmental and sustainability strategies of their own. In this stage of development and learning, governments can work with suppliers to understand environmental impacts, align environmental priorities, and influence each other's programmes by sharing experiences, information, and improving the overall supply chain performance.

4.3.4 Interest by the Investment Community and Lenders

The investment community is becoming increasingly interested in the environmental and social performance of organizations (e.g., Dow Jones Sustainability Index with fund managers). A number of rating schemes to evaluate this performance include Green Procurement criteria.

Other stakeholders such as communities, customers, advocacy groups, and shareholders are pressuring governments and private organizations for sustainable procurement.

4.4 Challenges

Several challenges exist for organizations in implementing and stimulating Green Procurement programmes all across the supply chain.

4.4.1 Uninformed Advocacy Groups

One important challenge to Green Procurement as a whole is that well-intentioned environmental groups may not understand the full picture and will send conflicting messages. This can lead to frustration on the part of procurers and undermine the effort. There appears to be a need to facilitate communication among environmental groups to ensure that their advocacy efforts send a consistent message to procurement managers.

4.4.2 Lack of Clear Definitions

Many procurement professionals and their organizations are still unaware, uncertain, or at best struggling to define the term "environmentally preferable". This becomes particularly difficult when organizations need to balance multiple environmental attributes in their decision making.

4.4.3 Integration into Management Systems

Decentralized organizations require consistent management systems to ensure consistent application of environmental initiatives; indeed, many Green Procurement activities in the public sector have been bottom-up, initiated by small groups or individuals.

Integrating Green Procurement activities within a quality or environmental management system can help ensure that objectives, targets, and measurement procedures are established throughout an organization.

4.4.4 Educating Marketing and Sales Professionals

For organizations that are selling and marketing Green products, educating sales people about the environmental attributes of a product or services is a challenge. This is especially important in industries with high employee turnover. Stimulating customer demand for environmentally preferable products is the key here, but if employees are not actively communicating this information, an opportunity to raise consumer awareness is lost.

4.4.5 Potential Barriers to Trade

Globalization and international trade issues pose potential barriers to establishing procurement programmes for both governments and private organizations. Ecolabels have in the past been, and likely in the future will be, discussed as a "barrier to trade" issue. There have already been instances where ecolabelling has been designed to support certain products within specific markets (e.g. the overwhelming demand by consumers in the UK for labelling of genetically modified foods).

As a result, labelling organizations tend to use clear, science-based, environmental criteria when establishing their programmes.

However, the Municipality of Kolding, Denmark, have reported they cannot request that products do actually have an ecolabel (such as the Nordic Swan or the EU-Flower) when they tender, as under EU procurement directives, they see this can be interpreted (the key word here) as limiting the number of suppliers who can respond and would therefore be seen as a closed and not an open "to all bidders" tender.

4.4.6 Changing the "Only Cost" Mindset

A key challenge identified by many public and private sector organizations is changing behaviour in their purchasing departments. In many instances, procurement is based on established supplier relationships coupled to personal or brand preferences.

Cost only can be the prime decision factor in purchasing. Many organizations do not have purchasing practices that factor in the more holistic concepts like total acquisition cost, total cost of ownership, or full life cycle costs approaches.

Such approaches recognize that "price alone is not the whole" and that Total Acquisition Cost (TAC) is the price paid, plus all of other costs involved in acquisition, for example:

- Quality: poor quality causes rework, returns, rejects, etc.
- Delivery cost: ex works or delivered, transport mode used, etc.
- Delivery performance: late delivery, damaged goods, etc.
- Lead time: unreliable lead times cause variations that disrupt planning and scheduling leading to "contingency" stock holdings, etc.
- Packing: point of display packs, etc.
- Warehousing: extra handling, storage, etc.
- Inventory: wastage, excess stocking, product obsolescence, etc.
- Administration: order processing, etc.

The question to be fully answered by a TAC analysis is: exactly what are all these costs, beyond the price paid? This enables a comparison of "apples with apples".

The Total Cost of Ownership (TCO), Whole Life Costing (WLC), and Life Cycle Costing (LCC) methods are all very similar approaches that are normally used for the purchase of capital equipment and can be defined as:

"The systematic consideration of all relevant costs and revenues associated with the acquisition and ownership of the asset."

Essentially therefore, these are a means of comparing options and their associated cost and revenue over a period of time where the elements to be costed include the following:

- Initial capital/procurement costs: e.g. the design, construction, installation, purchase, or leasing fees and charges.
- Future costs: e.g. all operating costs (rent, rates, cleaning, inspection, maintenance, repair, placements/renewals, energy, dismantling, disposal, security, and management). It should be noted that any unplanned and unexpected maintenance/refurbishment may ultimately amount to more than half of the initial capital spent.
- Opportunity costs: e.g. the cost of not having the money available for alternative investments, which would earn money, or the interest payable on loans to finance work.

The importance of TAC, TCO, WLC, and LCC is that they go beyond looking only at the cost price and emphasize that there is more involved than say the lowest cost.

Factoring in other Green considerations and total cost tradeoffs along with providing information and tools that will change the low-cost alone behaviour of some buyers is key to overcoming such narrowly focused practices.

As has been said, if everyone purchased on a lowest cost price basis, then every car on the road would be the cheapest one on the market. We will further examine Green TCO below.

4.4.7 Insufficient and Incomparable Environmental Information

There is often not enough environmental information available on certain products/services and there is therefore a requirement for information on the built-in and pre-existing energy for all supplied materials and services. Most suppliers however do not have this information, so making this available in a manner that is relevant to procurement managers for the finalizing of the initial specifications is a further challenge.

Specifications are critical in procurement and follow after someone has a need or requires a product/service. Specifications are therefore a description of what a customer/user wants and therefore communicate what is required to meet the needs.

Specifications do need to be clear and to communicate; they may therefore take the form of industry standards, or of coding/classifying products; they can also identify potential sources to provide materials and products.

Specifications additionally sets the users'/customers' expectations and the contractual arrangements, and, usually, unconsciously and by default, the Green product/service aspects.

Specifications are therefore the cornerstone document for procurement and, for example, "80% of costs are committed by the specification"; therefore ensuring Green aspects are considered at the specification writing stage is critical. For instance, the Bank of America had to work hard to convince a standards-setting committee for the financial industry to accept recycled paper for cheques and other encoded banking documents.

4.5 Factors Affecting Green Procurement

4.5.1 Collaboration

Going Green doesn't mean you have to spend a lot of money on new products or solutions. One way to create a sustainable supply chain is through collaboration with each trading partner. Organizations can get more return on their Green initiatives if they involve their partners and examine the entire upstream and downstream supply chain and not just their own part. When organizations begin to look outside their four walls and collaborate with their partners, they will often see an even stronger supply chain that is also friendly to the environment. As has been noted:

"Managing a dependent process in isolation and managing it independently is plain folly. The supply chain is a process; therefore managing it without the collaboration of the other players is a fruitless strategy. But it will be hard for many to make the paradigm shift that is needed to collaborate and to adopt new ways of working."

(Source: Emmett and Crocker, *The Relationship-Driven Supply Chain – Creating a Culture of Collaboration through the Chain* (2006))

The evidence for collaboration even in "normal" supply chains is overwhelming, (and is extensively covered for example in the above book); yet single unitary supply chain views generally prevail, where more arm's length transactional relationships are the norm.

The essential aspect involved in collaborative relationships is trust; indeed, any relationship is determined by trust as when there is no trust it means there is no relationship. Trust has varied levels, depicted on the following page in Table 4.1 as levels one to three.

Changing from the transactional approach to collaborative approaches goes far beyond the technical issues, of say ICT connectivity, and fully embraces the soft skills, as the following stereotypes between transactional and collaborative approaches show.

Transactional approaches are:

- Short-term
- Separated/arm's length
- "What is in it for me" (WIIFM), effectively an "I-me" orientation

Table 4.1: *Levels of trust*

Level one trust	Level two trust	Level three trust
Boundary trust	Reliable trust	Goodwill trust
Contractual	Competence	Commitment
Explicit promises	Known standards	Anything that is required to foster the relationship
Standard performance	Satisfactory performance	Success beyond expectation
Mistakes bring enforcement	→	Mistakes give shared learning for advantage
Exchange data for transactions	Cooperate on information for mutual access	Cognitive connections and joint decision making
Animal brain	→	Human brain
Symbonic	Share	Swap
Time bound (as far as the contract says)	→	Open-ended, ongoing, and leaving a legacy

- "One-off" deals
- Low contact/closed
- Little trust
- Price dominates
- "One night stand"
- Power-based
- Win/lose
- One-way
- All risk is with the supplier, the buyer/customer risks zero
- Power-based "spin" approaches
- Adversarial and inefficient
- Hierarchical with strict rules and procedures
- Blame culture
- Many formal controls
- Rigid contracts
- Alienated employees
- Predatory
- Technical performance specifications "rule".

By contrast, collaborative relationships are typified by the following:

- Long-term
- Close/alliance

- "What is in it for us" (WIIFU)
- "For ever"
- Shared vision/open
- Trust/risk/benefits
- Shared destiny
- "Marriage"
- Equality-based
- Win/win
- Two-way exchange of sensitive data
- Mutual approaches to reduce costs, times, and waste
- Shared risk and benefits
- Pragmatic trust
- Challenging to implement and continue with
- Equality
- Problem solving culture
- Self-controlled
- Flexible contracts
- Motivated employees
- Proactive
- Work beyond just "one" technical view.

However, many people and therefore organizations will not subscribe to a mutually sharing collaborative supply chain management approach. A major reason for not doing this is that procurement has often been traditionally founded on power and therefore two-way collaboration sits here as an uneasy concept.

Another major reason however is that soft skills are actually the hard skills for many people in organizations. Indeed, supply chain management collaboration between companies is unlikely to succeed without appropriate recognition that soft skill development is a prerequisite. (This is explored further in Part 8, Case Study 2, Collaboration in Supply Chains.)

Strategic collaborative alignment and operational integration are therefore two areas organizations should focus on first. When organizations focus on collaboration and integration, they can bring their partners on board to create a cohesive Green strategy that streamlines all of the multiple aspects of the supply chain right through the "design/source/make/move/sell" processes and through materials management to physical distribution

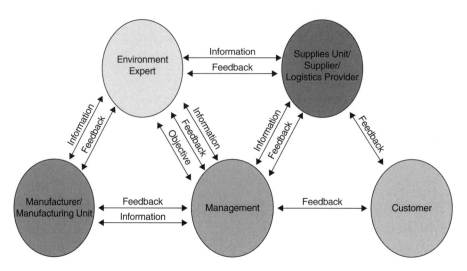

Figure 4.4: *Collaboration among key stakeholders*

management. These strategies will support the processes that will create the foundation of their programme and will help the organization drive continued improvement; Figure 4.4 illustrates one way to do this.

Green Procurement therefore must start with collaboration among key internal as well as external stakeholders of the end-to-end supply chain.

An environmental expert is involved in interpretation of the results, performing/suggesting modifications of the analysis, providing suggestions to design team and management, and again performing diagnosis and scenario analysis, if necessary.

The manufacturer provides design-related feedback and implements suggestions given by management and environment experts, e.g. Electronic Data Interchange (EDI) to be used instead of paper; encourage suppliers to follow Green Processes.

Based on the directions from those above, the suppliers and logistics providers can then optimize their processes in an environmentally friendly way.

Collaboration must also extend to collaboration with end consumers. In many cases, Green may mean more concentrated product in smaller packaging or even increased prices. Manufacturers must create an awareness programme that ensures consumers feel that they are getting value for cost while supporting Green. Customers use products and services and provide feedback to manufacturers and service providers.

Manufacturers and their customers are realizing that improving production processes reduces the use of valuable and expensive resources. They are starting to see that technology can lead to better resource utilization of plant and equipment and reducing transportation costs, plus reducing carbon emissions and fuel consumptions. The reduction of product packing can also lead to more shelf space availability for retailers.

4.5.2 Incentive Alignment

Incentive alignment is necessary for the involvement of all key stakeholders in implementing Green objectives. Consumption of indirect materials sold by a supplier to its customer for use in the production process can be reduced by involving both suppliers and manufacturers. Traditional supply contracts, however, provide no incentives for the supplier to make such efforts.

Substantial savings and waste reduction can be achieved by providing incentives to suppliers to find ways that will help reduce material consumption. Shared savings contracts typically combine a fixed service fee with a variable component based on the consumption volume and performance.

In these types of contract the parties decide how much effort to exert by trading off the cost of their effort against the benefits they will obtain from the reduced material consumption which gives an easy apportion of savings.

Suppliers' compensation should be based on value added services (e.g. high productivity, eco-friendly etc.) and not on the volume of material they sell to customers. Similarly, service providers can be rewarded with appropriate incentives for reducing raw material consumption, increasing productivity, and decreasing waste.

In order to align incentives, a model can be used in which a service or product is sold, but ownership remains with the supplier, with customers paying for the use and any maintenance. This aims to reduce environmental impacts by lowering the volume of resource inputs and in preventing wasteful resource use, while still allowing clients to enjoy the equivalent value. Here, suppliers will need to change their approach from selling materials and products to selling services, for example plant and equipment such as road freight vehicles are sold by some truck manufacturers on a cost per kilometre driven basis.

A supplier contract specifies how buyers pay suppliers, and contracts can be based on a variety of criteria on the basis of incentives for supplier or manufacturer or both, for example:

- Volume: unit price of product × volume of product
- Service: unit service fee × amount of service
- Volume and service (mixed contract): (unit service fee × amount of service) + (unit product fee × volume of product)

Incentives for suppliers and manufacturers are aligned in mixed contracts as they offer more returns in less consumption of raw materials.

4.5.3 Supplier Development

Effective procurement departments will normally regularly study the supply base and evaluate the extent to which current procurement activities are meeting the needs of the organization and, for example, key suppliers will be rated according to their current performance and also rated with the ideal, or preferred, performance by making a comparison to other suppliers. This will then identify those suppliers requiring supplier development.

Supplier development involves:

"Any effort of a buying firm with a supplier, to increase its performance and/or capabilities and meet the buying firm's short and/or long-term needs."

Supplier development is therefore of major importance in terms of improving procurement (and supply chain) performance and Emmett and Crocker (2009) identify the following reasons why supplier development may be undertaken:

- improving supplier performance;
- reducing costs;
- resolving serious quality issues;
- developing new routes to supply;
- improving business alignment between the supplier and the buying organization;

- developing a product or service not currently available in the market place;
- generating competition for a high price product or service dominating the market place.

The selection of suppliers for development will depend on:

- category strategy, for example based on the earlier mentioned Kraljic procurement portfolio;
- scale of value/improvement opportunity;
- cost, complexity, and duration of value attainment;
- supplier cooperation.

Before selecting suppliers for development, purchasing/supply management should clearly identify the reasons and have an understanding of why supplier development should be undertaken and what it involves.

There are a number of methodologies for prioritizing which suppliers are most suitable for development including a range of portfolio analysis techniques. A reasonable way to begin is to identify those products, goods, and services which are procured from the critical and bottleneck strategic suppliers and decide how these should be improved.

Selecting the best supplier for development may not always be the automatic choice. In most of the cases, it is the "less than best" suppliers which are most appropriate for development. Supplier development is normally undertaken with existing suppliers that can be, and agree to being, improved. The supplier's performance against agreed criteria must be measured in order to identify the scope for development at the outset and, once the development process has started, to monitor and manage improvement.

Success with supplier development has been identified in Emmett and Crocker (2009) as needing the following:

1. Define and develop a strategy to meet the business and end customer needs.
2. Secure agreement between both parties on how the supplier can help achieve these needs.
3. Establish clear measures to gauge the supplier performance.
4. Ensure regular, detailed, and action-focused feedback to the supplier.

5. Agree on the supplier's current performance gap and expected performance requirements.
6. Obtain acceptance and commitment from the supplier's senior management.
7. Develop and agree a time plan with the supplier to close the performance gap.
8. Get commitment on the part of the buyer to transfer knowledge and potentially best practice to the supplier.
9. Get commitment to invest significant procurement resource in the programme.
10. Establish a multifunctional customer team that will (a) adhere to a common sourcing strategy and (b) share knowledge.

Supplier development can therefore be a resource intensive process; however it needs to be undertaken only with a few selected suppliers and it should only be undertaken with those suppliers from which real organization benefit can be derived.

Supplier development can therefore be a one-off project as well as ongoing activity that may take some years to come to fruition. At any time, then, existing suppliers can be categorized as:

- being developed;
- on hold as a potential for development;
- identified as not being worth the investment of development.

Supplier development should ideally be a two-way process and can be thought of as being a joint buyer/supplier development activity. Some suppliers may be resistant to being developed; this is usually a function of their position in the market place and the way in which they perceive, and therefore "position", the buying organization. This is another reason why purchasing and supply management embarking on supplier development will require good interpersonal and influencing skills (the soft skills once again).

Purchasing and supply management managers should always be aware of the way in which a key supplier positions their buying organization; Figure 4.5 represents one view on this.

The clear point here is that suppliers are not necessarily "hungry" for a buyer's business and do take decisions on how to handle their customers.

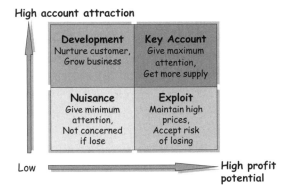

Figure 4.5: *Supplier's view of a buyer's business*

Such views may not of course be openly revealed, but most certainly will impact on how business is conducted.

It may therefore be necessary to give incentives to suppliers to encourage their commitment to supplier development, such as a reward of shared benefits or achieving a "preferred supplier" status.

In many cases, the development of the supplier will also be of benefit to the supplier's other customers, some of which may be the buying organization's competition. This in itself may be an incentive for the supplier to participate in a supplier development project, i.e. they can improve relationships with all their customers as a consequence.

This may not matter if the development is in terms of improved service, greater quality, value added, and management information for instance. For example, if the supplier's product has been developed to meet a particular competitive advantage of the buying organization, the purchasing and supply management should consider the implications of this at the outset.

Finally then, as a summary, the following best practice in supplier development has been adapted from Emmett and Crocker (2009):

- In selecting suppliers, use the predominance of quality/value over cost.
- Buying from a limited number of suppliers per purchased item.
- Sourcing from a few dependable suppliers.
- Providing education and/or technical assistance to suppliers with possible secondments.
- Longer term contracts with suppliers.
- The buyer provides clarity of specifications.

- Supplier performance evaluation and feedback.
- Parts standardization.
- Supplier reward and recognition.
- Plant visits to suppliers.
- Intensive information exchange with suppliers (i.e. sharing of accounting and financial data by the supplier and sharing of internal information such as costs and quality levels, by the supplier).
- Collaborating with suppliers in materials improvement and development of new materials.
- Involvement of suppliers in the buyer's new product development process.
- Investment of money, if needed.

4.5.4 Energy-Efficient Procurement

Energy-efficient procurement applies to:

- the design, construction, and management of buildings;
- the procurement of energy-using equipment, such as heating systems, vehicles, and electrical equipment;
- the direct purchase of energy, e.g. electricity.

It includes practices such as life cycle costing, mentioned in section 3.1.2, the setting of minimum energy efficiency standards, and all of the measures that will promote energy efficiency across the organization.

Energy-efficient procurement therefore offers social, economic, and environmental benefits, such as the following:

- Efficient use of energy will reduce costs and save money. As the market price of energy is expected to increase, then so will the financial benefits of energy efficiency.
- Energy-efficient goods, such as light bulbs, have a longer lifetime and are of higher quality than their cheaper alternatives. Purchasing these will reduce valuable time and effort involved in frequently replacing equipment.
- Reducing CO_2 emissions, as a result of energy-efficient procurement, will help public authorities minimize their contribution to climate change.

- Energy-efficient procurement requires transparent and rational decision making which contributes to good governance.

Energy-efficient procurement framework

The following diagram (Figure 4.6) shows what needs to be considered, where a framework is formulated to identify the status of implementation of energy-efficient procurement in any organization.

The methodology here is as follows:

- Review each column of the matrix, one at a time, and mark the place in each column which best describes the current situation of the supply chain; this part must be done by one person only. If different departments are responsible for different areas affected, there is the need to ensure that all are given the opportunity to complete the matrix. This will help determine what others think are the strengths and weaknesses of the implementation plan. If several people in the organization are involved, then a comparison of all matrices needs to be done so that results can be merged into only one matrix.

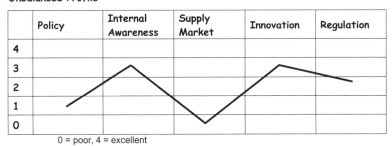

Figure 4.6: *Mapping the energy efficiency implementation status of a supply chain*

- Join up the marks to produce a graph line to create a profile of the supply chain. This line indicates how balanced the different aspects of the implementation of the energy procurement policy are, across the supply chain, and which are the strong and weak points.
- Once the status is recorded, appropriate measures can be taken to improve the weak points identified.
- Recommended actions will need to be included in the revised action plan and given priority by allocating more resources to them. The eventual aim is to move the supply chain up through the levels towards "best practice" performance whilst aiming for balance across the columns.

Sustainable sourcing and specifications

Organizations do stand to gain from pursuing Green and sustainable procurement strategies, yet despite the savings from cost avoidance and the risk reduction benefits, traditional sourcing approaches and mindsets often fall short of what's necessary to achieve results.

The primary reason is that some of the traditional strategic sourcing models, such as sealed bids, multi-round negotiations, and reverse auctions, can limit the options to achieving Green and sustainable savings and returns.

By forcing a rigid process onto both their own organizations and their supply base (e.g. gathering specifications, sourcing suppliers, issuing RFI, pre-qualifying suppliers, issuing RFQ, conducting negotiations, awarding to the supplying organization), then the procurement managers can place themselves into a fixed and possibly high cost corner, from which it can be difficult to escape. This is because some traditional sourcing approaches like tendering can limit the ability of suppliers to suggest or propose alternatives to the effectively mandatory standard technical (also known as conformance) specification that says simply "this is what we want, nothing more, nothing less".

As we now explore there are alternative ways to issue specifications, these being statement of need from internal sources that is to be satisfied by the procurement of external resources.

From the internal users' specifications, procurement will:

- provide information on available supply;
- provide a supplier appraisal;

- identify risks on suppliers and products;
- identify where the business is able to standardize.

Ultimately procurement aims to procure products and services which are fit for purpose and therefore the characteristics that give this are determined by the specification.

Specifications can really be seen as the cornerstone of the whole procurement process, as everything that happens after the specification will be dependent on, and result from, the specification. Getting them right is therefore critical, so specifications must be clear, communicate and should comply with the following criteria:

- Are the requirements stated clearly, unambiguously, and with only the essential characteristics stated?
- Will it enable suppliers to decide and cost their offer?
- Will the supplier's offer be able to be evaluated against the specification?
- Does the specification enable opportunity for all suppliers to make an offer?
- Does it include any legal requirements?

The development of the final specifications will usually require liaison between users, procurement, and maybe potential suppliers. It is in this liaison that procurement, for example, can suggest alternatives, such as Green options.

In Table 4.2 we can see an overview of two broad types of specifications that are substantially different. These are either technical specifications or performance specifications and Table 4.2 on the next page shows the important differences between these two types of specification.

Whilst the use of rote standard and bureaucratic processes ("if this, then that") may be acceptable for standard and unchanging requirements, they do give a limited internal analysis and allow for no brainstorming and scenario modelling, as this is seen as being outside of the specific preordained rule-bound process steps. Effectively, therefore, this limits the amount of creativity and analytical rigour that could actually be deployed throughout the sourcing stage.

Table 4.2: *Specifications*

	Technical specifications	Performance specifications
Supplier	Receives an exact and clear specification	Responds to the outcomes required in the customer's required operating conditions and environment
Buyer	Has certainty of what is being bought. However these may not the "best", as other options that may satisfy the need are excluded	Must very clearly specify the requirements and outcomes needed
Technical risk	With the buyer	With the supplier
Supplier innovation	Low/little	Highly likely
Examples	Simple and branded products	Services and complex projects

Some strategic sourcing models – and sometimes for good reason – do isolate the procurement function from the rest of the organization at specific points, so that this enables a more open and transparent market and pricing; for example, the 700 people working in one large procurement department we know are internally known as the company's spending police. The reasoning for such isolation is that buying was being previously over-influenced by certain internal and external stakeholders, with negative consequences on total cost.

However, it is still possible to have sourcing organizations limit this type of third party "meddling" in certain specific areas without negatively impacting the total cost. Indeed positive cross-functional contributions from internal and external stakeholders are actually needed to enable effective total and holistic "end-to-end" supply chain management.

In short, some traditional sourcing processes and tools, for example those that only using technical specifications and tendering, will actually limit options. Also such processes and tools will actually represent an "invisible" structural barrier and a blocker, instead of providing ways to investigate new possibilities that ultimately lead to improving and changing the traditional processes and tools.

It is, as often, a matter of getting the balance right. Sustainability is all about both fostering options and staying flexible, whilst taking into account the "soft factors" such as safety, quality, environmental concerns, and the overall supplier stability.

One organization we know suggested that sustainability initiatives also include maintaining and sustaining access to resources of all kinds such as commodities, feedstock, talent, and innovation. For organizations like this, sustainability comes down to changing internal philosophies on the role of sourcing from one of being only the process order placer or a trusted gate-keeper, towards being one of an options creator. This approach, however, requires changing more than just the overall philosophical orientation with the procurement function. To take advantage of sustainability, procurement teams, and the entire organization, must become more quantitative in how they examine and develop hypotheses and options.

In today's competitive business and global climate, organizations that fail to take a collaborative and sustainable approach to working with both suppliers and internal stakeholders will face numerous risks. These risks range from being placed on allocation (which can jeopardize that most basic tenet of procurement, continuity of supply) right through to lost sales.

Without the examination of newer yet often challenging options, like sustainable procurement, and by maintaining blindly the old methods and ways, this will ultimately create damaging problems, especially as sustainable sourcing is not just about reducing risk; it can also dramatically lower costs: the best of both worlds.

4.6 Moving towards Green Procurement

Green Procurement needn't necessarily be complex. The following action plan can be used to implement Green Purchasing in any organization through this simple step-by-step process:

- Question the need for the purchase in the first place. Can existing products or equipment be used instead of buying new goods? Can the requirement be met by hiring or sharing instead of purchasing?
- Appoint an environmental champion to spearhead your Green Procurement strategy.
- Agree Green Purchasing objectives and integrate them into a simple Green Procurement policy that clearly states your intentions. Ensure this fits in with your environmental policy.
- Get top-level support for your objectives from the chief executive or finance director.

- Communicate strategy and processes to staff and suppliers so they are clear on what is expected of them.
- Regularly audit purchases.
- Develop Green specifications and contract weighting tools.
- Assess the environmental impact of purchases against emissions to air and water, waste to landfill, resource use and environmental quality.
- Engage existing suppliers who may be able to provide products or services to fit in with new procurement policy. Seek their feedback before targeting new suppliers or contractors. Ask suppliers for sample products.
- Incorporate Green Procurement criteria into all key contracts focusing on those which have a high spend, a high environmental impact, and are easily influenced.
- Incorporate environmental specification into contracts including energy and water efficiency, recycled content, reusable packaging and products, no hazardous chemicals, and sustainably managed timber such as Forest Stewardship Council (FSC) certified. See also the Local Environmental Management Systems and Procurement (LEAP) toolkit or the European Union Green Public Procurement website for examples of environmental criteria.
- Award new contracts on the basis of value for money and total cost of ownership/whole life costing, not just the lowest price. This takes into account the whole life costs for Green purchases that may have lower operating or disposal costs. Additionally, choose products that use less energy (i.e. minimum A-rated energy-efficient) and have a long life span as they can be easily repaired or reused.
- Implement contract and monitor performance, including the environmental benefits of new product and services.
- Improve performance such as reducing packaging along with minimizing delivery frequency and miles.

4.7 Reflections on Green Procurement: Joined-up Thinking

Many organizations do now count Green issues as being critical in their strategy and their total supply chain. There are simply two major reasons for this: legislation drivers and consumer/customer drivers, where the latter pressure and demand may focus an organization to grow sales, as Green can be a source of competitive advantage.

However, Green efforts affect organizations in other ways. As noted in a PricewaterhouseCoopers analysis, *Achieving Superior Financial Performance in a Challenging Economy* (2008), those organizations in the food, drinks, and consumer products sector who reported their sustainability data performed better, delivered a higher return on assets, had a stronger cash flow, with better shareholder returns and higher gross margins.

A Green Procurement perspective extends beyond Corporate Social Responsibility (CSR) and includes the following:

- Supplier compliance with auditing and ethical sourcing procedures, such as the producing factories' use of energy-efficient production, considering social issues like wages and whether "sweatshop free" etc
- Buying products, materials, and services that are Green, such as recycled products, use made of energy-efficient materials etc.

Above all else, suppliers and all of the other supply chain players in any specific supply chain must duplicate the "end" buying organization's Green practices. Without this, then Green remains merely a singular "with me" from the initiating organization.

There are parallels here with the principle of just-in-time (JIT). This has, in some applications, been of limited value, as whilst the end buyer may have JIT supply from their first-tier supplier, these first-tier suppliers may now have to hold local stocks nearer to the customer to meet the need for JIT from their customers. This most likely results in extra waste in the upstream supply chain that is effectively invisible to the downstream end supplier, who of course, may not be "bothered" and chooses to ignore this upstream waste that they have actually created.

With Green it seems unlikely that such denials will work, because the real end here is the consumer's pressure; the consumer is the final, ultimate, originating end demand in any supply chain. As we shall see later, retailers are increasingly growing and developing their efforts to be Green, retailers of course being right next to consumers and so directly face the "first wave attack".

Any organization that is exposed by campaigners or the media represents, at least, an embarrassment, at worst, lost sales and ultimately, closure.

How Green therefore is your supply chain? The reality is, it could certainly be Greener, and waiting for pressure from customers/consumers may be too late.

So what should procurement professionals essentially be looking for when wishing to undertake Green Procurement? There is no simple one-line answer as it involves balancing multiple demands from internal and external sources, where besides the usual cost and value for money tradeoffs along with risk, there are also the legislation and consumer/customer pressures.

The influences on Green Purchasing in an organization will therefore comprise the following usual procurement considerations, but overlaid with a Green perspective, for example:

- Risk: e.g. buying biofuels that are not as readily available/accessible as oil-based fuels.
- Cost: e.g. buying biodegradable bottles.
- Performance: e.g. energy efficiency.
- Product development: e.g. organic cosmetics.

Whilst the normal procurement assessments and evaluations tools (as mentioned above) like total acquisition cost (TAC) and total cost of ownership (TCO) will continue to be used, Green Procurement will add in specific Green considerations. Accordingly a Green TCO will add to the normal life cycle or whole life costs the following environmental and social consequences costs, for example:

TCO environmental costs

- Compliance with legislation
- Risk of incidents, such as spillages, pollution
- Waste disposal.

TCO social consequences

- Health and safety of employees
- Customer relationships
- Society relationships
- Supplier relationships.

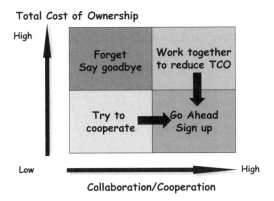

Figure 4.7: *TCO variables*

We have mentioned before the use of collaboration with suppliers and the degree to which suppliers have relationships that collaborate and coop-erate with a buyer's Green demands. This adds in another set of variables to TCO that can be illustrated as in Figure 4.7.

As is clearly seen, those suppliers who will cooperate on Green issues are critical for Green Procurement initiatives. It is also worth noting here that suppliers are often in touch with many other buyers on Green issues; indeed some suppliers will have Green as a key competence and differentiator.

As has been said, "You are only as good as your suppliers" and Green Procurement really emphasizes such linkages, as customers/consumers only deal with the one supplier and are not really interested in any supplier's supplier's problems. With Green, an end supplier's ignorance of what a sup-plier is doing upstream from them is of no concern or interest to customers/ consumers; accordingly with Green Procurement and Green Supply Chains, the whole is clearly greater that the parts where ignorance is not an option.

We really do need to join up all of the thinking.

PART 4

Green Supply Chain Execution

GREEN SUPPLY CHAINS			
GREEN SUPPLY CHAIN PLANNING	**GREEN PROCUREMENT**	**GREEN SUPPLY CHAIN EXECUTION**	**CARBON MANAGEMENT**

1. Life Cycle Engineering
2. S&OP
• Demand Planning
• Supply Planning
  o Production Planning
  o Inventory Planning
	• Collaboration
	• Incentive Alignment
	• Supplier Development
	• Energy-Efficient Procurement
	• Sustainable Sourcing
		• Green Production
		• Green Logistics
		• Green Packaging
		• Green Marketing
		• Supply Loops
			• Carbon Footprint Minimization

Green Supply Migration Strategy

Green Supply Chain Continuous Improvement

Green Supply Chain Performance Evaluation

5

Green Production

Green Production incorporates the search for and the deployment of alternatives to existing manufacturing technology, strategy and design, whilst taking into consideration the internal and external requirements and constraints, risks, safety measures, regulations, and the environmental impacts.

Green Production is therefore an organization strategy that focuses on profitability through using environmentally friendly operating processes.

The prime purpose of Green Production is to reduce the environmental impact of the manufacturing process at every stage and has three fundamental objectives:

- Decrease emissions, hazards, effluents, and accidents.
- Minimize the life cycle cost of products or services.
- Reduce the use of virgin materials and non-renewable forms of energy.

Green Production initiatives will not only work towards the optimization of production processes but will also seek to reduce costs and waste through life cycle costing, life cycle engineering, and process design. The manufacturing of eco-friendly products through traditional processes can be extremely expensive and unprofitable, if not impossible for many. Hence process re-engineering, technology upgrades and process design are very important to Green Production.

While designing Green Production systems, the following considerations must be taken into account:

- Refurbish and reuse as much product and parts as possible without compromising on quality.
- Minimize the consumption of raw materials and energy.
- Consume energy in a sustainable manner.
- Promote the use of renewable energy.
- Increase product life cycle.
- Reduce waste.
- Recycle waste.

None of the above will be a surprise to most readers as most people believe they are already doing the maximum possible both to reduce waste and to maximize recycling. However, a closer examination of an organization's production processes, technologies, and material flows reveals constraints that most people actually accept as fixed. Therefore these constraints are holding them back from moving towards real Green Production.

This chapter will look at several ways of moving past the constraints of existing technologies, existing infrastructure, and existing supply chain relationships in order to move towards real Green Production. While some of these methodologies are themselves quite well known, their application to create Green Production is still in development and it is this that we will emphasize in these methodologies.

5.1 Benefits of Green Production

A legitimate question at this stage is: why Green Production? Is it worth the bother?

In a supply chain, up to 50% of the total emission of greenhouse gases is a result of manufacturing and therefore Green Production is vital to achieve Green Supply Chains. Green Production acts as a vital link between supply side and demand side of a supply chain (Figure 5.1).

Green Procurement on the supply side is instrumental in creating the environmentally efficient and timely supply of raw material to Green Production. At the same time, Green Marketing creates the demand for

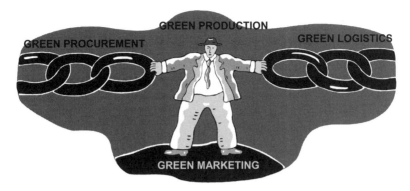

Figure 5.1: *Green Production – a vital link*

Green products. On the other hand, Green Logistics creates an environmentally sound outflow of goods from the organization.

Green Production in the middle therefore links supply and demand to optimize production and minimize waste.

Green Production works towards making organizations more responsible by prompting them to take steps to:

- prevent pollution;
- enable product stewardship;
- streamline internal processes for efficient outcomes;
- technological innovation;
- waste reduction at each stage of the production cycle.

Though many managers and policy makers have postulated that environmental regulations can negatively impact on an organization's bottom line, recent studies focusing on the impact of Green Production show that organizations that develop Green Production processes can not only offset the costs of regulations, but can also reap a series of tangible and intangible benefits.

Adoption of Green Production has also become necessary to stay ahead in a competitive market. Where competitors are moving towards Green Production, it becomes imperative for the organizations to keep up and to try and stay ahead of the competition.

There is also a growing consumer awareness of the environmental impacts of purchased products. Consumers are not only increasingly aware of the products' production processes, but are demanding that these be updated in order to reduce any environmental pollution and material wastage. Old processes are therefore seen as uneconomical and at times unusable in producing eco-friendly products.

For this reason, the adoption of Green Production helps organizations to enhance their image in the eyes of all stakeholders such as the public, consumers, employees, governments, and policy makers.

In addition to this, the adoption of Green Production gives:

- better working conditions, for example, safety and hygiene, and advantages with insurance organizations due to lower premiums as a result of a better safety, health, and environmental track record;
- lower long-term and intangible liabilities incurred due to past environmental claims from the public, employees, and policy makers;
- efficient and enhanced internal processes;
- lower regulatory costs;
- improved market opportunities;
- pre-empting regulation;
- reduced supply chain risk.

5.2 Drivers of Green Production

Management philosophers argue that Green Production, on one hand, benefits the natural environment and, on the other hand, helps to build a fundamentally sound strategy for the organization that will form the basis for competitive advantage in coming decades.

There are two main categories of drivers of Green Production:

1. The economic incentives to adopt Green Production methodologies.
2. The legal and regulatory compliance can bring in the adopting of the very same production methodologies due to the need to phase out older technologies by the increased environmental compliance burden, the increased probability of detection of non-compliance, and the increased cost of non-compliance.

These are explored further below.

5.2.1 Economic Drivers

- Lower consumption of raw material and energy results in reduced costs.
- Reduced medical expenses, due to reduced liabilities to employees, consumers, and the public surrounding the production locations.
- Savings in waste management, treatments, and/or disposal.
- Overall cost savings in production over the entire life cycle of products, due to more efficient production processes, reduced rework, reduced overall waste, and increased recycling.

5.2.2 Legal and Regulatory Drivers

- Increasingly stricter regulations with longer regulatory planning horizons plus a broader, internationally harmonized approach to regulation of the most noxious production processes and products.
- A more alert public, better non-compliance detection technologies, better funding to compliance agencies, more proactive NGOs, and 24-hour media are all contributing to make it virtually impossible for non-compliance to go undetected for long.
- Increases in possible civil and criminal liability, due to non-compliance, are forcing organizations to spend money to ensure their compliance with appropriate regulations and to modify processes as soon as a potential issue and surface. This is not only due to the increased penalties for non-compliance, but also due to the hawkish juries awarding damages of increased amounts to the victims of such environmental degradation. Directors and officers of the organizations can also personally face civil and criminal legal action, in turn making them wary about risking turning a blind eye to potential non-compliance issues.
- At the same time, many countries have streamlined the process for obtaining permits and have simplified the proceedings for proving compliance in order to make it easier to facilitate Green Production, thus creating an additional incentive.

5.3 Challenges of Green Production

If Green Production was easy, then everybody would be already doing it, rather than talking about it. Managers will have many challenges when looking to move towards Green Production and below we outline some of the main challenges to be found.

5.3.1 Installed Industrial Capacity with Outdated Technology

Just because newer, cleaner production technology becomes available, all of the existing installed production capacity does not disappear. Frequently, the sunk costs are too high and will act as anchors holding back the organizations to the outdated technologies. Even when the old dirty production machinery is phased out, another buyer, perhaps in a developing country, is found to buy and use it for many more years to come. Hence the problem does not disappear, it just moves to another location.

5.3.2 Perception of Extra Costs

There persists a perception that Green Production is expensive. All the retooling, new technology, and process re-engineering is seen as a very costly exercise. These costs may also be exaggerated in order to persist with the status quo and, at the same time, the benefits may be discounted or ignored for the same reason. However, Green Production can create a massive cost advantage in the medium to long term; so, therefore, smart organizations will start with small steps so that Green Production pays for itself, as they gradually then escalate their commitment to the programme.

5.3.3 Gaining Cooperation of Supply Chain Partners

This is frequently a problem because the supply chain partners have their own priorities and perceptions of Green Production. In many cases, and as in common with many other supply chain approaches, without the cooperation and collaboration of the supply chain partners, the drive towards Green Production will remain only partly done.

5.3.4 Lack of Clarity on Green Impact of Different Technologies

In an ideal world it would plainly be clear to everyone that new technology is cleaner and Greener. However, this is not always the case. Sometimes, it is merely greenwashing and at other times, it is merely shifting the dirty problem to someone else's backyard. Sometimes, even what appears and is promoted to be clean, Green technology is more harmful to the environment and human health.

5.3.5 Customer-centric Supply Chain Evolution and the Underlying Assumptions

The centrepiece of every company's strategy is the customer. All the product features, benefits, and associated services are designed in order to satisfy customers' expressed or assumed demands. However, sometimes there is a conflict between customers' demands, for example between demand for having a product available when they visit the retail store, versus the demand for Green products that are manufactured with the least amount of environmental footprint.

In such cases, organizations will make tradeoffs based on their own assumptions of a customer preference. Here, however, customer education and choice is paramount so that they can make personal educated tradeoffs and release the organizations from impossible expectations and any consumers' accusations of providing them with false information.

5.3.6 Trend of Outsourcing to Non-transparent Manufacturing Locations

As manufacturing is increasingly outsourced to China and to non-transparent locations, organizations are frequently out of touch with the production practices and environmental footprint of their own supply chains. Sometimes, despite their best efforts they are unable to fully monitor these due to distance, language problems, or other more important priorities, as well as occasional deceptive conduct by some contract manufacturers.

A false belief can be born that says, 'If we cannot see it, then it does not exist'. As such, organizations can then claim to be Green, if they outsource every carbon producing activity and ignore the responsibility of monitoring the environmental impact of any of their outsourced service providers. This belief is obviously wrong and also somewhat dishonest, but the fact that it happens does limit the drive towards Green Production.

5.3.7 Change Management and the Difficulty in Changing Attitudes and Thinking

Like any other change, Green Production is not without its own change management issues. Some of the most common change management issues encountered here are as follows:

- Insufficient top management leadership or commitment.
- Misplaced expectations or the lack of sufficient planning.
- Weak internal supply chain coordination within organizations and with the supply chain partners.
- Organizational inertia.
- Poor diffusion of Green Production best practices.
- Consumer and investor inability to recognize and reward Green organizations.

5.4 Key Components of Green Production

Despite the above long list of challenges, Green Production is steadily moving towards cleaner, Greener manufacturing as it is driven by economic incentives and regulatory structures. Needless to say that consumer proactivism is also playing a major role in this drive.

A systematic approach to Green Production has, however, so far been missing. A typical change cycle is reactive, for example, initiated by the availability of some new technology, which is then adopted after much debate and hesitation within the organization.

Most organizations will not proactively go out in search of ways to make their production the Greenest possible using the available technology. Neither do they strive to keep their production at the cutting edge of Green, despite the benefits it brings them.

We attribute this reactive approach to Green Production to the lack of understanding and availability of methodologies for systematically turning the whole production Green. One such methodology that can be used is our Green Production Framework, as shown in Figure 5.2.

Figure 5.2: *Green Production framework*

5.4.1 Supply Chain Parameters

As is shown, Green Production works on multiple levels within and outside the organization. At the lowest level of the pyramid, the underpinning of Green Production is provided by the overall drive towards Green Supply Chains.

Collaboration with supply chain partners

In this regard the primary driving force is the effort to collaborate with supply chain partners across the entire supply chain. Without this collaborative effort, the efforts towards Green Production can easily fail by simply outsourcing production to another, less environmentally proactive, company or location.

Efficient Green Leadership

This refers to taking the collaboration efforts across the entire supply chain to a whole new level, as different functional groups across multiple organizations work together to create Green products. Similar to Efficient Customer Response methodology (ECR) of the 80s, this methodology has the design to implementation time reduced greatly; this as a result of cutting across several silos in order to co-design, co-produce, and co-market Green products.

The reason for this change in model is very simple. As shown below in Figure 5.3, the traditional supply chain collaboration model relies on sales staff of one company interacting with the procurement staff of another company (their customer) in order to understand all aspects of the drive towards the Green Supply Chains.

No matter how efficient this communication is, something is bound to get lost in such a traditional, tightly bound communication model.

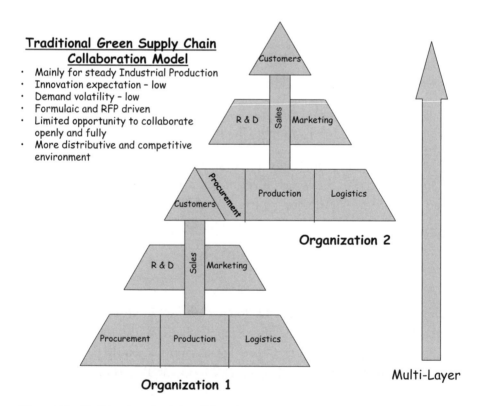

Figure 5.3: *Traditional supply chain collaboration*

Efficient Green Leadership (EGL) Model
- For rapid collaboration and change
- Innovation expectation – very high
- Functional areas collaborative openly and pro-
  actively to create Green Supply Chains

Figure 5.4: *Efficient Green Leadership model for supply chain collaboration*

In contrast to the above model, the Efficient Green Leadership (EGL) model is designed to encourage collaboration at multiple layers within the organizations. As shown in Figure 5.4, each functional layer communicates with its own counterpart in other organizations. They talk the same language and collaboration is much easier to procure.

The key benefits of this approach are many. The customer facing teams, marketing, R&D, and sales, collaborate with each other across multiple organizations in order to work out the details of the product features, packaging, communication message, channels, and other key aspects of customer strategy.

At the same time, the production back office functions of procurement, production, and logistics will collaborate with each other and then the customer facing teams will deliver those features in the most environmentally responsible manner.

It should be noted that initiative for environmentally sound projects can come from anywhere within this system, including the customer or top management itself. Because the whole system is dedicated towards creating this change then the results are rapid, sustainable, and bring in a real Green change. (We will discuss this model in further detail in Chapter 11 on implementation.)

Network remapping

One aspect of supply chain parameters is remapping of the entire supply chain network in order to create a fresh picture of a Green network. Frequently, organizations will find that the network would look markedly different than their existing network, when the imperative to reduce total network costs is married to the imperative to reduce the environmental impact.

This is particularly the case if customer re-education is possible or is envisaged in order to reduce the delivery frequency by increasing the lead times.

Transportation and logistics realignment

Transportation and logistics realignment leads to reduction in air, water, and land pollution prevention. Chapter 6 on Green Logistics covers this aspect in much more detail. However, it is mentioned here to highlight its primary importance in forming the overall supply chain underpinnings for movements towards Green Production.

Carbon tracking

Carbon tracking refers to tracking the amount of carbon dioxide emitted to the atmosphere by organizations' activities. By tracking their carbon footprints organizations can measure the social and environmental impact of all the products they produce and sell.

This pollution prevention approach is adopted by central authorities where only a certain amount (called a cap) of pollutants can be emitted to the atmosphere by their operations. Organizations, or a group, are issued emission permits and are allowed certain carbon emission credits or allowances. Organizations can only emit pollutants within that cap or that limit.

If a company wants to emit more pollutant than they have credits for, then it would need to exchange or trade its credits with a company that has used fewer carbon emission credits than it was allowed for.

In this way an organization that is polluting the environment can buy more credits or spend more money, and organizations that are introducing fewer pollutants can sell their credits or spend less.

This is an economic incentive for organizations to save the environment and still be in a development state. The growth in this market is very fast indeed and carbon will move on to become the single biggest commodity ever traded. It also provides a solution to the problem of "global warming" and we will discuss carbon management a lot more in Chapter 10.

5.4.2 Organizational Parameters

These include those parameters that are mainly at an organizational level. Examples are as follows.

Risk and reputation management

It is obviously important for all organizations that they manage their reputation with the public, with the government, and with the customers. At the same time, risk management is paramount because of the potential liabilities, not only at the time of production, but also at times long after production (for example, as has been found with past employees who worked openly with asbestos).

Most organizations are now taking both risk management and reputation management very seriously indeed and employ dedicated internal or external staff for this purpose. However, most such staff are often totally ignorant of the massive risks and reputation issues faced, as a result of apathy towards Green Supply Chains and Green Production. Boards are therefore increasingly setting the agenda in this respect in order to mitigate their own personal and official liabilities.

Product stewardship

Product stewardship is an environmental management tool where every organization that is responsible for the product from its design to its manufacturing is also responsible for reducing its environmental impacts right up to and beyond its disposal. For example, a manufacturer would need to plan for recycling or disposal of the product at the end of its life.

Hence it enforces involved parties to produce as little waste as possible and to use less toxic substances during manufacturing, so that at the end of a product's life it produces less toxicity and environmental degradation.

Product stewardship therefore provides a framework to understand total costs of a product from design to end-of-life.

Product stewardship activities have been around since the early 1990s and in this environment management practice, the responsibility of minimizing environmental impacts lies with whoever in the entire supply chain is responsible for environmental degradation during the processes, or whoever in the supply chain has maximum capability to do so.

This means that large retailers in particular, though not directly responsible for manufacturing the product, will still retain significant responsibility for making sure that the environmental impact of the entire supply chain is minimized (see Figure 5.5). Most large retailers have indeed already taken this on board and are taking steps in order to be responsible corporate citizens.

In this environmental management approach, everyone who is involved in the lifespan of the product is responsible for minimizing its impact on the

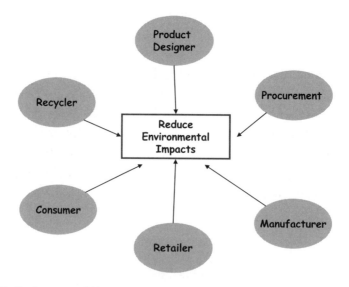

Figure 5.5: *Product stewardship*

environment. It could be as producer in the design, procurement, and manu-facturing phase, or retailer and consumer in the demand phase, or recycler.

Used oil recycling is one example where the consumer takes back the used oil from their motor vehicles to a used oil facility, run by their local council. Here the used oil is collected, reprocessed, and put to other uses. Disposing of the used oil in an irresponsible way would pollute land, water, and infrastructure, hence the used oil from vehicles and machinery is reclaimed and refined and used in other areas such as burner fuel or hydraulic oil. Another example is a container/bottle deposit charge. One pays a deposit for a bottle separately from its contents. If the customer returns the bottle, the deposit collected initially is paid back. Otherwise the deposit money retained presumably pays for subsequent litter control measures.

Product stewardship is not just all about the impact of waste on the environment. It takes into account end-to-end impact of a product on the environment throughout the supply chain. Thus product stewardship results in conservation of resources and environment efforts with the involvement of everyone in the supply chain. The responsibility of protecting and saving does not only lie with the public sector or producers but with everyone who is involved – producer, seller, and the user.

The success of product stewardship hinges upon the principles, shown in Table 5.1 overleaf.

External and internal communication

Seamless communication internally within the organization and externally with all the supply chain players is the key to the success of Green Production process.

All the parties have to work as a team to achieve the Green objectives and meet regulatory requirements. Contribution is required from everyone and benefits will be reaped by mankind now and in future and while this is an obvious conclusion, so often the root cause of problems with introduction of Green can be traced to lack of communication, whether this is in format, content, or frequency either within the organization or with external stake-holders. Media relations departments can be perhaps the worst culprits, as the spin emerging from these departments will frequently lead consumers to make allegations of greenwashing.

Table 5.1: *Product stewardship principles*

Principle	Details
Accountability	Everyone is accountable for environmental impacts of a product.
	Government: should provide infrastructure to aide recycling or disposal; promote product stewardship.
	Producers: conserve on resources used in manufacturing of the product, use material that is less toxic and readily refurbished or recycled.
	Retailers: prefer products from producers who produce environmentally friendly products, encourage consumers to return the goods after consumption for recycling or refurbishment.
	Consumers: choose environmentally safe products and recycle.
Integrated and transparent cost	The cost of recycling or disposal should be part of the total cost.
	Thus manufacturers to consumers will have drive and incentive to reduce their cost.
Management support	Management should support the initiatives to produce goods that reduce environmental impacts; eco-friendly production that uses less resources (energy and material) and produces less waste.
Government support	Government should provide incentives for product stewardship.
	Provide information needed to make an informed decision on environmentally safe purchasing, usage, recycling/disposing decisions.

A consistent, integrated, strategic approach to communications is needed to produce effective results.

Incentives alignment

Frequently one of the barriers to the introduction of Green Supply Chain and Green Production efforts is misalignment of incentives, either within the company or within the supply chain. It is therefore imperative that organizations take a more thorough and deliberative approach to align incentives across the supply chain. Obviously, the incentives should be used to create and maintain the impetus towards change, and we will discuss this in detail in Chapter 11 on implementation.

5.4.3 Production Parameters

At this level we address those issues that are directly related to the production. Examples include the following.

Manufacturing efficiency

For production people especially, this is obviously the crux of the Green Production effort, to get the maximum output from minimum utilization of resources while creating the least amount of waste.

Technological innovation, process re-engineering, systemic review, and execution attention all play important roles in this effort.

Waste reduction

There is no doubt that waste has tremendous impact on the environment which goes far beyond what is visible to most consumers. Table 5.2, overleaf, highlights some of the key environmental impacts of wastes.

While waste of material results in an excess usage of the Earth's resources without increasing the well-being or quality of life in any way, the wasting of land space results in actually degrading the quality of life for the population by making less space available for humans, parklands, and habitat.

One of the key means of achieving Green Production is cutting out waste of materials and space. We will examine the methods to reduce waste at the next level in the model, process parameters, where we discuss Lean manufacturing and other ways of cutting out waste.

Packaging

While in this book we have included packaging under a separate chapter (Green Packaging – Chapter 7), for practical reasons we have also included it here as packaging falls into a "no man's land" in most organizations, because there are multiple functions responsible for it, for example, marketing and R&D for design, procurement for ordering, and manufacturing for using it. Who then, within the whole organization structure, carries the accountability for making sure that the environmental impact of packaging is minimized?

Table 5.2: *Environmental impacts of waste*

Material related environmental impacts	Space related environmental impacts
Excess Production • Use of additional raw materials and energy unnecessary good • Product obsolescence or spoilage resulting in more waste and disposal activities • Extra emissions, waste, disposal, worker exposure, etc	Excess Production • Additional space required to store excess goods • Additional requirement of lighting, heating and cooling
Faults and Damages • Consumption of materials and energy in producing faulty/damaged goods • Recycling of faulty/damaged goods • Additional space for rework and repair	Faults and Damages • Additional space for rework and repair • Space and energy required for storing faulty goods
Excess and Outdated Inventory • Waste from deterioration or damage to stored work-in-process (WIP) • More materials needed to replace damaged WIP • More energy used to heat, cool and light • More waste from outdated WIP	Excess and Outdated Inventory • Additional space and packaging to store WIP
Transportation • Additional packaging required to protect components during transportation • Special shipping and packaging required to transport hazardous material	Transportation • Damage and spills during transport • Emissions from vehicles

We have asked this question in many organizations and the answer is almost always a very confused reply about shared accountability and with no effective measurement at all of "just what is going on".

Production is however the best placed to take leadership and ensure that in practical terms packaging is most environmentally sound, simply because many organizations regard packaging as part of the product. Hence it is imperative that production optimizes packaging and uses reusable packaging or packaging that produces the minimum amount of waste.

5.4.4 Process Parameters

Green Production processes are designed in such a way as to minimize the lifetime impact on the environment affecting the cost and quality. These processes use less energy and material, reduce and eliminate by-products, use clean process technologies, and strive to extend the life cycle of the products.

Process parameters towards Green Production can be divided into two key areas: Lean (cutting waste) and Six Sigma (quality control through variance reduction).

While some of the objectives and results of these two do not actually directly support environmental proactiveness, we nevertheless believe they are useful process parameters that can be incorporated in every organization's driver towards Green Production. The reasons for this are many, as Lean and Six Sigma are both widely known and utilized, and they have practitioners and thinkers who have already devoted a lot of time to development and refinement of methodologies, which will produce results if they are implemented properly.

Lean production

Lean production, which is often known simply as "Lean", is a competitive practice that reduces costs, improves environment and quality, and improves the bottom line. Lean production is aimed at the elimination of waste in every area of production. Here any expenditure that does not create a value for the customer is a waste and must be eliminated. This could include activities from various processes such as customer relations, product design, and supplier networks to factory management. Its goal is to incorporate less human effort, less inventory, less time to develop products, and less space whilst being highly responsive to customer demand and, at the same time, producing top quality products in the most efficient, environmentally responsible, and economical manner possible.

Lean production is closely associated with Green Production as there is an overlap between the goals and drivers for both processes. As seen in Figure 5.6 on the following page, in fact the strategies to create Lean supply chains can easily be adapted and deployed for greening of supply chains as well.

Before we discuss Lean in more detail, a word of caution is in order.

Lean effectively can be traced back to W. Edwards Deming in the USA in the 1930s; however his principles and methods to change and improve processes remained unused in the USA at that time. Deming eventually took his ideas to Japan in the early 1950s, where they were taken up by

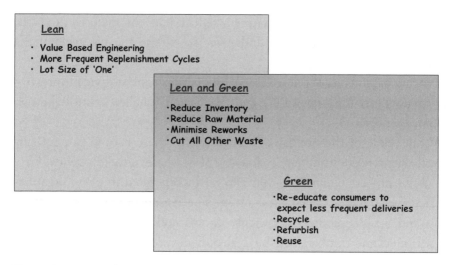

Figure 5.6: *Lean and Green*

Toyota and grew into the Toyota Production System (TPS). This targeted anything that does not add value with four clear implicit rules:

- How people work: all work shall be highly specified as to the content, sequence, timing, and outcome.
- How people connect: every supplier/customer connection must be direct with unambiguous communication.
- How the production line is constructed: every route must be simple and direct.
- How to improve: improvements use the scientific method, guided by a teacher and undertaken at the lowest level possible.

The actual word "lean", however, is a 1990s Western repackaging of the Toyota Production System and is covered in the book *The Machine that Changed the World* by James P. Womack, Daniel T. Jones, and Daniel Roos, which reported on the success of the Japanese automotive industry.

Lean has various definitions, of which the following are short examples:

- "No fat"
- "Eliminating waste"
- "Doing more with less"

- "Working smarter not harder" (as the goal is to meet demand and use fewer resources)
- "Flowing not stopping"
- "Adding value" (by streamlining the non value adding processes)
- "A system for creating thinking people".

Daniel T. Jones has recently defined Lean as:

"It is about ensuring a common steady rhythm across the supply chain in line with demand; guarded from supply disruptions and real fluctuations in demand by (holding) just the right amount of inventory, possibly held off line. Little and often is right thinking."

(Source: Daniel T. Jones 13 February 2007 e-letter)

Lean has been highly effective in streamlining supply chains in a variety of industries, ranging from automobiles to chemicals, with the following being reported from a variety of manufacturing industries:

Increases of:

- 57% in productivity
- 45% more capacity

Reductions of:

- 83% in lead times
- 54% in set up times
- 67% in space requirements
- 38% in supply chain costs

As the benefits of Lean were rolling in, another revolution was taking place, the so-called China effect. China was taking over many of the manufacturing capabilities from other countries from across the world; global supply chains were initially stretched and actually snapped in some places.

Entering into the late 2000s, to the eventual bewilderment and consternation of some organizations, the gradual and slow increase of sales and stock turns in all kinds of industries then stagnated and sometimes reversed.

Why?

Well, one view is that many executives had missed making the connection between globalization and inventories as the growing globalization of supply chains, coupled to the wrong "toolkit only approach" application of Lean principles, had caused unacceptable risks.

However, what can now be done, and is done by some organizations, is to adapt the Lean principles to suit the environmental goals. This means that we must not see Lean as being only a "toolkit" application with the "tools" giving us a quick fix. As has been noted:

"Many are unsuccessful as they concentrate on the explicit tools and not on the implicit principles; they want the tools but not the thinking behind them."

Therefore what works is to apply the principles to fit your ways and to not blindly copy others or just use the tools. We must not ignore the critical thinking that is behind Lean and that requires a change to our existing thinking; difficult maybe, but 100% critical to do.

Whilst each organization will therefore have to really sit down and think how to work out the details that will fit their own production processes, in essence Lean basically involves cutting out the seven types of waste:

- Inventory: stock in waiting and excess stock.
- Movement: unnecessary people or machinery movement, poor ergonomics, goods moved more than required.
- Time: waiting, idle people and machinery, inactivity.
- Inappropriate processing: non added value activities, like storage, too many steps in processes.
- Defects/rework: frequent errors.
- Overproduction: worst of all, as this has elements of all the above.
- Intellect: not using people's brains, no cross-training.

Sustained, systematic thinking is advocated to first identify the waste, then to identify the root cause of the waste, and then to develop ways to cut out the waste. Organizations that have devoted resources and management attention to this type of sustained, systematic thinking have reaped, and will reap, significant financial and environmental benefits.

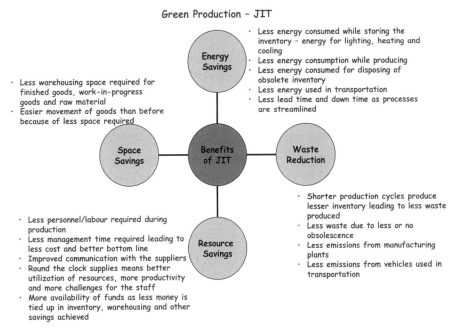

Figure 5.7: *Benefits of just-in-time (JIT)*

Just-in-time (JIT)

A key component of Lean principles is just-in-time (JIT) inventory strategy, which deserves a mention of its own. It focuses on reducing inventory and provides material, energy, and space savings.

JIT as part of Green Production provides the following benefits (Figure 5.7).

To achieve the full benefits of JIT, internal and external communication within the organization must be very efficient. Internally an organization should know what is happening elsewhere within the production process, so that the right inventory can be made available to the right process at the right time with replenishment reorders made accordingly. Externally, there needs to be seamless communication with the vendors so that they can fulfil the needs of production in a timely manner.

Six Sigma

Six Sigma is another management methodology which became very popular. It supports Green Production by primarily eliminating defects from manufacturing processes and, hence, cutting waste. Through exercising greater care and management control minor investment defects are caught as early as possible through the process. As a result, significant savings can be made by reducing the number of defects, rework, and spending time on defective pieces.

Though it was originally developed to eliminate defects from manufacturing processes it has also been adapted for a variety of other business processes. Six Sigma projects involve the utilization of statistics based on quality management tools, to train a group of people within the organization who become experts in these methods. These Six Sigma specialists are designated Black Belts, Yellow Belts, and Green Belts based on their level of expertise in implementing Six Sigma projects.

Six Sigma projects have quantifiable financial targets to make more money and, at the same time, satisfy customers and improve efficiency. They focus on customer requirements, error elimination, cycle time reductions, and cost reductions. Elimination of defects or errors from products or services being delivered has, therefore, a direct impact on the bottom line of the business. Six Sigma projects aim to cut out the waste of fixing the errors or defects by rework or disposal which wastes a significant amount of an organization's resources.

Six Sigma methodologies

DMAIC and DMADV are the two key methodologies of Six Sigma. There are many similarities, though there are some differences as well:

- DMAIC – utilized to improve an existing process in an organization.
- DMADV – utilized to create new product or process design.

DMAIC

DMAIC process is widely popular across industrial corporations worldwide. Depending on the way it is implemented, it has given a wide variation of results. Some sceptics have claimed that it is not as successful as originally envisaged, but our view is that the primary reason for lack of success has almost always been incorrect application of the tool.

DMAIC consists of the five steps detailed in Table 5.3.

Table 5.3: *DMAIC 5 steps*

Define	Goals are set for process improvement taking into account customer requirements and business strategies.
Measure	Measure the existing processes/system and collect relevant data to determine the factors that influence the process and form a baseline for measuring whether or not the defects/errors have been reduced or eliminated.
Analyse	Analyse data collected above to determine the defects or errors, the causes of the errors or defects, and their effects. Analyse the data to find ways to reduce the gap between current performance and desired performance set above.
Improve	Improve and optimize the process/system so that defects are lowered or eliminated and the processes are streamlined. There are various techniques such as Design of Experiments (DOE), Taguchi methods etc.
Control	Control mechanisms should be put in place to monitor the process on a regular basis so that peak performance continues and processes can be improved continuously.

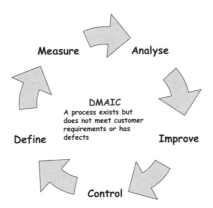

Figure 5.8: *DMAIC process*

Six Sigma is a continuous improvement process. Little improvements are achieved on a regular basis by resetting the goals once the cycle has been completed and measurement and control methods then identify further potential for improvements (see Figure 5.8).

DMADV

DMADV is also known as DFSS (Design for Six Sigma) and consists of the five steps shown in Table 5.4 overleaf.

Table 5.4: *DMADV 5 steps*

Define	Goals are set for the new process taking into account customer requirements and business strategies.
Measure	Identify characteristics that are Critical To Quality (CTQs), product capabilities, production process capability, and associated risks.
Analyse	In this phase different design alternatives are developed that can reduce defects. Then high-level designs for these design options are developed. These options are then evaluated to determine the one that is best.
Design Details	The design is optimized to achieve the peak performance. Various simulation techniques are used to accomplish this. A plan for verification of the design is also generated at this stage.
Verification	After analysis and testing, the design is verified using pilots run. Once verification is criteria is met the process is implemented in production and handed over to process owners.

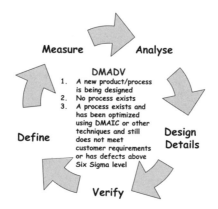

Figure 5.9: *DMADV process*

DMAIC should be used when the existing process is unable to meet customer requirements or it has many defects. DMADV meanwhile should be used when no process exists, or an optimized process does not meet customer requirements, or the process has defects above Six Sigma level (see Figure 5.9).

We have sketched above the elements of the Six Sigma process in very brief outline in order to explain their role in Green Production processes and their importance for environmentally conscious production. They can be adapted by each organization to meet its environmental goal quite easily. However, for more details on Six Sigma itself, the reader is referred to one of many books devoted entirely to this topic.

5.4.5 Product Parameters

This is the obvious apex of the pyramid, the reason for the entire Green Production effort. It is however, also the simplest part of the whole puzzle. If everything else in the entire Green Production pyramid has been adequately addressed, the two main relevant considerations that remain are:

1. Make sure that the product is created in such a way that when its useful life is over it can be easily recycled or reused by the consumer/customer.
2. Package it appropriately in order to minimize waste while safeguarding the product in transit.

Green products are designed in such a way that at the end of their life, the maximum amount can be reused, reclaimed, and recycled. In a design for the disassembly approach to product design, the main principle used here is that at the end of its life, any product or its part should be reusable, recyclable, or remanufactured. Therefore, everything that is produced should have an environmentally safe disposal plan at the end of its life. If no such plan exists, then the product should not be produced in the first place.

To summarize:

- Green Production encourages innovation, integration, and improvement of products, services, and processes.
- There is an opportunity to streamline the processes, improve efficiency, and differentiate products and services, and build the organization's image.
- The initial costs to convert existing production infrastructure to allow "Green Production" can be offset by gains from the efforts.

6

Green Logistics

Before we talk about Green Logistics, it is important to clearly differentiate between Green Supply Chains and Green Logistics. This is necessary because despite that fact that what we know today as the discipline of supply chains has been in existence for over 25 years, there is still a misconception that logistics and supply chains are synonymous. This misconception is particularly strong in senior circles where CEOs, financiers, and boards will frequently construe supply chains to be same as either procurement or logistics.

While both procurement and logistics are subsets of supply chains, they are, by themselves, only links in the total and complete supply chain.

This remains confusing for some people when one person understands a term to mean one thing, but then another person understands the same term differently. Whilst logistics in the UK, for example, was used originally to encompass the whole supply chain, during the 1990s, logistics began to be used as a new name for transport or for warehousing/stores.

Logistics in this usage was previously called distribution by some; this is about delivering the right goods to the right place at the right time and at the right cost. This definition is the "rights of distribution" and represents, in a simple way, the objectives for distribution. Distribution therefore involved the combining of transport with warehousing.

Logistics can therefore remain a confusing word as, additionally, some people use the term logistics to describe their own internal company process, and use the supply chain term when they are dealing with external suppliers/

customers. At the risk of further confusion, others also call their internal logistics processes their internal supply chain!

Logistics is however very commonly used today to cover the management of the movement of goods through the supply chain. It is therefore one of the key factors that influence the environment as it is responsible for significant amounts of emissions of greenhouse gases. Transport and warehousing industries are at the heart of logistics and hence most of the developments in greening logistics have centred around reducing the impact of transportation and warehousing activities on the environment.

Green Logistics has attracted by far the most attention when looking at all of the elements in a Green Supply Chain. Regulators have been readily able to focus on the control of emissions as the concern about smog and its impact on human health was raised since the 1950s, for example, the UK clean smoke campaigns to replace coal power and then again, more recently, with vehicle emissions and the realization of global warming.

Emission control standards and their application to the freight industry have put Green Logistics at the forefront of the 'greening' movement and newer technologies for generating energy for movement of goods and people are constantly being sought. However, despite some very powerful lobbies with entrenched existing interests, these newer technologies are gradually coming forward.

In this chapter we will not delve too deeply into new vehicle engine technologies; rather we will look at the drivers, benefits, and challenges to Green Logistics before examining a comprehensive framework for 'greening' of logistics with essentially existing technologies. New technologies will obviously result in much better results but organizations need not wait for those new technologies before doing something. Every day spent waiting for new technologies is a day wasted; "winners" will always start before the "laggards".

6.1 Drivers of Green Logistics

These are the key drivers of Green Logistics:

- Organizations are under increased pressure to provide customers with environmentally friendly logistics services. As discussed earlier, the emissions from transport vehicles such as road trucks, ships, trains, and aircraft are the most visible contributors to air quality problems in most urban areas. Emission standards are now in existence in most parts of the world for significant amounts of working time. Consumers, governments, industrial customers, NGOs, and many other stakeholders consistently exert significant pressure for Green Logistics.

- There is a very high cost of non-compliance with environmental legislation to all organizations. The emission standards are being imposed increasingly strictly as authorities are also aware of citizen activism. Popular media and films have shown ways in which ordinary citizens have organized to fight again powerful industry lobbies and government apathy and corruption and this has increased awareness and knowledge and encouraged more activism.

- Transport is perceived as one of the main contributors of greenhouse gases and hence logistics is a most obvious activity for greening supply chains. This, coupled to a greater hunger for means to "Green" logistics, and a better understanding of these means, is achieved by using the cutting edge methodologies that are being developed, tested, and refined. Willingness to experiment and learn, to devote resources, and to change is creating a powerful movement towards Green Logistics.

- Some government programmes offer financial incentives for lowering emissions and improving energy efficiency. Organizations can use these incentive programmes to not only reduce greenhouse gas emissions, but, at the same time, to achieve internal and external logistics efficiencies which will provide benefits in the long run. Again, governments are using appropriate motivators, such as capital cost write-offs, taxation benefits, and grants, to create the necessary action for Green Logistics and the incentives offered are often strong enough to create a powerful drive towards Green Logistics.

- Spiralling and frequently fluctuating fuel prices create an incentive to minimize the impact of these on the overall cost structure of the business and this can be greatly achieved by moving towards Green Logistics. Moreover, policies that have discouraged the use of fossil fuels have had a large impact on the transport industry.

- There is ever increasing pressure from voluntary and mandatory programmes, such as Green groups, governments to execute reverse logistics, and design products and packaging that will facilitate the efficient, safe and cost effective product recovery.

6.2 Benefits of Green Logistics

Green Logistics offers numerous benefits to environment, society, and organizations. These can be viewed as follows:

- The first and the most important benefit is the reduced impact on the ecosystem, the reduced environmental degradation, and the resultant enhanced quality of life.
- At the same time Green Logistics frequently results in lower costs due to fewer trucks, better vehicle utilization, better maintenance of equipment, efficient routing, reduced congestion etc.
- Green Logistics will help to mitigate risks of legal action and financial impacts of avoidable environmental incidents and the ever increasing sterner environmental regulations. It therefore provides an organization with the ability to proactively respond to any scrutiny and due diligence in its environmental and social practices.
- Green Logistics also provides health benefits to the community through better air quality and less noise pollution, particularly to those urban neighbourhoods that are located near busy freight zones, such as freight transfer points, airports, seaports etc.
- At the same time, Green Logistics results in enhanced safety and health conditions for employees, contractors, and logistics partners.
- Green Logistics increases customer loyalty and brand goodwill as such Green active organizations display noticeable proactive steps of managing the environmental and social consequences of their operations.
- Involvement of community, customers, and vendors in devising sustainable solutions and product/waste take back programmes will help in strengthening customer relationships and building brand image. It demonstrates corporate citizenship and responsiveness to community, employees, public interest groups, supply chain partners, and regulators.

6.3 Challenges in Green Logistics

The fundamental characteristics of logistical systems and sustainability are sometimes contradictory; therefore the resultant key challenges are discussed below.

6.3.1 Cost and Externalities

Cost minimization is one of the main objectives of logistics optimization. In addition, other objectives like faster and more flexible deliveries enhance customer service and reliability. However these objectives can be in contradiction with environmental considerations.

Freight distribution organizations focus highly on strategies that will enable them to reduce cost. For example, to reduce cost, organizations often choose to use cheaper varieties of fuels or decide to delay maintenance that impacts on roadworthiness. Such tactics to reduce cost have an adverse impact on the environment. The cheaper fuels and road unworthy vehicles emit greenhouse gases, increase noise pollution, and reduce air quality.

While some of these means of reducing costs are just short-term fixes and will also have large cost impacts on the organization in the long run, many of the other environmental costs are often externalized.

This means that the benefits of logistics are realized by the users and consumers, but the cost is actually being largely borne by the environment. As many people do not recognize such environmental costs, the onus is on governments and organizations to include sustainability considerations in logistics activities. Regulations around the world are often uncoordinated, contradictory, and even misguided. For example, in some countries diesel is often subsidized and cheaper than gasoline, even though diesel engines have much more negative environmental implications.

6.3.2 Response Time, Flexibility, and Reduced Inventories

For many years, logisticians have been taught that reducing the time to deliver is crucial, as it increases the efficiency of the distribution system. Trucks and aircraft are the most popular modes of transportation for reducing shipment time, but they generate high pollution and are not energy-efficient. In recent years there has been a significant increase in air freight and trucking activities due to time constraints imposed and the need to improve response times and reduce stock holdings.

Providing flexibility in production with strategies like just-in-time (JIT), or improving customer service with emergency or overnight deliveries have taken their toll on the environment. Frequently such urgency would be unnecessary, if the activity had been planned well in advance; however, urgency due to a lack of preplanning results in half truck loads and more frequent trips and hence more implications for the environment.

Most consumers are also not yet trained to wait for products and often have an "I want it now" mentality that sponsors, for example, the retailers' "must have" product availability on shelf. Yet consumers also want companies to minimize the environmental impact of their activities. Organizations therefore need to communicate clearly the reason why some items may be temporarily out of stock, or will need longer lead/wait times so that they can reduce the environmental impact of having to satisfy the demand instantly.

Many supply chain and logistics strategies focus on reducing inventory with frequent, short, speedy, and reliable shipments. These strategies also remove the need to stock and store excess inventories and consequently one of the major advantages of these strategies is a reduction in warehousing demands. However what this effectively means is that if the inventories are not in the warehouses, then they are very likely to be in transit in the transportation system, thus contributing further to existing congestion and pollution and putting an additional burden on the environment and society.

6.3.3 Reliability

Service reliability is one of the prime objectives in logistics and its success hinges upon the ability to keep promises and remove uncertainty. For example, one of the key factors here would be to deliver goods on time with no shortages, breakages, or damage, this being measured by the commonly used KPI of "on time in full" (or OTIF).

Logistics providers often realize these objectives by employing the transportation modes that are perceived as being most reliable, for example road and air transport. However, these modes are the most polluting and, conversely, the least polluting modes are often less reliable, such as railways that have a poor reputation on customer satisfaction in most countries when compared to road trucking. Shipping can also be prone to port industrial action in some countries, although on many important and competitive trade routes, it does offer fixed and known departure/arrival times with excellent records of reliability. However, this is not universal, as for example with transport between the east coast and the west coast and Australia where other modes are frequently used to ensure reliability.

6.3.4 Excess Product Movements due to Customization, IP Protection, and Process Specialization

Frequently additional movements are introduced in the supply chain to facilitate product customization, intellectual property protection, tax optimization, or process specialization. While these steps add value to the supply chain, they increase the carbon footprint of the logistics chain.

For example in the computer manufacturing industry, intermediate plants, between manufacturing and consumer, are set up for assembly of certain parts. This facilitates product customization but puts additional movement of goods in the production line. Consider also the following globally reaching (partial) supply chain for Lee Cooper jeans that has customers worldwide and sells to agents, wholesalers, and retailers who have received finished products from a factory in Tunisia that gets supplies of:

- denim cloth from Italy, using dye from West Germany and cotton from Benin, West Africa, and Pakistan;
- zips from West Germany, using wire for the teeth from Japan and polyester tape from France;
- thread from Northern Ireland, using dye from Spain and fibre from Japan;
- rivets and buttons from USA, using zinc from Australia and copper from Namibia;
- pumice (used in stonewashing) from Turkey.

Similarly many companies, especially FMCG multinationals are setting up global supply centres in tax optimization locations to reduce the overall tax burden. Frequently this increases the number of movements and hence the carbon footprint.

There is therefore a direct conflict between the profit motive and the Green drive; the profit motive frequently wins.

With the growing trend towards outsourced production, organizations are often wary of the risk of having a single manufacturer produce the whole product and may also be concerned over potentially competing products being launched by the contract manufacturer or its allies. Despite the most watertight contracts and the use of intellectual property protection through patents, most practical companies realize that the most effective means of protecting their intellectual property is to make sure that no one single entity has access to the information about the full production process or the bill of materials (BOM). Elaborate supply chains movements can therefore be designed across different continents in order to protect the intellectual property by carrying out parts of the production process in disparate locations. This could also be done for other reasons such as process specialization, skills, or installed production capacity. In any case, the result is always the same: excess movements and hence excess carbon production.

6.3.5 e-Commerce

The explosion of the information highway and emergence of e-commerce markets has changed the landscape of many industries with retail and logistics being two highly affected industries. The logistics activities that have benefited the most from consumers' direct from home retail buying e-commerce are the parcel shipping organizations such as DHL, UPS, and Federal Express who very largely use road trucking and air transport. The knock-on impact to retail outlets selling products like books and CDs/DVDs has been dramatic as they have been replaced in many medium sized cities by home deliveries for goods bought online. So instead of people buying goods from shopping centres or retail stores and bearing the cost of transportation, now with e-commerce the final distribution of goods has to be integrated with the supply chain.

This drastically increases the amount of packaging required and number of frequent and shorter trips to the households. This reverse of more recent decades spent pursuing consolidation of retailing and distribution efforts is therefore putting an additional burden on the supply chains, on road transport, on waste from packaging, and on the environment.

6.3.6 Road Congestion

Both money and carbon are wasted by road congestion. So, for example, carbon efficiency would be improved by reducing car usage, but political implications when restricting car usage present a high barrier.

As pointed also out in *Excellence in Freight Transport* (Emmett, 2009) in the UK, road congestion is a major growing concern and journeys that take longer mean more vehicles are needed to carry the same freight volumes. Road congestion can mean late arrivals, delayed deliveries, missed book-in times, rejected deliveries, stock-outs, lost sales, and loss of customers; leading to higher costs, falls in productivity, unreliability and leading on to that major supply chain disrupter: uncertainty.

In recent times in the UK, road building has not kept up with the growth in road traffic and in the last 50 years, the number of cars has increased by some 15 times, whereas goods vehicles have increased fivefold (although large goods vehicles have become much larger during this time). The freight industry meanwhile has noted that there are around 26 million cars licensed compared with around 450 000 freight vehicles and believes that the way forward is to determine a combined transport policy aimed at encouraging motorists onto public transport, especially at peak times.

The car issue is an important one here. Brought about by improved quality of life and the personal freedom that such transport brings, car growth was virtually exponential in the late twentieth century. As more cars are used, then more road space is used; this causes road congestion as the extra cars need more road space but this is not provided. Less car parking space availability, due to the growth in car usage, in turn causes congestion in urban areas, leading to increased journey times with less reliability and predictability, a vicious circle that in turn leads to actually lowering the quality of life. Also the perceived "saviour" of public road transport is affected and is slowed down by the increased use of personal car transport, which then means fewer people use it. Public transport then attracts less investment leading to an inferior availability: another vicious circle completed.

This car problem is therefore a complex one and is not a "one solution fits all" issue. In a market economy the price mechanism is usually brought into play, for example responses like the congestion charge are found in Central London. How far such market pricing level activities will continue is beyond the scope of this chapter. It suffices to wonder, however, how soon it will be before road congestion causes freight transport costs to increase, which in turn will then be passed on to the consumer in price increases on, say, their packet of cornflakes. After all, as is said in the UK, "If you have it, then a truck has brought it".

6.4 Moving towards Green Logistics

Our intention with the previous section describing the challenges to Green Logistics is not to discourage readers, or to convince them that nothing can be done. Rather, it is to highlight the various objections and barriers they are likely to encounter on their journey towards Green Logistics; indeed we are of the view that such a journey is not only possible but necessary. Without Green Logistics, the drive towards Green Supply Chains will be missing a crucial component and hence it will fall short.

So the key question is: despite the above challenges, what is the best way to ensure success in the drive towards Green Logistics?

This section therefore describes a systematic way towards Green Logistics.

As mentioned earlier the transportation and warehousing activities are of paramount importance in logistics, and greening of logistics involves greening these activities. This section covers various ways of achieving sustainable transportation and warehousing. Figure 6.1 shows the wheel of Green Logistics.

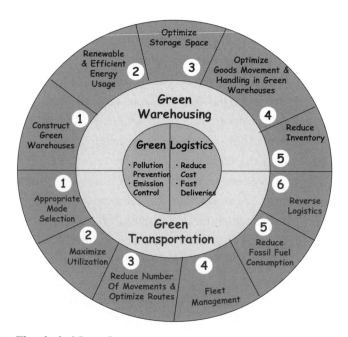

Figure 6.1: *The wheel of Green Logistics*

6.4.1 Green Transportation

Movement towards Green Logistics starts with Green Transportation. For many people Green Logistics and Green Transportation are interchangeable concepts. However, this is not necessarily true since Green Warehousing is equally important, and there is frequently a tradeoff between Green Transportation and Green Warehousing. For this reason, during the Green Supply Chain Planning stage (as discussed in Chapter 3), a holistic view of the entire supply chain is essential when planning a move towards Green. Assuming that the Green Supply Chain Planning is carried out effectively, we can look at the greening of logistics through a sequence of activities that are designed to build on each other.

Firstly, effective use of the most appropriate transportation mode will not only reduce cost, but also reduces the adverse impact on the environment. Organizations should use the most effective and efficient mode of transportation and, wherever appropriate, sea transport should be the primary mode of transportation to give effective Green Transport. The next choice on a Green basis should be by rail and then road and air transport. In general, the cheapest mode is also the most energy-efficient with the consignment size and distance being two key determinants in the transport mode selection, along with the service/reliability aspect discussed earlier.

Having selected the most appropriate mode, it is crucial to make sure that the carrying capacity is utilized to its maximum on a weight or cubic basis both on the journey out and on the return journey. Frequently road transportation companies quote prices on the basis that they will be backhauling empty, however efficient transport organizations will try to ensure round trip vehicle fill.

Aligned with the above objective of maximizing utilization is the drive to reduce the number of movements through better planning of overall supply chains. Better load planning should result in maximizing the throughput of the transportation assets. Optimum route planning will reduce the distance travelled while still achieving the same throughput. A reduction in the number of trips to deliver goods whilst using use the shortest route will usually contribute to greening the transportation activities. This, at times, might mean pooling the deliveries to one destination to optimize the number of trips and thus delaying deliveries. The resultant delays can be communicated and negotiated with the customers alongside the benefits this provides to the environment. Ultimately of course, this will be a customer decision, which in turn may well be sponsored by consumer pressures for Green Transport, and of course those supplying transport organizations which operate in a competitive supply market may also find they have to respond to such pressures.

Efficient fleet management contributes significantly to reduce environmental impacts and the cost of transporting freight. Some simple measures such as turning off the engines during pick-up and deliveries, proper tyre pressure, and appropriate vehicle speed will all reduce fuel consumption and subsequent emissions. When sourcing vehicles fuel efficiencies and design improvements should be taken into account. Appropriate driver training programmes can help reduce fuel consumption. Some organizations implement driver incentive programmes to recognize and reward fuel efficiency gains or fuel-efficient driving techniques. Timely inspection and maintenance of vehicles can reduce break-downs and lower fuel consumption and emissions.

As a way of amplifying these points, in recent years, UK major fleet operators have reported the following savings:

- mileage reduced by 15%;
- CO_2 omissions reduced by 23%;
- driver training brought a massive improvement in fuel economy;
- reduction of 1200 TEU (twenty foot equivalent) freight container loads, per year by better container fill;
- plans to reduce CO_2 by collaboration to improve vehicle utilization, two-way full loading, improving routing, increasing vehicle fill rates, and scheduling in real time.

Many of the above initiatives are means of reducing the usage of fossil fuel as organizations should always be looking at ways of reducing the usage of fossil fuels and hence eventually contributing to the reduction in emission of greenhouse gases.

This could be as simple as switching to biofuels or other Green energy sources for transportation. Newer technologies are being trialled all the time and organizations should remain on the cutting edge in their quest to reduce the fossil fuel dependence. Indeed in some countries, like the UK, the reduction of fossil fuels and improving fuel consumption remains the critical aspect of their road transport operations. This is given full coverage in Emmett *Excellence in Freight Transport* (2009).

Finally, the integration of reverse logistics to a holistic view of Green Logistics is essential, in order to ensure that it does not remain an afterthought that causes serious greenhouse gas impacts from inadequate planning and inefficient execution. In most companies reverse logistics is still an activity that is not planned. Many activities are still being arranged on ad hoc basis and negate the valuable work done elsewhere towards Green Logistics. In fact once the focus is put on proper integration of reverse logistics in Green Logistics, it is a relatively simple exercise to execute reverse logistics. This is covered more fully in Chapter 9.

6.4.2 Green Warehousing

Green Warehousing starts with a Green Building. New warehouses should be built keeping the Green Building principles at the forefront during the design and construction stage. Existing warehouses can be converted into Green warehouses by incorporating the same principles as much as possible.

Green Building is not a new concept. It has been steadily gaining momentum, especially as a result of analysis that revealed that more than half of greenhouse gases are released as a result of poor building temperature optimization.

A significant body of work is available on this topic, especially targeting those people who are charged with design and construction of buildings. Suffice here to note that these principles are equally applicable to warehouse buildings. This is particularly so where warehousing needs include significant temperature control, either due to requirements of the products stored, or due to the climatic conditions of the location of the warehouse.

Aligned with the Green Building of the warehouses is the drive towards renewable and efficient use of energy. As the renewal energy technology is hitting an inflexion point, it is steadily becoming more and more competitive with the traditional energy sources. Warehousing is an ideal application due to availability of large roof spaces, for example, to install solar panels. Efficient use of energy is required on a daily basis in warehouses, whether it is heating, cooling, lighting, or plant/machinery operation; accordingly this aspect must be given the appropriate attention during the warehouse design and construction.

Within the warehouse, the storage space needs to be utilized in the most effective and efficient manner in order to maximize utilization and minimize usage of energy. Appropriate warehouse planning is a prerequisite in order to achieve this end. At the same time the movement of goods to, within, and from the warehouse needs to be optimized in order to reduce the energy consuming activity and optimize energy usage. For example proper airing will establish good indoor air quality and eliminate sources of indoor air pollution. Similarly, cartons, pallets, and racking configuration should be such as to make full use of available height. Reusable shipping containers have standard shape and size and are designed for more efficient stacking, retrieval, and automation. Some of the other considerations are:

- Efficient planning of loading dock space reduces energy consumption in those months when there are extreme external temperatures and provides more endurable working conditions for workers.
- Energy-efficient lighting fixtures, such as timed lighting systems or motion sensors, should be used.
- Use of natural light where feasible.
- Heat generated by refrigerated storage systems can be recovered to heat water, provide space heat, or power other processes.
- Use of energy efficiency of materials handling equipment, for example, fork lift trucks, conveyors/sorters, and automated storage/retrieval systems (AS/RS).

Additional considerations are:

- Integrated sales and operational plans (S&OP) should be developed with involvement from sales, marketing, operations, and logistics departments to help forecast demand, production, and inventory levels more accurately.
- Engaging external supply chain partners such as customers, suppliers, and 3PLs to develop a collaborative plan and exchange forecast information enhances information flow, coordination, and estimates.
- ICT software and tools will help in the real time exchange of point-of-sale data, inventory levels, and reorder status updates. In addition the

up-to-date production and delivery schedules are readily available and can be communicated internally and externally to foster better collaboration and cooperation. This helps to improve the visibility of forecasts that can reduce speculative orders, excess production, unnecessary shipments, and waste.

Inventory should be readily available and retrievable as and when required. It should be stored using the minimum amount of energy and effort. The quantity of inventory required and stored is determined by accuracy of forecast techniques used to determine demand and by the reliability of the supply lead time.

Improving the accuracy of supply lead time and the demand forecasts will help to reduce inventory and therefore the storage space, labour and machine time, resource usage including energy, waste, and recycling efforts.

Effectual inventory management is of prime importance to any organization as it results in less waste, better warehouse utilization and decreased capital, labour, and utility costs. Below are some of the ways to achieve better inventory management:

- Accurate forecasting of demand will keep the inventory levels lower.
- Fixed and known supply lead times enable better planning and remove variability/uncertainty.
- Optimizing replenishment policies for the players of a supply chain help optimization of total cost along the supply chain.
- Supplier managed inventory programmes and goods return policies for suppliers lower incentives to carry excess inventory.
- Storage space and stock obsolescence are reduced by consolidating storage of inventory within controlled sites. Reduction in obsolete or degraded inventory translates to reduced waste generation and thus lower disposal and recycling effort. This also means lower raw material requisitions.

Automation of processes that are paper or labour intensive provides economic and sustainability benefits.

7

Green Packaging

Packaging is perhaps the most visible element of a Green Supply Chain. In most cases, a typical consumer sees the packaging long before they get to see or touch the product. From the packaging we derive clues about how environmentally conscious the organization has been during the production, procurement, and logistics processes.

It is quite easy to underestimate the impact of Green Packaging on the overall supply chain's environmental performance.

Traditionally, packaging's primary function was to safeguard the product during movement and storage prior to its consumption or use. Somewhere along the way, marketing then figured that packaging was also conveying ideas of product attractiveness to the buyer or to other influencers (such as young children accompanying their parents on shopping trips). Since then packaging has acquired a life of its own, one that assigns multiple functions to the simple wrappers or packaging. Figure 7.1 on the following page, discusses these in detail.

At its basic core, the function of packaging is still to:

1. Protect products
2. Enable storing the product
3. In addition to the storage function, provide the function information about the product, including the nature of the product, usage of product, ingredients in the product, country of origin etc.
4. Also draw attention in a retail location to the product while it is displayed in the window or on the shelf. This is particularly true in busy

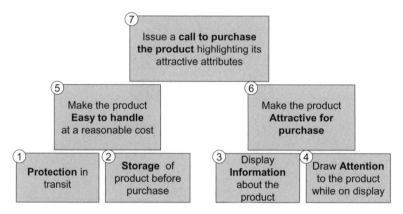

Figure 7.1: *Packaging hierarchy of functions*

shopping areas, with numerous products clamouring for customer attention and spend.

5. 1 and 2 above also make the product easy to handle in the logistics transport/warehousing functions, at the retailers, and for the end customers.

6. 3 and 4 above combine to make the product attractive for the end customers.

7. 5 and 6 above serve the end purpose by issuing a call to action for product purchase by highlighting the attractive attributes, including the price.

Traditional marketers tend to be still focused on overuse of packaging to attract the customers, while many of the consumers have meanwhile moved on to recognize that over-packaging results in:

- wastage
- excessive costs
- resource overuse and misuse
- environmental degradation due to landfills.

Astute marketers now therefore realize that the consumers have awareness that many of the above functions of packaging can actually be undertaken by other means, or have now become redundant. For example, information can be disseminated via electronic means, reducing the need for massive user manuals accompanying many products. Similarly, the benefits of drawing consumers' attention to products by using attractive packaging, so that they will make an impulse purchase, have to be counterweighed against any backlash from consumer perceptions that over-packaging is one of the main causes of environmental pollution.

Hence Green Packaging has become exceedingly important.

Green Packaging results in less damage to the environment than the traditional forms of packaging as packaging waste is one of the highest sources of environmental degradation; there are therefore big opportunities for improvements. Green Packaging can also affect the rest of the Green Supply Chain Process and any additional logistics cost can be more than recouped by the reduced consumption of raw materials for packaging.

So, how does Green Packaging differ from traditional packaging? Figure 7.2 highlights some of the key initiatives.

The four key differentiators highlighted above are:

1. **Reduce packaging:** Consumers increasingly have a belief that organizations are overusing packaging. This places great obligation on the consumers to dispose of the packaging in an appropriate manner and may even result in feelings of overconsumption. In addition to minimizing the use of packaging to its bare minimum, there is still a need to convey a message saying that the prime reason is to reduce environmental impact and also increase the product acceptance by an environmentally proactive population.

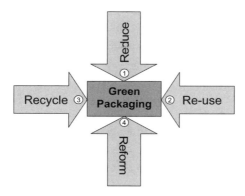

Figure 7.2: *Green Packaging – key differentiators*

2. **Reuse packaging:** This is probably the best way to deploy packaging. In contrast to other methods, here the organization takes full responsibility for taking the packaging from the consumer and putting it back in reuse in a closed loop chain. This is particularly relevant in products where the company is responsible for delivery of the goods to customer premises, such as the deliveries to industrial/business customers or to end consumers for goods such as furniture or white goods. Because the goods are delivered to customer premises, the delivery personnel are in a good position to take the packaging back without much additional cost. There is also clearly no reason to deploy large amounts of single use packaging for products where the packaging has no other purpose than the safety in transit and in storage.

3. **Recycle packaging:** Where the packaging cannot be collected and reused by the company due to the nature of the transaction or of the packaging, then it should be easily recycled through the most efficient and environmentally friendly method of putting it back in use for either the same or similar products. Recycling programmes are now operating in many countries for most recyclable products and much packaging also now carries instructions on how to recycle it. Organizations can go one step further to provide information on websites and by other means to define the full recycle chain to facilitate and assure appropriate recycling activities.

4. **Reform packaging:** This is perhaps the most far reaching differentiator. Reforming packaging includes going to the very core of reasoning of why packaging is used and examines just how the same function can be fulfilled without any accompanying environmental impact. This can include changing to biodegradable packaging material, changing to other more environmentally sound packaging material, and changing the method of service/product delivery (for example, e-books instead of paper books). Neither the technology, nor the imagination can limit innovation in this area and we are just beginning to see such packaging reformations.

7.1 Benefits of Green Packaging

As this book is being prepared the world is going through a global financial crisis, commonly called the credit crunch as there is a severe credit shortage. While the situation is expected by analysts to improve shortly, it is also apparent that changes are very likely in the world of business. The cost consciousness that has become embedded into organizations' patterns of behaviour will make it imperative to continue to look at all ways of saving costs.

For many organizations, packaging presents one of the most readily available opportunities to both reduce costs and reduce overall environmental impact. By enabling suppliers to suggest design, material, and other related changes as a part of the sourcing process, organizations can often achieve significant savings. For example, a retailer was able to make significant savings on direct packaging costs with the help of its supply chain partners; furthermore as a result of modified packaging, it was also able to switch to using standard pallets and moved away from the previous inefficient method; it also saved on cleaning charges and water and significantly reduced the number of shipments. It was then able to pass on part of the savings to its customers.

As is clear from this example, once the main constraints are removed, the savings are frequently cumulative as they build on each other, such as the unwieldy package size in the above example.

However, benefits of Green Packaging are not restricted to cost reductions only. As discussed earlier, packaging is frequently the first thing that consumers notice about a product and there is a large primary impression made on the consumer. This is before they see, feel, touch, or use the product itself. So just what does your packaging say about your organization? Do the consumers perceive your company as an innovative trendsetter constantly inventing new ways to reduce costs for them and save the environment? Or, do they perceive it as still persisting with outdated ways of presenting products?

7.2 Drivers of Green Packaging

In today's organizations, packaging represents one of the ideal categories to prioritize and target with strategic sourcing and with redesign/re-engineering. This is especially true in the midsize organizations that do not have resources to do anything more than to just keep the company ticking over. Savings, though, can be significant and in the case of packaging, 20% to 30% savings are routinely achieved through better sourcing, and 40 to 50% is possible, if this incorporates redesign and re-engineering.

Many organizations are caught in a tightening vice of lower demand and high overhead costs. With spare capacity and high overheads, the fixed costs are not moving down. Funding costs and credit costs are on the increase too. Meanwhile, however, many suppliers continue to look for higher prices across a range of commodities from energy to transportation to raw materials/ingredients. At the same time, retailers are expecting continual price decreases and better service levels.

Given this situation, CEOs and CFOs must ask themselves if they can afford to ignore large packaging cost savings in one of the few areas where they can influence cost reduction.

It is ironic that whilst organizations will often negotiate hard for many other inputs, they often still continue to neglect looking at packaging costs critically. The procurement methods remain routine. They obtain a few quotations on a biannual basis, and then negotiate to extract single digit concessions from the selected supplier. But this is frequently suboptimal and the options to re-design, reform, and re-engineer are commonly ignored. However, for this to happen, a much closer working relationship with the suppliers is needed. They will need to understand the underlying purpose of packaging, the logistics operations involved with packaged product transportation and storage, and the disposal mechanisms for the packaging. Most suppliers lack the ability or the willingness to go so deep into their own products' life cycle, and, for example, will not involve suppliers in suggesting improvements. Internally, some procurement teams may lack the expertise or willingness to carry out the analysis. Hence the sales or marketing perspective is accepted; however, this could be far from the reality as the marketing perspectives will often lack appreciation of the relative impact of the varied packaging options on logistics (transportation and storage), and on the environment. Only a Green Supply Chain analysis could reveal the true picture to all of the stakeholders and, in the process, save significant costs and prevent environmental degradation.

Meanwhile, some of the other drivers of Green Packaging are as follows:

- A desire to reduce the cost by recycling and reusing waste packaging material to reduce the raw material required for packaging.
- A desire to eliminate excessive cost by removing the unnecessary packaging of some goods.

- The public demand for the use of safe and appropriate packaging materials that will benefit the environment.
- Increase in customer satisfaction through having clean neighbourhoods as Green Packaging results in less waste accumulation and easier recollection.
- Enhanced goodwill and perception as a socially and environmentally responsible organization to end users.

7.3 Getting Started with Green Packaging

We frequently face the objection that the Green Supply Chain is just too big to tackle. The change involved is indeed seen as such a massive one that most CEOs and boards, despite their best intentions, are comfortable doing nothing and stay with the status quo. The second big objection is of course the cost involved with the initial analysis and diagnostic that is required in order to figure out the best way forward.

We counter both the objections with the same answer: start with Green Packaging. Why is the answer to both the objections the same? Because not only does it allow starting a thousand-mile journey with a single step, it also pays for itself. As discussed earlier in this chapter, Green Packaging mostly results in significant cost reduction. This allows companies to become comfortable with the results of the analysis and their ability to carry out the project on a long-term basis.

Figure 7.3 overleaf shows an outline of the path towards Green Packaging.

Step 1: Redesign

This step involves redefining the packaging requirements through a reassessment of the purpose of packaging and then the redesign of packaging based on this purpose. While redesigning the packaging the four key differentiators of Green Packaging are kept at the forefront: reform, reduce, recycle, and reuse, as these will lower the environmental impact of the new packaging significantly.

It will be useful at this stage to get third party support and outsourcing providers who have deep domain knowledge in the packaging arena. For larger organizations, this third party support might make less sense, especially if they have dedicated sourcing and engineering professionals.

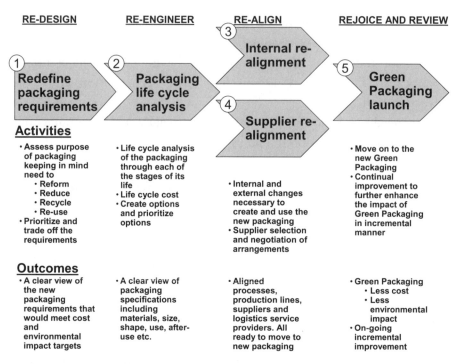

Figure 7.3: *Moving towards Green Packaging*

However, many packaging professionals inside larger organizations are focused mainly on new product roll-outs and cost containment, rather than on Green Packaging redesign. While the expertise might be there, years of disuse might make it less available when the need arises. Moreover, a holistic and strategic Green Supply Chain perspective may be missing despite having the technical expertise in engineering and packaging design. For this reason, even for larger organizations, an outside set of expert eyes could lead to significant cost and environmental savings.

An organization must develop an understanding of its true requirements and expectations so this will lead an organization to question its prior assumptions. This incorporates significant rethinking about how each of the purposes of packaging can be fulfilled, while reducing the environmental impact and costs. Multifunctional teams of engineers, marketers, logisticians, and sales staff may need to be formed and assisted by external service providers. This drive to reform can lead to making breakthroughs in environmental impact reduction and cost reduction.

However, the drive to reform packaging needs to be followed up by an equally vigourous drive to reduce, recycle, and reuse packaging. Packaging redesign should take these aspects in consideration as well, though they will become far more important in Step 2: Re-engineer.

A vastly overlooked aspect of the move towards Green Packaging is the ability to communicate the optimal set of requirements both internally to the organization and to the potential supply base, in time. The aim is to prepare people for internal re-engineering and to find, not just a low cost supplier, but the right long-term partner for the packaging materials.

For organizations used to traditional procurement practices, it can be a big change to define and share requirements in an open transparent manner. Traditional procurement in a production environment is focused on making sure that the production line does not shut down due to a supplier quality problem or a late delivery. However, the level of sophistication and communication protocol required to gather and disseminate information at this stage of movement towards Green Packaging may be beyond the capacity of traditional procurement personnel. A dedicated project management team is therefore required to make Green Packaging a success.

Step 2: Re-engineer

This step takes the output from Step 1 further to the next stage of re-engineering, where there is a complete packaging life cycle analysis (discussed in detail earlier in Chapter 3). This is carried out in order to clearly determine the whole life cycle of the packaging and the relevant costs. The outcome of this stage is a clear view of all relevant specifications and steps in the life cycle of the packaging. This step must be carried out in close cooperation with all of the potential suppliers of packaging, in order to make best use of the information available upstream in the supply chain.

When it comes to maximizing returns from packaging re-engineering efforts, the most successful organizations are those that focus on creating mutually trusting relationships with their supply chain partners. In reaching out to suppliers, organizations should focus first on getting their potential partners excited about the opportunity. If they do buy into the process, the supply chain partners will not only provide valuable information for the life cycle analysis, but also will be instrumental in bringing up new ideas for redesign and re-engineering. Moreover, their close cooperation will be required in the next two steps, and their involvement at this phase will therefore ensure that having provided input during the redesign and re-engineering phases, they will take a lot more ownership during the re-alignment and implementation phases.

In most cases, partner suppliers will not only create material cost savings, but will continue to work over the course of the relationship on ways to reduce cost and environmental impact. Indeed, the innovative suppliers will look at an opportunity not just to initially fill their available capacity but will also look at what the relationship might bring them in the longer term. For this reason, innovative suppliers will be excited to join in the efforts towards re-engineering Green Packaging. The experience, knowledge, and expertise provide them with competitive advantage and a continued source of profitability. It also provides a long-term relationship with customers who cannot be replicated easily, due to the high switching costs and a significant learning curve for new suppliers.

The outcome of this step is a clearly articulated specification for the packaging in its entirety with the focus on minimizing environmental impact and costs. The specification includes material, size, shape, dimensions, colour, markings, printing, etc. Alternatively, a performance rather than a technical or conformance-based specification can be used. This simply says what the required performance output is and leaves the design and solutions to the supplier's specialist knowledge.

All specifications will take a tremendous coordination effort to bring together multiple viewpoints from production, engineering, marketing, logistics, procurement, and suppliers; therefore, an effective project management team is required to carry out the process and see it to fruitful conclusion.

Step 3: Re-align

By this time there should be absolute clarity in the minds of all the internal and external teams about just what Green Packaging means for this particular supply chain. All aspects of the Green Packaging – materials, shape, form, size, dimensions, colour, printing etc. – will have been decided by the multifunctional teams who have been brought together to create this level of clarity.

The next step is to prepare the associated supply chain of both internal and external participants for the switch to Green Packaging. In practical terms Step 3 is the most action-oriented step. For example, the production lines might need to be retooled, pallets, trucks, storage spaces, handling equipment, and other machinery may have to be re-aligned or changed. There is usually a one-off cost involved in all this preparation, but in most cases its pays for itself in a short period of time.

Next, it is time to move to the deployment phase by introducing phased engineering and operational changes into packaging operations. The first step here is to consider engineering factors that balance the ease of implementation with the overall potential disruption for the organization. At the same time, it is also essential to adjust for other determinants that might prioritize certain initiatives over others.

While sometimes the changes might be as simple as just switching from one supplier to another, at other times, major internal changes might be required in production or packaging lines. Making sure all the changes are carried out without causing disruption in the processes and while meeting all the operational goals is a challenge in itself. However, most production planners and engineering staff are well versed in planning for and executing these changes.

Internal and external storage areas, transportation equipment, and handling equipment may need changes as well. External logistics service providers will need to be involved in making sure that their infrastructure can cope with the proposed packaging changes.

All this re-alignment and preparation must be tested through pilot projects in order to carry out fine-tuning. This will ensure that the project is a success once launched.

Step 4: Rejoice and review

By this time there should be significant momentum towards change. All the business processes, facilities, equipment, and suppliers have been re-aligned for the Green Packaging. Pilots have been carried out, key lessons examined and incorporated into the project.

It is time to change over to Green Packaging. New packaging is put in place and the response carefully observed in the first few months in order to make sure any teething issues are promptly settled. It is a rare project which will not have any teething issues. However, the team must keep the long-term perspective in mind and keep everyone focused on the end goal. Equally important is communicating and celebrating success. This will build the momentum towards expanding the Green Packaging programme and other Green Supply Chain projects.

Finally, it must be kept in mind that what is cutting edge today will be out-of-date in perhaps a few months. Hence there is a need for continual improvement. New materials, processes, technologies, suppliers will come on line and create both possible additional cost and environmental savings. An effective Green Supply Chain programme will therefore have built into it an ability to continually innovate and improve.

8

Green Marketing

A legitimate question is frequently asked: "Why is Green marketing a part of Green Supply Chains?"

We answer this by saying that the Green Customer is increasingly very well informed about the supply ecosystem aspects of the product they are buying. Therefore, unless all aspects of the marketing are fully integrated and aligned to communicate a correct and honest "Green" message, then many customers will regard any superficial Green PR as merely "greenwashing". Almost any organization can claim to be 100% carbon neutral by outsourcing all carbon producing activities. However, to effectively "go Green", an organization has to credibly communicate that it has gone through its entire supply chain in its attempt to reduce the environmental footprint.

As we explain in Part 8, Case Study 1 (Making an End-to-end Supply Chain Green: the GFTN/WWF initiative), very few supply chains are yet integrated, organized, and controlled in such a total end-to-end way.

The term "greenwashing" has actually become very popular in the past two to five years. While most traditional dictionaries have yet to incorporate this term into their collection, online reference dictionary.com defines greenwashing as "*the practice of promoting environmentally friendly programmes to deflect attention from an organization's environmentally unfriendly or less savoury activities*".

Media, NGOs and transnational environmental organizations are now continuously on alert for greenwashing attempts by organizations trying to promote their Green credentials. Such false PR can include baseless or false claims (for example, claiming to be phosphate free when they are actually not), making useless claims (for example, claiming to be sulphate free when phosphates were traditionally the problem with the product category), or making exaggerated claims.

8.1 Importance of Green Marketing

The core issue here is that we have limited resources on the Earth with which we then endeavour to satisfy unlimited wants.

By haphazardly consuming Earth's air, water, forests, minerals, and agricultural capacity now, we are actually condemning future generations to substandard lives – a sad legacy indeed. There is therefore a clear tradeoff between consumption now and consumption at a later date (or by future generations). Some do accept that the Earth is no longer a resource at the disposal of human beings to be exploited and discarded; rather it is held as a "collective custodial trust" that is to be preserved, enhanced, and passed on to the next generation in a better shape than we found it. This objective is increasingly being held sacrosanct by the more progressive nations, populations, and organizations.

From this viewpoint, as consumers and organizations grapple with the problems of limited natural resources, they are now developing newer technologies and methodologies of satisfying their unlimited wants. The purpose of Green Marketing is to broadly communicate this objective and provide the chosen means to achieve this objective. Green Marketing communicates and monitors how organizations are striving to change their internal and external processes, supply chains, infrastructure, systems, and technologies in order to achieve the above objective. Not only is it an integral part of the Green Supply Chains, but it is also an important contributor to ensure that organizations thrive in future.

Meanwhile executives have given us the following reasons for their Green Marketing efforts:

- "Organizations believe they have a moral obligation to be more socially responsible."

- "Organizations perceive environmental marketing to be an opportunity that can be used to achieve its objectives."
- "Governmental bodies are forcing organizations to become more environmentally responsible and proactive in communicating their efforts."
- "Competitors' environmental activities pressure organizations to change their environmental marketing activities."
- "Cost factors associated with waste disposal or reductions in material usage forces organizations to modify their behaviour."

8.2 Drivers of Green Marketing

Most customers (both consumers and industrial producers) are becoming increasingly aware and concerned about the proper stewardship of Earth's resources. In a 1992 study of countries, more than 50% of consumers in each country said that they were concerned about the environment. A similar study in Australia alone has concluded that 84.6% of the people surveyed had a belief that all individuals had responsibility to care for the environment and 80% of this sample said they had modified their behaviour, including their purchasing behaviour, for environmental reasons.

As the nature of demand evolves, most progressive organizations can take Green as opportunities for creating or enhancing competitive advantage. There are numerous cases of organizations that have become much more environmentally responsible while searching for ways to better satisfy their consumer demand. McDonald's, for example, phased out its clam shell packaging in most cases and replaced it with waxed paper because of increased consumer concern about polystyrene packaging and ozone depletion. Many organizations, including Xerox, produced recycled super high quality photocopier paper to satisfy the demands for less environmentally harmful products.

Of course, some organizations take short cuts to Green Marketing and resort to greenwashing. However, increasing consumer sophistication, rapid availability and dissemination of information through the internet, and the exploding popularity of new social media online make it increasingly difficult to create any sustainable competitive advantage through greenwashing. In most instances the perpetrators do get found out and are then shunned by proactive consumers. In many instances, though, the greenwashers are so far away from the Green Consumers, mainly due to supply chain complexities, that they just do not have knowledge of how consumers regard them.

Some of the key drivers for Green Marketing are as follows.

8.2.1 Social Responsibility Culture

Organizations now accept that they are members of the wider community and must behave in an environmentally responsible fashion; here the profit motive is now supplemented by an environmental stewardship motive. Environmental safeguards are now integrated into many organizations' cultures. Not only that – this environmental proactiveness is now a tool for organizational self-promotion. Indeed, organizations such as the Body Shop have based their entire marketing strategy around the fact that they are an environmentally responsible organization.

However, many other organizations still do not adequately promote their environmental initiatives. For example, Coca-Cola has invested enormous time and resources in various recycling activities around the world and has moved towards Green Packaging by modifying its packaging to minimize its environmental impact. However, this message rarely comes out as strongly as the Body Shop's environmental message. Similarly, Walt Disney World (WDW) has an extensive waste management programme and infrastructure in place to reduce environmental impact; however, this effort is rarely focused upon during marketing or promotional activities.

On the whole, this drive towards social responsibility is producing a move towards Green Supply Chains as well as towards Green Marketing.

8.2.2 Government Pressure

Governmental regulations regarding environmental marketing are normally being framed to protect consumers and they aim to:

- reduce production of harmful products or by-products;
- reduce consumer and industry use of harmful products;
- ensure consumers have the information and ability to evaluate the environmental impact of products they are using.

Through regulation which is similar to all other such efforts of governments, they want to "protect" consumers and society. This includes efforts to control the amount of hazardous waste, air pollution, effluents, solid waste, and other environmentally detrimental material produced by organizations. At the same time, governments try to motivate consumers to become more environmentally responsible in their consumption habits. For this they will often mandate facilitation and information dissemination. Facilitation includes such efforts as the introduction of voluntary curbside recycling programmes, waste recycling programmes, and various other programmes that make it easier for consumers to reduce their environmental footprint. Information dissemination includes Green Marketing to enable consumers to make informed choices. In this way, government pressure is actually increasing a drive towards Green Marketing.

8.2.3 Competitive Pressure

Frequently, the strongest market competitor introduces Green Marketing efforts in order to enhance its competitive position and create a competitive advantage. However, other players in the same market do not want to be left behind, and soon introduce their own programmes of a similar nature. The public's perception here then turns to the laggards, who are now seen as organizations that are incapable of keeping up with their competitors and are perhaps on the verge of failure.

For market leaders, the introduction of a Green Marketing programme is an excellent means not only of creating significant competitive advantage, but also of removing the bottom end players from the specific industry. Further enhancement in such programmes will also allow market leaders to consolidate their leadership position and enhance their market share in the long run.

8.2.4 Profit Enhancement

Organizations are increasingly concluding that Green Marketing programmes lead to higher profits. In many instances this is a direct result of higher revenues and lower costs at the same time.

Many consumers are actually willing to pay a somewhat higher price for a demonstrably superior Green product. Time and time again this has been shown by real life cases such as recycled greeting cards, organic produce, "Green" timber etc. However, not many organizations are adept at Green

Marketing that requires the creation and communication of a coherent Green message to the consumers. Such organizations will then frequently blame the consumers for a lack of interest in Green products.

Conversely others, such as Coca-Cola, neglect to communicate their Green credentials, perhaps because they do not want to diffuse their core message.

In either case, this is a missed opportunity to enhance revenue through Green Marketing.

At the same time, during attempts to minimize all types of waste, organizations are often forced to re-examine their entire supply and production processes and infrastructure. In many cases they will develop vastly superior production processes that not only reduce waste, but will also reduce the need for several raw materials. For example, by reducing the production of environmentally harmful by-products, such as polychlorinated biphenyl (PCB) contaminated oil (which is becoming costly to dispose of), the overall costs are reduced. In other cases however, instead of minimizing waste, organizations will attempt to locate end-of-pipeline sinks by finding markets for their waste materials, so that their waste now becomes another organization's input for production. An example here is of a company that produces acidic waste water which it sells to another organization who then use it to neutralize base materials.

8.2.5 Desire for Innovation

The final driver for Green Marketing is the innate desire for innovation that is built into the DNA of many progressive organizations. As a result of innovation then, new products, new services, or even new industries are being constantly developed to market to Green Consumers. This can happen in many ways and some examples are given below.

An organization develops a technology for reducing waste and sells it to other organizations. There are many examples of such technologies that were firstly developed for internal use, but were subsequently sold in the external market as they had discovered more general applications.

A waste recycling or removal industry has developed out of a service that was initially provided as an additional step. For example, organizations that clean the oil in large industrial condensers so that this will increase the condensers' life, find they can remove their clients' requirements for replacing the oil, as well as the need to dispose of the waste oil. This reduces the operating costs for those owning the condensers and generates revenue for those organizations cleaning the oil.

As regards specialist Green Marketing developments, specialist Green Supply Chain and environmental consulting organizations are now selling facilitation services to assist an organization's effort to "go Green".

8.3 Challenges in Green Marketing

There are a number of potential problems that must be overcome in order to make Green Marketing a success. One of the main problems is that organizations using Green Marketing must ensure that their activities are not misleading to consumers or industry, and that they do not breach any of the regulations or laws dealing with environmental marketing. Green Marketing claims must clearly state environmental benefits.

A problem that the organizations frequently grapple with is that consumers' perceptions are sometimes not correct. For example in McDonald's case, where it has switched from using polystyrene clam shell packaging to using plastic coated paper, there is now some scientific evidence which suggests that when taking a cradle to grave approach, polystyrene is actually less environmentally harmful. If this is the case, then whilst McDonald's bowed to consumer pressure, they may actually have chosen the more environmentally harmful option. This highlights the problem of undertaking inadequately rigorous research and analysis in order to prove hypotheses beyond a reasonable doubt.

This highlights another problem whereby despite the best intentions, managers and consumers are frequently confused about the science behind the environmental impact. This is because of the way in which the environmental impact information is created and disseminated and who controls such activities. Frequently, the distinction between science, government, NGOs, and the corporations becomes blurred and a narrow self-interest can take over. The result gives massive amounts of misinformation, disinformation, or phoney science which is followed by withdrawn conclusions and frequent repudiations. As a result of such confusions, many organizations face a dilemma.

In an attempt to become socially responsible, organizations may face the risk that their environmentally responsible action of today will be found to be harmful in the future. For example, the aerosol industry switched from CFCs (chlorofluorocarbons) to HFCs (hydrofluorocarbons) but later discovered that HFCs were also greenhouse gases. This may explain why some organizations, like Coca-Cola and Walt Disney World, are trying to become socially responsible without publicizing the point; they may be protecting themselves from potential future negative backlash if it is then determined they have made a wrong decision in the past.

Governmental attempts to protect the environment may result in a proliferation of regulations and guidelines, with no single central controlling body. Moreover, if the regulations are based on misinformation derived from phoney science, they could backfire, exacerbating the environmental catastrophe. Addressing all the environmental issues through regulations might not even be possible due to lack of information or ability to formulate appropriate regulations based on available information.

Companies may also find that following the leader is not always a sound strategy either. A large US oil corporation followed the competition and introduced "biodegradable" plastic garbage bags; whilst technically these bags were biodegradable, the conditions under which they were disposed of did not actually allow biodegradation to occur. This then led to allegations of misleading advertisement claims and suits by several US states.

Finally, the push to reduce costs or increase profits may not force organizations to address the important issue of environmental degradation. Some end-of-pipeline solutions may not actually reduce the waste but rather shift it around. While this may be profitable or even environmentally sound in the short run, it does not necessarily address the larger environmental problem in the long run. Ultimately more waste produced will enter the waste stream.

8.4 Elements of Green Marketing

There persists a mistaken belief that Green Marketing rests exclusively with the promotion or advertising of products with environmental characteristics. Popular expressions such as phosphate free, mercury free, 100% recyclable, 100% CFC free, ozone friendly, and environmentally friendly are seen by most corporations as being the core of their Green Marketing initiatives. However, Green Marketing is a much broader concept that can be equally applied to manufacturing, consumer goods, and industrial goods and services. An extreme example is from the service industry where around the world there are resorts that are now promoting themselves as "ecotourism" resorts. They provide an experience as close to nature as is possible, providing promised comfort/luxury whilst operating in a way that minimizes their environmental impact.

The full range of activities and considerations incorporated in Green Marketing are shown in Figure 8.1 below. We will then use this to discuss Green Marketing in a comprehensive manner as, whilst the changes envisaged in this framework are fairly far reaching, it can be safely said that no organization following this framework could be accused of merely "greenwashing". At the same time, if done properly, most companies will also have a net positive financial impact as a result.

Green Marketing can be defined as:

A series of activities planned and executed to generate and facilitate exchange intended to satisfy human needs or wants in a manner that causes minimal negative impact on the Earth's environment.

The emphasis here is on the minimal negative impact on the Earth's environment.

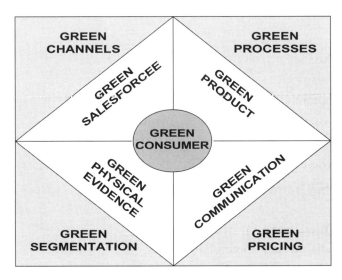

Figure 8.1: *Green Marketing framework*

Another key point is that the focus is on the satisfaction of human needs and wants, rather than on products and features. This is because such wants and needs might be satisfied by substituting a harmful product with a harmless product, or even with no product.

Let us now examine the elements of Green Marketing in more detail.

Green Consumer

The focus of all Green Marketing activities is in the centre of the framework – the Green Consumer. While other stakeholders are important and need to be catered to as well, the underpinning reason of all Green Marketing, and indeed of the whole Green Supply Chain, is to satisfy the needs and wants of the Green Consumer in a manner that causes minimal harm to the environment.

Green Marketers are already spending enormous amounts of money trying to get into the heads of Green Consumers so that they can understand and then influence their buying process. It is, however, ironic and paradoxical that many business leaders and supply chain leaders would rather wish for their organizations to be left alone – in so doing, they pass up on the enormous revenue enhancement of Green Marketing to consumers.

Surrounding the Green Consumer are the first core customer facing Green elements, as follows:

- Green Product
- Green Sales Force
- Green Communication
- Green Physical Evidence.

Each of these customer facing Green elements has a corresponding organizational element. These are as follows:

- Green Processes for Green Products
- Green Channels for Green Sales Force
- Green Pricing for Green Communication
- Green Segmentation for Green Physical Evidence.

As we look below at each of the pairs above, it will be clear that Green Marketing actually goes well beyond greenwashing and into changing the core of the organization's ways and methods of conducting business.

Green Processes and Green Products

These form the backbone of Green Marketing. Entire supply chain processes, including procurement, production, and logistics, are covered under Green Processes. Green Product will not only be manufactured and serviced by utilizing Green Processes. It will also be completely transparent to the Green Consumer that the product has been so made.

We have covered the Green Processes in detail in the rest of this book and it is sufficient to note here that unless the differences between the traditional processes and the Green Processes are made crystal clear to the consumer, then there will always be some suspicion about the "Green" credentials of the product.

To augment the Green credentials of the product, the packaging, product design, delivery, and other aspects of the product can be varied in order to reinforce the difference between the traditional products and the Green Products. However all these efforts without the solid underpinning of Green Processes will be merely seen as greenwashing and such attempts are very likely to backfire.

Green Channels and Green Sales Force

All the attempts to change to Green Processes and products are futile if the customer facing parts of the organization are not truly on board with the Green objectives. Traditional sales channels to customers and the staff operating them may require substantial retraining to equip them with a Green mindset and give them the information necessary to communicate this mindset to the consumer. Occasionally new channels will have to be created because of the mismatch between the Green message and the existing channels.

A Green Sales Force is even more important than the Green Channels as unless the sales force truly believes and lives the Green message, it will remain impossible to communicate the significance of Green Processes and

Products. It is equally difficult to understand and communicate all the intricate details of Green Processes and Products unless the sales force is interested in the message itself, as the cognitive dissonance between the beliefs and the messages would show through, and negatively undermine the message, the product, and the organization.

Green Pricing and Green Communication

Green Pricing sends a very important signal to the consumer about the quality, attention to the environment, and innovative spirit within the company. Many times we are asked the question: "Will the consumers pay the extra amount necessary to go 'Green'"?

We ask two questions in return:

1. How did you arrive at the conclusion that going "Green" will result in net higher costs?
2. What pricing strategy are you using currently in order to maximize your revenues from your current product/customer base and how can you adapt this strategy to incorporate Green Products and Green Consumers?

Generally, the answers to these two questions answer the original question quite well.

However, occasionally there is some confusion around the pricing strategy. In such cases no amount of clarity around incremental cost/benefit of Green Products would resolve the confusion. In order to clarify the confusion we would therefore recommend a thorough analysis of pricing drivers, such as cost, competition, and customers as well as analysis about basic demand and supply determinants, analysis that is beyond the scope of this book. We can however note here that the pricing signals are extremely important and need to be carefully orchestrated in order to enhance the reputation, credibility, and revenue of the organization.

Green Communication, on the other hand, is using the right medium and conveying the right message using the right channels and media to reach the target audience, the Green Consumers; the channels and media here are Green Channels, Green Sales Force, Green Media, traditional media, or new media.

In order to create and execute a cohesive communication strategy, the choice of media and matching the message to the selected media is vitally important.

Intangible and subliminal communication are equally important, whether in choice of colours, fonts, packaging materials, printing materials (if any), or the texture and feel of the medium. Green Promotion, which is related to Green Communication, covers the entire scope of public relations and exposure strategies that will create momentum towards adoption of Green Products.

Green Segmentation and Green Physical Evidence

Traditional segmentation, targeting, and positioning is the art of dividing potential customers into groups with similar characteristics, so that they can be offered bespoke and tailored value propositions that appeal to them. Green Segmentation takes this one step further by dividing Green Consumers into segments of like-minded people so that products, processes, communications, and channels can be tailored to each group. As one example, we show below a Green Segmentation attempt for a paint manufacturer (Figure 8.2).

In this example Agnostics and Penny Pinchers are two categories of potential buyers who are low in environmental sensitivity while the True Greenies and Value Seekers are two categories of potential buyers who are high in environmental sensitivity.

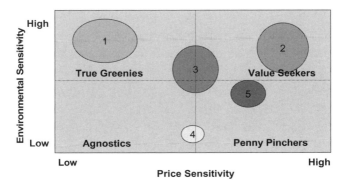

Figure 8.2: *Green Segmentation; paint industry example*

When the total pool of consumers is next segmented based on their psychographics, it appears that segments 4 and 5 are fairly small and they would not care much for a Green Product. However, segments 1, 2, and 3 are all fairly big segments and need very different marketing strategies, both in terms of pricing and of communication. Segment 1, for example, would be willing to pay a much higher price and may need a different channel than segments 2 and 3, who are much more sensitive on price.

As is clear from the above example, it is erroneous to assume all consumers, including Green Consumers, think alike and can be offered the same value proposition through a uniform marketing strategy. It is both an art and a science to isolate the right psychographic and/or demographic factors to make the segments. Further, it is an art to design an appropriate value proposition and communicate it to the segments without any cross-contamination of the message. Finally, it is an art to execute the marketing strategy based on segmentation.

However, it is imperative that no matter what the value proposition is, ample physical evidence be given to the Green Consumer so as to convince them that the offering is a genuine proposition, rather than just another attempt at greenwashing. Most Green Consumers are fairly sophisticated and sceptical at the same time and they are constantly on alert against being hoodwinked into believing that something is true when it is not. They will therefore continually look for physical evidence to support all claims of "Greenness".

9

Supply Loops

Throughout this book, we have frequently used the term "supply loops" when describing supply chain models that take into a process inputs which are outputs from another process. It is now necessary to look at supply loops in more detail, as it is important for the reader to gain a good understanding of what supply loops are, how they are configured, what their benefits are, and how important they are for the overall Green Supply Chains.

The term "supply loop" refers to those parts of an overall supply chain that recycle or reuse the materials, products, or by-products from either the same supply chain or from another supply chain. While most supply chains, when looked at in detail, have some supply loops built into them, it is fair to say that use of the words "supply loops" can be usefully expanded far more than is presently the case.

No two supply chains are alike, and no two supply loops will be exactly the same. Every organization configures its supply chain to suit its current needs and uses supply loops when it becomes cost effective to do so. However cost is only ever one part, as cost and service and cost and value are two high-level examples of tradeoffs that go beyond taking only "single" cost views. With Green Supply Chains, then, the lack of knowledge and the lack of continual and relentless thinking to work hard towards properly configuring Greener supply chains will ultimately lead to an acceptance of the status quo and maintaining the current thinking, making little use of the supply loop concept.

9.1 Examples of Supply Loops

Below we give three common examples of supply loops that are frequently encountered in the industrial supply chains. These include

- a manufacturing process supply loop
- a forward logistics supply loop
- a forward and reverse logistics supply loop.

9.1.1   Manufacturing Process Supply Loops Examples

In this kind of supply loop the by-products of one process will be input to the next process and so on, until the by-product or the waste cannot be reused in any way, the waste being then finally disposed of in an environmentally friendly way. The industries where these types of supply loop are encountered are numerous, and include, among others, chemicals, fast moving consumer goods, petroleum products, pharmaceutical, agri-business etc.

Of course, each industry, indeed each organization, will have its own characteristics in terms of how the supply loops are configured and used.

We will look at Figure 9.1 as a generic representation of a supply loop.

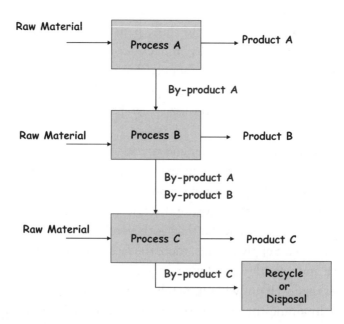

Figure 9.1: *Manufacturing process supply loop structure*

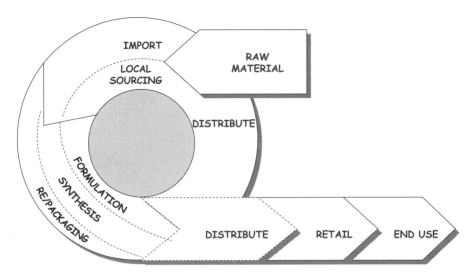

Figure 9.2: *Forward logistics supply loop structure*

9.1.2 Forward Logistics Supply Loops Example

These are simple supply loops where the output from one process is then distributed either directly as an end product, or is further repackaged, reformulated, or taken through other value added steps, in order to make it usable to the end customers.

Here, a considerable amount of manufacturing is avoided by making use of an end product from another process which is primarily aimed at a completely different application. Most of the examples of this type of supply loop are in fast moving consumer goods or the chemicals industry.

Again the examples will vary for each organization and it is also common to see combinations of this type of supply loop with the other two types of supply loop. Figure 9.2 has been adapted from a case study in a speciality chemicals business.

9.1.3 Forward and Reverse Logistics Supply Loops Example

These are integrated supply loops with multitiered structures and multidirectional movements of rejects from one process, that attempts to move it, for use as an input into another process.

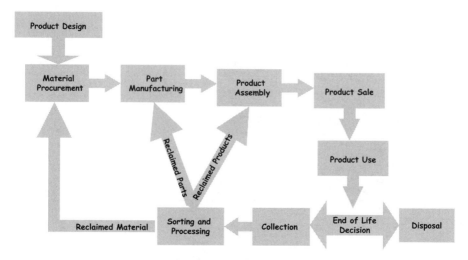

Figure 9.3: *Forward and reverse logistics supply loop*

More and more industrial organizations are now starting to think along these lines because of the focus on Green Supply Chains across the industrial spectrum and the cost pressures. It almost always pays to ask the question, *"What could we be discarding as a by-product that is material that we need as an input into our process?"* With some lateral thinking and following up the resulting ideas with preliminary analysis and some investigation, it is quite possible to come up with some real applications of supply loops to create loops within loops with the overall supply chain.

A continual improvement mindset is essential in order to create an optimized multitiered/directional supply loop. Rarely is such a supply chain created in a single iteration (see Figure 9.3).

As new technologies become available, as newer applications are discovered for the by-products, and as new sources of materials are discovered, the supply chain needs to be continually reviewed and realigned in order to keep it at its most environmentally sound level.

9.2 Components of Supply Loops

The above three examples show that whilst each supply loop will be different from others, there are still some commonly encountered elements among most supply loops:

- Circular supply chain: at least for some parts of the supply chain.
- Reverse logistics: a major decision is required to recycle or reuse at some step in the supply chain.
- Disassembly lines: these have well developed processes and infrastructure to facilitate disassembly and/or redeployment of by-products or end-of-life products.

9.2.1 Circular Supply Chain

Circular supply chains are those where the output (for example as a by-product, a residual, or the actual product) from one process is utilized as the key input for a totally different process.

In this context it is important to distinguish between the many differences in terminology. We have seen the terms in Table 9.1 overleaf and many other terms used in a loose manner, sometimes interchangeably. Clearly, there is difference, not only in the shades of meaning, but also in the processes, equipment, infrastructure, and the outcomes.

Examples of all of these abound, but none of these have yet been used to the extent that is possible. Also the amount of energy and time used on each of the processes will vary tremendously, therefore leading to varying cost outcomes for the Green Supply Chain. It is clear that in this context there is a matter of degree of change that is a key determinant of the type of process (see Figure 9.4 on page 171).

9.2.2 Reverse Logistics

Reverse logistics, as the name suggests, is the movement of goods in the reverse order, from destination to origin, to enable reprocessing, remanufacturing, repairing, reusing, recycling, disassembling, or disposing. The term "goods", used here, stands for raw material, work in progress/subassembly's inventory, and also finished goods. The term "destination" stands for manufacturing plant for raw material, warehouses for inventory, and the consumers, retailers, or distributors of the finished goods.

The reverse logistics process also includes the management and the sale of surplus as well as any returned goods, equipment, and machines (this is often called Returns Management). As logistics is related to bringing the product to the customers, then reverse logistics is related to returning the

Table 9.1 *Terminology variations in circular supply chains*

Term	Explanation
Remanufactured	A full manufacturing process is carried out to produce goods using a combination of material that is new and from used goods. For example, mobile phones and other similar goods are remanufactured from parts of returns combined with new parts.
Reconditioned	Total overhaul of the product but not full manufacturing process. The basic structure remains the same but the worn out or failed parts are removed and replaced with new ones and oil is replaced then with reassembly and inspection. For example Bosch recondition machines and tools and sell them for a discounted price with warranty.
Refurbished	Most of the structure of the product is untouched, the product gets its "as new" condition via cosmetic changes such as minor repairs, new paints, cleaning, removal of stains, scratches etc. For example, the refurbishing of furniture.
Re-process	The process is repeated because the previous run of the process did not result in desired outcomes; in effect this is the rerunning of a production process.
Reclaim	Reclaiming the oils or fluids after a process so that these reclaimed oils or fluids can be used elsewhere in the same process or a new process.
Repair	Replacement of faulty or failed parts to make the product usable again.
Recycle	Collection of used or faulty products so that they can be used again, either in the same form or in a different form. For example, Nike collects worn out athletic shoes at any Reuse-A-Shoe collection centre or shoe drive event. At their recycling facilities these shoes are sorted, shredded, and processed into three types of raw material; rubber from the outsole, foam from the midsole, and fabric fibres from the upper, collectively called Nike Grind. Nike Grind is then used in playgrounds, running tracks, and basketball courts.
Reuse	Use the product again with or without any alteration, e.g. packaging, totes, and pallets Another example reuse of the white goods was launched at Daventry District Council in England. With this initiative the council collects broken and discarded white goods such as washing machines, dishwashers, etc. as part of household waste collection. They are then checked and repaired, and distributed to low-income families who need these items but cannot afford them.
Disposal	Disposal to landfill after only non-salvageable material is left.
Disassembly	Removal of parts from used products without damaging the parts. These parts are later reused or recycled, the rest of the product being either recycled or disposed.

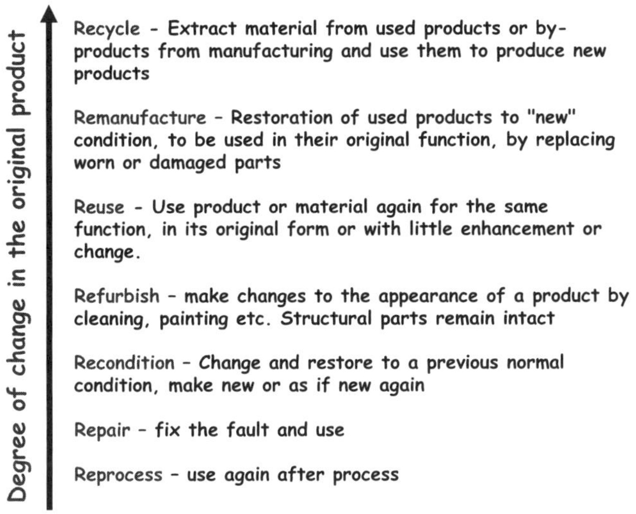

Degree of change in the original product

Recycle - Extract material from used products or by-products from manufacturing and use them to produce new products

Remanufacture – Restoration of used products to "new" condition, to be used in their original function, by replacing worn or damaged parts

Reuse - Use product or material again for the same function, in its original form or with little enhancement or change.

Refurbish – make changes to the appearance of a product by cleaning, painting etc. Structural parts remain intact

Recondition – Change and restore to a previous normal condition, make new or as if new again

Repair – fix the fault and use

Reprocess – use again after process

Figure 9.4: *Circular supply chains – Degree of change*

used, faulty, or unwanted product from the customer to the provider. The customer here can be the end user, retailer, or distributor depending upon the return policies. The provider can be the retailer, distributor, or producer depending upon where and how the product was bought and again the return policies. However it is not just returns management – it also includes returns prevention, gate keeping, collection, disposal, and other end-of-life concerns.

Reverse logistics is therefore a very important part of supply loops and it is discussed in more detail next.

Reverse logistics activities

Efficient "gate keeping" is of prime importance in reverse logistics. It is the point of entry of goods into the reverse logistics process and it requires the careful screening of returned goods to see whether they are defective, damaged, or unwarranted. Generous return policies have been found to draw in customers and increase sales, but they can also lead to abuse by the customer if they are not handled properly.

Once the goods are returned to an organization then various disposal options are available. The adapted case is shown in Figure 9.5 overleaf. These are some of the many options available depending on the nature of

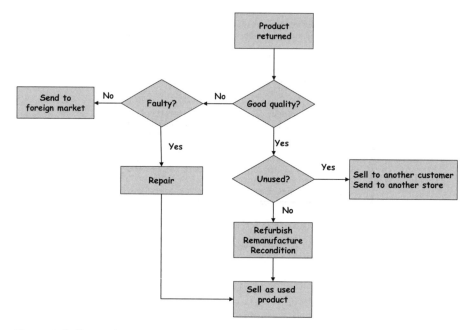

Figure 9.5: *Reverse logistics*

the business, kinds of good offered to the market, and end user characteristics. There are many reasons for return of goods, for example, faulty goods or channel overload – after stocktaking when retailers/resellers may return goods to the suppliers as they are deemed to be outdated products.

In this example, the product can be returned to the supplier for a full refund, it may be resold to a different customer, or it may be sold through an outlet store if it has not been used.

There are other options:

- If the quality is not good, then it can be sold on to another foreign market where lower quality products are acceptable.
- If a used product has some working life left, then an organization can choose to recondition, refurbish, or remanufacture the product before selling it directly or selling it to an organization which performs such activities.
- If the product is faulty then it will be repaired and resold.
- If the product is not functional and cannot be used in any way, then an appropriate cost effective disposal method with minimal environmental implication is adopted.

Before sending goods away for disposal, then the following checks should be made:

- Any usable materials that can be reclaimed will be reclaimed, e.g. packaging, totes, and pallets. Broken totes and pallets can be refurbished and reused many times before a time comes that they are beyond repair; when this happens they are then disposed of.
- Any recyclable materials will be removed.
- Anything remaining will be disposed of, for example to a landfill.

Types of returns

As shown in Figure 9.6 the returns that an organization receives are either from supply chain partners or from consumers. As shown below, there are various reasons for returns.

Challenges with reverse logistics; retailer–producer conflict

Managing returns is not easy as both retailer and producer activities are driven by different objectives. Disagreements between a retailer and the

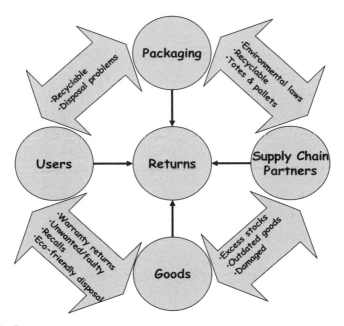

Figure 9.6: *Returns management*

producer could be related to value of product, condition of product, or when to show the return. The retailer may want the full credit for the returned item but the producer may have reason not to refund in full. They might disagree on the state in which the product reached the producer.

If the producer gets a damaged product, then they may believe that the retailer sent the damaged product, whereas the retailer may argue that it was sent in perfect condition and got damaged on the way. Also retailers would want to get the refund on the product immediately, whereas producers may want to credit returns at a later date.

Inefficient handling of returns

Many organizations have resources allocated to forward logistics but not to reverse logistics. First of all they do not have good gate keeping and then when the product is returned, it is not known what to do with it, whether for example, it should go to repairs, recycle, or landfill.

Organizations will often not have enough resources allocated to returns and those people allocated to returns may not be trained well and the decision rules may not be made clear. So employees often take longer to make decisions and as a result the reverse logistics cycle often takes longer.

Information systems

Lack of a good information system is a common problem that organizations face in the execution of reverse logistics. Few organizations have an automated return process and there are not many good reverse logistics information systems available, the first priority of most organizations being to build a core IT system where reverse logistics is not part of that core. Reverse logistics systems have to be very flexible and operate both externally between organizations and internally across many functions of the same organization. Developing such a system which interfaces between all the different systems involved is therefore very complex and difficult to develop and then integrate with the many existing individual core systems

Integrated supply chain system

There are not yet many integrated supply chain systems which can track the movement of goods as they move backwards through the channel.

Frequently, for these reasons, within many organizations reverse logistics is then relegated to the position of an afterthought in supply chain planning, with onerous results.

9.2.3 Disassembly Lines

One of the major innovations of the late twentieth century that led to heavy interest in Green Supply Chains was disassembly lines. Similar to assembly lines in nature, these are used to strip out usable parts, components, and/or material from products which have reached the end of their life cycle stage and they can do this in a systematic and cost effective manner.

Industrial engineers have now worked with fairly complex disassembly line models to create proper sequencing and line balancing in order to maximize output. The sequence and the line balance would be very different to those for the assembly line for the same product. Indeed there are now a variety of disassembly systems which either disassemble to order, or utilize just-in-time principles for the disassembly of products.

However, changes in nature or in the configuration of products lead to complication in disassembly lines which then need to be rebalanced and sequenced frequently. Moreover, the nature of the end-of-life products is often one where there is frequent variation in the quality of the material presented for disassembly. This high variability leads in turn to high variability of processing time and makes management, using, for example, statistical process control or Six Sigma, very difficult. Furthermore, the process of disassembly may require extreme heat, force, or other destructive elements, making it harder to configure and manage the process.

9.3 Drivers of Supply Loops

9.3.1 Return Policy and Competitive Pressure

Return policies in major retail chains have initiated a drive towards the better management of reverse logistics and hence a drive towards supply loops. On one hand, the returns help to pull in customers and encourage them to overspend, but on the other hand, they create the reverse logistics burden.

Faced with reverse logistics' massive costs, some organizations have now started to take stern steps to curb the number of returns. For example, most organizations still give a full refund on returned goods within a certain number of days; but if the product is returned after that predetermined period, then instead of issuing a full refund for the product, a credit note is issued. Other retailers will take returns on malfunctioning goods up to a certain number of months, but after the predetermined period the customers are then required to contact the manufacturers directly. A variable picture therefore, as this is all being frequently driven by specific countries' consumer legislation.

However, these customer service pressures pose a challenge, for example when the steps are too aggressive and the competitors have generous return policies. Usually with generous return policies the entire burden on returns falls upon the manufacturers and can turn into "Return Abuse" as the consumer shares the generous return policy with the retailer, and can therefore return anything to the retailer. The retailer and wholesaler may then return it back up the supply chain to the manufacturer, who is often then left to take on most of the risk for the returns.

However, with the growing trend of offshore manufacturing by contract manufacturers, the whole area of returns management and resulting supply loops is being redefined continuously.

9.3.2 Corporate Social Responsibility

Corporate Social Responsibility (CSR) means running a business in a way that has minimum impact on humans, animals, and environment. Government regulations, competitive pressures, corporate image, and increasing consumer awareness are the main drivers behind growing corporate social responsibility. While there are growing external pressures that force companies to be more and more responsible, some organizations use their supply loop capabilities for philanthropic reasons – for example, the Hannadowns programme developed by Hanna Andersson, a $50 million direct retailer from Portland, USA. Here, as the Hanna Anderson clothes will last beyond the needs of a growing child, instead of throwing away the clothes after use, customers were asked to mail back their children's Hanna Andersson clothes. These were then distributed to children in need, with customers who returned the clothes being given 20% off the sale price of new Hanna Andersson clothes. This programme was very successful with the returns being distributed to schools, homeless shelters, and other charities.

9.3.3 Customer and Channel Relationships

Supply loops help to improve channel relationships. While good channel relationships are important in every industry, this is particularly so in those industries where the products become obsolete very quickly, for example in auto consumer electronics. If the products returns are not in place then inventories at dealers will build up and funds will be tied up in obsolete inventories instead of in new products. Most dealers are family-based businesses and have limited funds and very basic inventory management systems. If the funds are tied up in inventories that are not selling then they will not invest in new products.

In such cases a generous return allowance from an organization will help to remove any old and outdated goods from dealers who can continually present a fresh product range to the end customer. Hence, the manufacturer has an incentive to structure supply loops in order to ultimately service the end user better. With fresh inventories a higher price can be charged and hence supply loops can also protect the margins. This helps to develop and grow good customer and channel relationships, increase loyalty, and improve customer satisfaction.

9.3.4 Legislation

Similar to all other Green Supply Chain efforts, legislation is playing a positive contributory role in the drive towards supply loops. As the avenues for the disposal of waste become more limited, organizations then have to search for better and more cost effective ways by utilizing the by-products and residuals.

9.3.5 Disposal Issues

Landfill fees are increasing; indeed it is becoming extremely difficult to dispose of hazardous waste at any cost. As a result, organizations have to search for better ways of using the by-products and residuals, and supply loops offer innovative, creative, and cost effective ways of doing so.

9.3.6 Asset Recovery Drive

Recapturing value and recovering assets are strategic to most organizations these days. Many organizations are finding the substantial proportion of their bottom line margins are the outcome of their asset recovery programmes. Materials extracted from discarded products, which otherwise would have been disposed of, are essentially free and hence add up to profit.

9.4 Benefits of Supply Loops

9.4.1 Waste Reduction

Waste reduction is one of the main objectives of supply loops. Whether this is found as a result of intra-process, inter-process, within a supply chain or across supply chains, then the main thrust of supply loops will be to keep the waste produced by activities to a minimum and hence reduce the environmental impact.

9.4.2 Use and Reuse of By-Products

The use and reuse of by-products also help to maximize the utilization of material with one process or manufacturing cycle, and also to maximize waste reduction. As mentioned before, the by-products can then be used in the manufacturing of a different product in the same plant or in the same supply chain or in a totally different supply chain. Sometimes all by-products can be put to use, whilst at other times, only one or two of the by-products can be used and the remainder will go through the waste processing or disposal process.

9.4.3 Reduced Costs

Use of recycled material helps to reduce the total cost of a manufacturing process. In addition, recycling of materials reduces the cost of disposal. We have already discussed this lowered cost due to the reduction in the manufacturing footprint and in the product requirements. This is actually the primary reason why supply loops have been very successful in almost all applications.

9.5 Moving towards Supply Loops

Moving towards supply loops is essentially a creative process and following, therefore, are some guidelines designed to assist organizations who are embarking on the journey.

9.5.1 Start Small

The magnitude of an envisaged task is perhaps the biggest obstacle facing managers embarking on this journey. We suggest here that the answer to the question of, "How do you eat an elephant?" is, one bite at a time.

There are many reasons for this "break it down into small parts" tactic, the main reason being that this is a creative process which is also a highly accretive process, building on its past success. That also means there will be several iterations, which should be expected and welcomed by the change agents. After all, every journey has to start with just one step.

9.5.2 Hypotheses Generation, Testing and Confirmation

Gather a team of experts from various departments and functions within the organization and use a brainstorming session to generate hypotheses on supply loops. During these sessions answer some basic questions such as:

- Who can utilize my by-products or residuals?
- Whose by-products or residuals can we utilize?

Keep track of all the ideas generated, and test these ideas with data. On conceptual confirmation of some of these hypotheses, next run trials and tests in order to confirm they work in practice before rolling them out.

9.5.3 Utilize Technologies

There is a lot of technology available which can be deployed in the right manner. Whether it is reverse logistics, or disassembly lines, or recycling, the level of sophistication is quite high. Most companies are either unaware of the full extent of the technological sophistication or think that it does not apply to their business due to a variety of reasons. We contend that this is not necessarily the case. Organizations must continually use the best available cost effective technology in order to create ever better supply loops within their Green Supply Chains.

9.5.4 Learn from Competitors, Suppliers, Customers, and Others

This is the best way to diffuse knowledge within supply chains and organizations. Organizations must actively keep an open mind so that they can learn from external parties who are already successfully configuring supply loops in similar situations.

9.5.5 Keep Expanding and Continual Improvement

This is a corollary to point 9.5.1. Having started small, it is imperative that the full benefit of the accretive nature of the process is taken. That means that companies should always be looking for better ways of creating more and bigger supply loops within their Green Supply Chains. That will help companies get the full benefit of supply loops and remain on the leader board of the Green Supply Chain players.

PART 5

Carbon Management

GREEN SUPPLY CHAINS			
GREEN SUPPLY CHAIN PLANNING	**GREEN PROCUREMENT**	**GREEN SUPPLY CHAIN EXECUTION**	**CARBON MANAGEMENT**

1. Life Cycle Engineering
2. S&OP
• Demand Planning
• Supply Planning
  ○ Production Planning
  ○ Inventory Planning
	• Collaboration
	• Incentive Alignment
	• Supplier Development
	• Energy-Efficient Procurement
	• Sustainable Sourcing
		• Green Production
		• Green Logistics
		• Green Packaging
		• Green Marketing
		• Supply Loops
			• Carbon Footprint Minimization

Green Supply Migration Strategy

Green Supply Chain Continuous Improvement

Green Supply Chain Performance Evaluation

10

Carbon Footprint Minimization across the Supply Chain

Perhaps no other topic in Green Supply Chains has been responsible for more carbon emissions than the topic of carbon management!

There are multitudes of papers, research reports, and surveys on this topic. Indeed it could be said that this is where the rubber hits the road for most organizations. With emerging regulations, then all organizations will be eventually affected by carbon management, therefore organizations are starting to sit up and take notice. Indeed, due to the amount as well as the quality of information available on this topic, it has become somewhat of a mystery for many in the business world.

We will therefore take a simple approach in this chapter in order to demystify the topic as much as possible so that we can sponsor a wider understanding; after all, with understanding comes action and the prime purpose of this book is to prompt action.

For many people the terms carbon management and Green Supply Chains are synonymous; however, rather obviously, the two are different. Carbon management, though a vast subject in its own right, is just one small subset of the overall Green Supply Chain framework. For example, an organization can outsource most of its carbon producing activities to locations in jurisdictions outside the regulatory purview of its own country. With free trade it may then reap the full rewards of such outsourcing, but without bearing any responsibility for the carbon impact of those outsourced activities. The obvious Green Supply Chain answer is then that the organization at the demand end of a supply chain should take on the full responsibility for the carbon impact of its entire supply chain.

What then is carbon management, and why is it important?

While most people are informed about the current debate on this topic, a historical perspective is important in order to understand the future regulatory direction. Indeed we believe there will be several rounds of new regulations in the coming years, with both international and national legislation. This regulatory evolution is likely to be a result of a mix of historical events with future economic and environmental policy at an international level.

It has long been recognized that the market price of the goods and services did not include the cost of what are known as externalities. This covers things such as polluting the air, effluents discharged into the water, noisy disturbance to the people living around the manufacturing location, traffic and other disruption to the people affected by production of those goods and services. It is impossible for any organization to find everyone who is adversely affected by its efforts to produce goods and services and to then compensate them. Indeed the queue will be a long one if any organization ever attempts to do so.

However in 2008/9, the problems with externalities were seen as one of the key failures of what many economists saw as an otherwise perfect mechanism to organize human activities through "The Market". The best market-based means of dealing with the problem of externalities was to internalize them through a trading mechanism. This would allow the free markets to allocate capital and organize human endeavour in the most efficient manner. However, as this book was being written many free market economists and bankers were in hiding. Many organizations (or industries) now existed solely because of state support/interference.

In such a scenario, at some time in the future, then we can see that policy makers are going to realize that a free market-based solution to the problem of externalities may not indeed be the most efficient. With this realization, there will surely be another round of national regulations and international negotiation to combat the problems of greenhouse gases and global warming.

It took nearly 20 years for the current set of suggested regulatory frameworks to take hold; however, whilst the shape and form of the next generation of regulations remains to be seen, we suspect it will come much more quickly and will perhaps be a lot more onerous for organizations.

In simple terms the current set of suggested regulations sees that carbon management has four key principles:

1. Carbon measurement
2. Carbon minimization
3. Carbon offsetting
4. Carbon trading.

The first two of these fundamental principles are at the core of the reduction of greenhouse gases (GHG) and are likely to remain unchanged. The last two are likely to see several iterations of negotiations as economic and political situations change on the geopolitical front.

Smart organizations will however have to be equally well prepared on all four key principles. However, in this book we will focus intensely on the first two fundamental principles for several reasons.

Firstly, they are the core principles that focus on tackling the problem head on, rather than on either apportioning blame for the problem or on dividing the spoils from funding directed at mitigating the problem.

Secondly, they are also inviolate principles which will remain a key underpinning of increasingly stringent regulations that are likely to evolve in future. In other words, the carbon problem needs to be addressed with or without trading or offsetting mechanisms.

If all countries in the world cannot agree on the currently proposed trading or offsetting mechanisms at Copenhagen, then a more direct intervention will be seen as necessary. Alternatively, if they are seen as inadequate to tackle the problem, then a more direct regulatory or fiscal control will be required. In either case the policy is likely to evolve much further beyond its current state in the not too distant future.

For our purposes, to fit in with the overall Green Supply Chains theme, we will use the slightly adapted model given below.

As shown in Figure 10.1 overleaf, carbon management, this is a cycle of four steps: (1) carbon measurement, (2) carbon minimization, (3) carbon monitoring, and (4) carbon reporting.

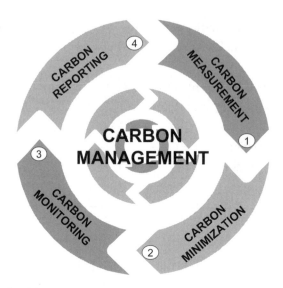

Figure 10.1: *Carbon Management*

10.1 Carbon Measurement

For the first time in human history we have undertaken to do something which is seemingly impossible, to measure all the carbon gases that emerge out of all the activities happening on the planet. Some of these activities occur naturally, such as livestock breathing in the paddock. However most of them are a result of some industrial endeavour, for which examples abound.

At the global level, it is theoretically possible to take every emission of greenhouse gases and allocate it to an individual product or service. This would result in demonstrating the carbon footprint of various products and services. Indeed many reputable think tanks and universities have done such an exercise and the results provide valuable information in making tradeoffs between those products and services which will provide a similar utility or satisfaction to consumers.

However, when we focus on individual products and on individual organizations, then the picture becomes rather more complex as several key questions must be answered, very precisely, before we can establish the carbon footprint.

10.1.1 Where Does the Organization's Boundary Start and End?

The first question that needs to be answered is "Where does the organization's boundary start and end?"

Obviously, if we are measuring the carbon footprint of an organization then we do need to understand the extent of its coverage. This, in itself, is nearly an impossible question to answer as in today's world of global trading, almost all large organizations will subcontract production and also outsource some of their own activities to third party service providers. So should these be included or excluded from their carbon footprint?

The contractual arrangements, the degree of control, the geographical locations of the outsourced activities, and most other criteria on which the decision to include or exclude can be based, will all vary greatly. In such circumstances it frequently becomes a meaningless exercise to measure the carbon footprint of just one organization. For example when Pepsi wanted to measure the carbon produced for making a carton of orange juice and it had to include:

- the cost of the activities it undertook itself, such as squeezing juice out of the oranges;
- the carbon produced for growing the oranges;
- the carbon produced for manufacturing the cartons;
- the carbon produced for transportation of empty cartons and oranges to its facility;
- the carbon produced for transportation of full cartons from its facilities to the distribution centres and further on to the retail outlets.

Most of these activities were obviously undertaken by third party providers, such as growers of oranges, contract manufacturers of cartons, transporters, and warehouse owners etc. A holistic view would include the carbon produced by all these service providers as well, which is the obvious answer.

But then we arrive at the carbon footprint of the entire supply chain rather than the carbon footprint of the organization, in this case Pepsi. The footprint belongs as much to the retailer who sells it, such as Wal-Mart, or to the grower who grows the oranges in Florida, or to the contract manufacturer who provides the cartons or juices the oranges for Pepsi.

This is why we emphasize that the most accurate and holistic way to measure the carbon footprint is to measure it for an entire supply chain.

10.1.2 Who is Responsible for Measurement of Carbon in the Entire Supply Chain?

The second question that needs to be answered is who is responsible for measurement of carbon in the entire supply chain?

Is it the party who owns the brand, say Pepsi in the above example, or the party who has the most influence on the supply chain, such as Wal-Mart? Or should it be the party who creates the most greenhouse gases such as the manufacturer of the fertilizer used for growing oranges, or the party who stands to gain the most from measurement of carbon, for example from offsets, trading, or publicity?

There are no obvious answers to these questions. The question is so difficult to answer because we believe that unless all the organizations in the entire supply chain take responsibility for the measurement and the accountability for minimization of carbon footprint, then the efforts are likely to result in mere greenwashing.

In practical terms, it seems clear that the organization which has the most influence over the entire supply chain should have the responsibility for taking on the leadership for carbon measurement and its minimization. After all with influence (and power) must come the duty (to use it for greater good). Organizations that do not recognize their influence, or refuse to exercise it, will soon find out that their influence is waning as consumers place their trust and custom elsewhere.

10.1.3 How to Measure the Carbon Footprint?

The third key question here is how to measure the carbon footprint? One would expect this to be a relatively straightforward scientific methodology, with one single answer for each activity. Alas, the world is not so simple. There are now a multitude of methodologies, each with their own pros and cons, which are deployed to measure the carbon emissions.

In Table 10.1, we highlight some of the various carbon emissions calculation methodologies currently available and no doubt there are many more available and others being developed. The impact of using different

Table 10.1: *Carbon measurement methodologies*

Organization's name	Description	Website
Carbon Footprint Business Calculator	Provide a comprehensive proforma enabling you to collect all Footprint's emissions. Experienced environmental consultants appraise your footprint, using traceable metrics (e.g. DEFRA), and deliver an easy to digest summary report to you.	www.carbonfootprint. com
Emission Statement	All emission statement audits follow the GHG Protocol corporate reporting guidelines, adhere to ISO Standard 14064-1, and are National Greenhouse and Energy System compliant. We follow a systematic approach to the Carbon Audit Process and its corresponding Audit Outputs, conducting a detailed calculation of the emissions associated with energy consuming activities at a business facility or across a full supply chain.	www.emissionstatement. com.au
Carbon Trust	Have developed the online calculator to help your organization calculate its carbon footprint, and the basic footprint indicator provides a rough estimate of your organization's carbon emissions based on your organization's energy bill and sector.	www.carbontrust.co.uk
Carbon Credit Environmental Services	No information about the methodology used for carbon calculation.	www.getcarboncreditco2. com
Carbon Conscious	No information about the methodology used for carbon calculation.	www.carbonconscious. com.au
Native Energy	No information about the methodology used for carbon calculation.	www.nativeenergy.com
Carbon UK	Have used the conversion data issued by DEFRA but have tried to make it a simple but accurate calculator.	www.carbonuk.co.uk
CarbonMe	No information about the methodology used for carbon calculation.	www.carbonme.org

Table 10.1: *Continued*

Organization's name	Description	Website
Pure the Clean Planet Trust	The PURE for Business calculator (currently an Excel spreadsheet) has been developed to allow you to easily determine your business footprint, answering a small number of questions related to your operations.	www.puretrust.org.uk
SAI Global	No information about the methodology used for carbon calculation.	www.saiglobal.com
The Green Office	The Office Footprint Calculator™ is primarily based on data published by United Nations agencies and the Intergovernmental Panel on Climate Change. Averages for US office resource consumption are derived using datasets provided by the US Department of Transportation, US Department of Energy, Lawrence Berkeley Laboratory, Oak Ridge National Laboratory, and other industry groups such as Special Coffee Association of America.	www.thegreenoffice.com
Verteego Carbon	Verteego Carbon is based on methodology Bilan Carbon ADEME as well as the GHG Protocol and makes it possible to identify the CO_2 emissions related to the consumption of energy, the production, waste, transport, the real estate, and the life cycle of products.	www.verteegocarbon.com
The Carbon Neutral Organization	The most widely-accepted measurement protocols are the WRI/WBCSD Greenhouse Gas Protocol (www.ghgprotocol.org) and ISO 14064. The Greenhouse Gas Protocol has been in existence for longer than ISO 14064 and is used by most large corporations – it is also the standard that we use for client assessments.	www.carbonneutral.com

Table 10.1: *Continued*

Organization's name	Description	Website
Terra Pass	A TerraPass Carbon Balanced Business advisor will guide you through the entire process. We'll analyse your business' carbon footprint using information you provide about your business' energy use, travel and commuting. You will then receive a report of your CO_2 emissions from each area of your business, which in turn helps you identify ways to reduce your carbon footprint.	www.terrapass.com
Renewable Choice Energy	Business Carbon Calculator offers a first-look GHG audit to help you meet your corporate responsibility and sustainability goals.	www.renewablechoice. com
Carbon Advice Group	No information about the methodology used for carbon calculation.	www.carbonadvicegroup. com

carbon calculator methodologies was shown very clearly in a chart that compared the results of various methodologies on a simple task of producing a glass of beer, where with the different carbon calculations, the resultant emissions varied by as much as 300%.

The easiest – and wrong – way of showing progress would be to measure by one methodology at the beginning and use another, less onerous one at the end. Perhaps some organizations are already resorting to such greenwashing in order to make claims that get them the most publicity. Needless to say, however, real progress will only be achieved by using the most suitable methodology over a time period of sustained effort where carbon emissions are shown to have been reduced.

The common theme across all methodologies is to create a detailed understanding of activities and their carbon emissions in order to add it up. Some of the more esoteric ones take short cuts which may not always be appropriate, but the short cuts do serve a purpose as they simplify the calculations and hence the discussion. For this reason, each organization must first establish the most appropriate methodology for its purpose, then work to customize it and use it (see Table 10.1). Most importantly, comparisons over time and space will only be valid if there is consistency in measurement methodology and in ensuring that this is maintained. This should always be borne in mind while making any comparisons.

At the individual product level, this supply chain approach has the potential to find significant emissions reduction opportunities and give large financial benefits by reducing the carbon footprint of the product. It can also help individual organizations to understand the carbon emissions across their supply chains and allow them to prioritize areas where further reductions in emissions can be achieved.

It can ultimately help all organizations to make better informed decisions by considering the costs and liabilities that exist whenever carbon emissions are generated in the supply chain, such as in product manufacturing, purchasing, distribution logistics, and product development.

As consumer attitudes change, it also allows forward thinking organizations to develop low carbon products to capture new markets and generate higher profits over time. This is the next step in the evolution of efforts to reduce carbon emissions and mitigate climate change.

10.2 Carbon Minimization

The key thrust of carbon management is to minimize the carbon emissions throughout the entire supply chain. This carbon minimization can include efforts such as emissions reduction, abatement, sequestering, and offsetting.

Reducing the carbon footprint of products across the supply chain is the first obvious step for organizations to take. For those organizations that recognize the need to reduce energy costs, and to play their part in mitigation of climate change, then an integrated supply chain analysis is the most logical means of reducing carbon emissions. There are several key drivers for this move:

- Lack of oil fears and energy cost volatility.
- Legislation: there is a growing political drive to regulate, tax, cap, or trade the carbon emissions.
- Consumers: with the growing demand for Greener products.
- Society: with the growing demand for a cleaner world.

In a carbon constrained world, organizations will look towards ways to provide for consumer needs and wants, while emitting fewer carbon gases. Energy efficiency and low carbon energy supply will continue to play an important role, but more fundamental solutions are also needed.

Having already established that we need to measure the carbon footprint of the entire supply chain, rather than any one organization within it, we need to minimize the carbon footprint at the entire supply chain level too. (Some people also call this approach carbon life cycle analysis, CLCA, or just carbon LCA.)

Traditionally, the key driver here for organizations is for energy efficiency, with carbon management initiatives analysing the operations of single organizations or even single sites. As mentioned earlier, our holistic approach allows the full carbon footprint for the entire supply chain to be measured, minimized, monitored, and reported.

A comparison of the traditional carbon minimization approach and the Green Supply Chain approach is shown in Figures 10.2a and 10.2b.

The results of a carbon reduction project across the entire supply chain would look like Figure 10.3.

Figure 10.3 clearly shows which activities the effort towards carbon minimization should be focused on and who, in the entire supply chain, is most

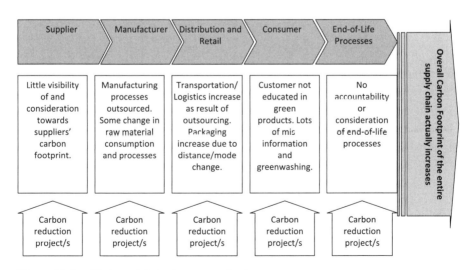

Figure 10.2a: *Carbon minimization at organization*

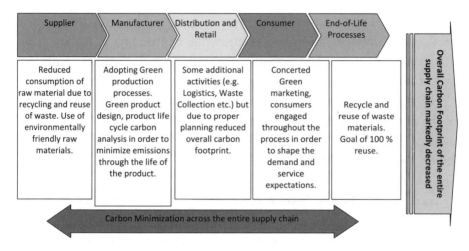

Figure 10.2b: *Carbon minimization for entire supply chain*

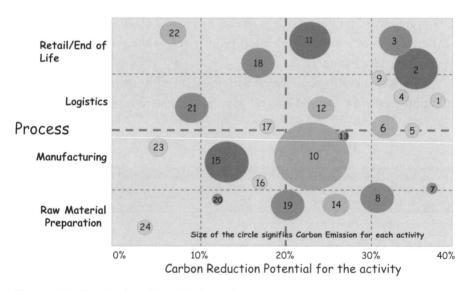

Figure 10.3: *Results of a carbon reduction project*

capable of focusing the effort. Such an effort, of course, will only be possible if all participants in the entire supply chain are totally on board with the analysis and minimization effort. This is why the party who is most influential in the entire supply chain should have the responsibility for taking leadership in the process.

10.2.1 Carbon Offsetting

Offsetting describes the practice of removing or avoiding the release of carbon dioxide emissions into the atmosphere by funding carbon projects that lead to:

- the destruction of greenhouse gas emissions;
- the prevention of their release into the atmosphere;
- the sequestration or storage of carbon dioxide in a solid material through biological or physical processes.

The Clean Air-Cool Planet and Forum for the Future believe that high quality offsets do result in genuine emission reductions, and recognize that they will play an important role in all carbon neutrality strategies. Organizations offsetting their emissions generally do this as a complementary activity to both creating a carbon footprint and implementing direct emissions reduction activities.

In practice, carbon offsets are generated as the result of a greenhouse gas emission reduction project that delivers measurable reductions in emissions through a variety of technologies, including renewable energy, converting waste gas to energy, and increased forestry. The projects create emission reductions by, for example, displacing more fossil fuel intensive activities, or by reducing the direct release of GHG (greenhouse gas) into the atmosphere.

Reducing emissions at source may require a long-term development, significant capital investment, and/or behavioural change, all of which take time. For example, an organization may want to upgrade all of its buildings to become more energy-efficient, but it may not have the capital to do so all at once. Offsetting, on the other hand, will provide short-term environmental benefits, and is an excellent way of balancing the carbon footprint that currently cannot be reduced by using only internal abatement measures.

It may then be appropriate for some organizations to develop a voluntary offsetting strategy. Carbon trading is where an organization buys credits as a way of offsetting their own carbon emissions and is associated with environmental projects that reduce emissions of carbon dioxide or other greenhouse gases around the world. For some service sector or consumer facing organizations, there may be PR and corporate social responsibility benefits from offsetting some of their emissions.

For any offsetting strategy to be successful, it is necessary that the offsets purchased are of high quality and from verified projects that create truly additional emission reductions.

10.3 Carbon Monitoring

Having measured and minimized carbon for the entire supply chain, it is still extremely important that the resultant gains made in greening supply chains are not dissipated through inadvertent changes. This means that a continual monitoring of changes is required, on a periodic basis, into the methodology or the intensity of activities in order to know the impact of these changes. Only by doing this can we be sure that the organizations and supply chains are reporting the most current information to the regulators and to the public. This is particularly important to avoid charges of green-washing for example, based on carbon reduction from one-off projects that were later reversed.

Monitoring is a relatively simple activity because all we are doing here is measuring the change from the last time the measurement was taken. It is not meant to replace those measurements which are more rigorous and are hence a less frequent activity. However, monitoring mechanisms can be easily built when the initial measurement process is initiated, as the models, the measurements, and the activities identified during the initial measurement process will all be useful for the ongoing monitoring.

10.4 Carbon Reporting

Different stakeholders have different information requirements. While the regulators may have a simple check list asking for compliance/non-compliance information, sophisticated consumers would like to know in detail about what an organization is doing in order to mitigate the climate change that has resulted from its activities.

Many corporate communications departments are still trying to find the carbon information requirements of the various stakeholders. Indeed, they are still trying to understand those various stakeholders who want to receive information about the impact on climate change as any excessive positive spin on the information will be seen as greenwashing by all but the most naïve consumers.

Many countries are now introducing, or have just introduced, legislation requiring the mandatory reporting of certain information pertaining to their greenhouse gas emissions and carbon footprint. While mandatory reporting requirements are mostly quite straightforward, organizations need to make sure that they do not breach the regulations, either by omitting to give certain mandatory information, or by the less than accurate reporting of information. Where appropriate, the measurement methodology should also be disclosed in order to mitigate any allegations of opaque reporting or greenwashing.

PART 6

Migration Strategy

GREEN SUPPLY CHAINS			
GREEN SUPPLY CHAIN PLANNING	**GREEN PROCUREMENT**	**GREEN SUPPLY CHAIN EXECUTION**	**CARBON MANAGEMENT**

1. Life Cycle Engineering
2. S&OP
• Demand Planning
 	
• Supply Planning
 	
  ○ Production Planning
 	
  ○ Inventory Planning
	• Collaboration
	
	• Incentive Alignment
	
	• Supplier Development
	
	• Energy-Efficient
		• Green Production
		
		• Green Logistics
		
		• Green Packaging
		
		• Green Marketing
		
		• Supply Loops
			• Carbon Footprint Minimization

Green Supply Chain Migration Strategy

Green Supply Chain Continuous Improvement

Green Supply Chain Performance Evaluation

11

Green Supply Chain Migration Strategy

Having discussed the components of Green Supply Chains in previous chapters we now come to the part where we discuss how to structure, manage, and implement those programmes that will take a large organization from having a traditional supply chain to creating a Green Supply Chain.

As indicated earlier, migration to Green Supply Chains will need the cooperation of all participants in the total and entire supply chain. Ideally all should work closely with each other to design products through their entire life cycle so that the carbon footprint and waste are minimized and the output is maximized. This will not only ensure the greenest possible outcome in the shortest period of time but also will minimize the cost for the output.

The key questions we are asked is *"How to gain co-operation of the supply chain partners?"* and *"How to engage them in the process in order to show them the benefits to their own businesses and to the society?"*

We advocate the use of our Efficient Green Leadership (EGL) model which we discussed briefly in Chapter 5. We now present this in more detail.

Efficient Green Leadership (EGL) model

The EGL model is a methodology devised in order to create rapid collaboration among supply chain partners for the purpose of creating, discussing, and finally adopting sensible Green Supply Chain solutions. The model facilitates open and transparent collaboration among functional teams at all levels within the organizations involved, in order to come up with the most cost effective and most environmentally effective solutions. This is because supply chains that adopt this model will now have functional teams of individuals from different companies working together who are speaking the same language, working towards common goals, and adopting the same mindset right from the beginning.

This is in a sharp contrast to the traditional supply chain mindset fostered by using only functionally driven supply chains, for example procurement driven. In Figure 11.1 below there are three organizations shown in the supply chain, whereas in fact there could be many more organizations

Figure 11.1: *Efficient Green Leadership model*

involved in the total supply chain process; however for ease and simplicity we have only shown three organizations.

The benefits of using the EGL model are a rapid dispersion of knowledge, fostering an extraordinary amount of mutual trust, ease of implementation, and the enthusiasm of the project teams. However, at the same time organizations have to watch for signs of teams becoming self-serving bureaucracies who may work more for their own good rather than for the overall purpose they set out to achieve.

So how do we go about adopting the EGL Model for creating Green Supply Chains?

Once the teams are formed and accountability and incentives are rigorously agreed upon, the rest of the effort can broadly be divided into five strategic segments:

- Process identification
- Development of system to measure performance
- Supply chain management system
- Prioritization of tasks
- Improvement procedures.

These are indicated in the Migration Strategy Framework in Figure 11.2 overleaf.

As shown below in Figure 11.3 overleaf and then explained fully, we recommend a 3×3 approach as a way forward to migrate existing supply chains to Green Supply Chains and this includes the following steps:

- Three waves of migration of three phases each.
- Each wave will be of 18+ months duration.
- Each phase will be of 6+ months duration.
- Waves help to migrate various elements of a supply chain in a steady and controlled way so that they are easy to manage, control, and improve, rather than using a "big bang" approach.
- Each supply chain should decide which components of its supply chain are to be part of each wave, based on several factors. However, we have found packaging, procurement, and logistics to be good candidates for wave one, production and marketing to be good candidates for wave two, and the rest of the components are well covered as part of wave three.

IDENTIFY PROCESS	DEVELOP PERFORMANCE MEASUREMENT	MEASURE THE SUPPLY CHAIN SYSTEM	PRIORITIZE AND DEVELOP ALTERNATIVES	ESTABLISH IMPROVEMENT INITIATIVES
Procurement and Supply	• Planning • Training • Implementation	• Mixed contracts with more profit in less consumption • Involving suppliers in decision-making process	• Prioritize the process steps in order of increasing the performance • Develop alternatives for performance improvement	• Organizational alignment towards continuous improvement • Involvement of suppliers/vendors in key decision-making process • Regular audit and performance review • Clear communication between suppliers and logistics providers • Aligned incentives
Production	• Environmental cost accounting • Life cycle costing • Process design • Life cycle engineering	• Categorizing and identifying environmental costs • Developing most economical and environmentally friendly process	• Achieve process improvement through conducting interviews with process personnel and suppliers	
Packaging	• Resource minimization • Reduced hazards • Recycling and energy recovery	• Financial savings • Local and global environmental benefits	• Usage of reusable and recyclable packaging • Customer collaboration • Waste reduction	
Product Sales and Marketing	• Creating awareness among consumers for Green products	• Consumers buying Green products	• Making eco-friendly products as prime organization objective	
Logistics	• Mode of transport used • 3PL performance evaluation	• More use of rail transport • 3PL collaboration	• Logistics optimization • Use of clean fuel • Optimized truck loads	
Product End-of-life Management	• Product design • Supply loop effectiveness	• Reprocessing end-of-life products	• Collecting waste material for economic value recovery	

Figure 11.2: *Migration strategy framework*

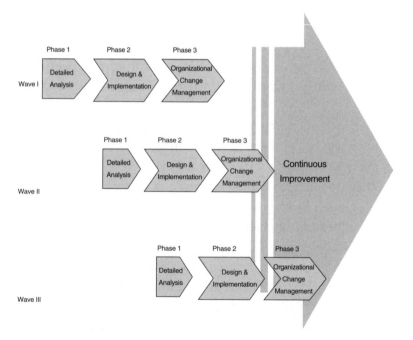

Figure 11.3: *Recommended approach for migration towards Greener Supply Chains*

11.1 Phase I, Detailed Analysis

The first stage and phase of the migration process involves a rigorous analysis that will kick-start the migration process. It formulates collaboration procedures among various stakeholders and needs the support of top management from each player/partner across the supply chain (see Figure 11.4 overleaf). These are two of the key hurdles while implementing Green practices.

Migrating towards Green Supply Chains requires management commitment from key stakeholders in setting up objectives and continually improving them; these will need the following:

- Visible management commitment, effective communication, and training to ensure environmental protection, and the safety and health of employees and the community.
- Measurable objectives that move the organization towards a Green Supply Chain in a balanced manner.
- Recognition by all participants in the supply chain, their employees, and subcontractors that a Green Supply Chain is one of the top management priorities of the business and is not just lip service or a PR exercise to keep the environmentalists happy, or to hoodwink the customers.
- Starting with compliance with all the applicable legislation, regulations, and relevant industry standards and then moving beyond compliance into setting up Green Supply Chain standards for the competing supply chains.
- Providing appropriate resources to implement the policy, including making it available to the public and employees.
- Involving all the departments that are potentially affected.
- Determining and formulating the main objectives and targets.
- Appointing a person with leadership capabilities responsible for developing and implementing the programme.
- Making available the technical and economic means required and preventing interference with other projects.
- Promoting relations with environmental institutions and authorities.
- Monitoring and evaluating progress.

In the next step, the teams will analyse the environmental impact of each process chosen for analysis during that phase; they will need to:

MANAGEMENT COMMITMENT AND SUPPORT	ANALYSE CURRENT PROCESES TO SELECT MIGRATION PROSPECTS	FUTURE STATE AND GAP ANALYSIS

- Buy-in from all stakeholders to migrate to Green Supply Chain

- Formulate Green Supply Chain Management objectives, and communicate these to the key stakeholders

- Define teams, roles, and responsibilities and align incentives for all stakeholders

- In-depth analysis of the current processes/products/services to be migrated

  – How do the existing processes work?

  – How can the inputs and outputs be greened?

  – Determine needs to be addressed in the eco-design of products and select eco-design tools accordingly

  – Document the results in a management system accessible by all key stakeholders

  – Identify areas where there is a lack of data and skills within the organization to meet the requirements

- Select the supply chain elements that will be greened during current stage. This may affect and include a number of partner organizations. It is recommended that instead of migrating one element fully e.g. migrating full production, it is better to migrate one subdivision of production process

- Define the future state and its required Green features

- For each product/service/process carry out an environmental profile, looking at their ability to meet the recyclability and restrictions on use of substances

- Perform a thorough gap analysis between current and future state

- Put together a cost plan identifying responsibilities, training, actions to obtain reliable data, and actions to ensure compliance with regulations

- Get the analysis approved by all the stakeholders

Figure 11.4: *Phase I framework for migration strategy*

- Analyse the chosen process and study the inputs, the processing, and the outputs. For example, if analysing the procurement process to enable production, then you would study the type and quality of raw material procured, the amount of pollution generated transporting the raw material, Green policies and practices of the suppliers and, once the raw material is consumed, the ways in which the residue is disposed of. The analysis parameters will differ from process to process, e.g. a procurement process will have different analysis parameters than packaging, and the parameters for packaging will differ from those of logistics.

- Document, if not already done, the inputs, the processing, and the outputs, so that they can be made available to all the key stakeholders at a later time and can be used in the next phase when developing a baseline for the Green metrics.
- Identify and document the areas where sufficient information is not ready, or, where it is hard to clearly identify the environmental effects due to the lack of data, resources, or understanding of the process.
- Identify the key risks and impacts associated with the current inputs, processing, and outputs that can be detrimental to the environment at different stages. These will include issues that can arise when recycling or disposing of an item in an environmentally friendly manner.
- Identify the key organizations and supply chain partners in key sectors and assess their environmental performance.
- Liaise with the supply chain partners to identify ways of improving their environmental performance and reporting.
- Provide line managers with appropriate environmental parameters to enable them to include environmental criteria in their process reporting.

After an in-depth analysis of the existing functionality of the product/process/service (we will now call it a supply chain entity or just entity), the next step is to define the desired Green state of the entity and highlight the gaps that exist. This will involve the following:

- Define the future desired state, detailing the features and components that will render it a Green Supply Chain entity, whilst adhering to the legal Green requirements, or, to the organization's Green policies, commitment, and objectives.
- Carry out an environmental profile for each component of the entity in its future Green state. Document how these components will conform to Green requirements in terms of use, use of restricted substance, waste management, and other applicable factors.

- Perform a thorough gap analysis between current state and future state detailing each and every parameter of the entity, whether it will be enhanced to meet Green commitments, or will maintain the status quo.
- Develop a proposal for the Green migration identifying migration costs, responsibilities, training requirements for internal and external supply chain partners, associated risks, degree of compliance with Green regulations, anomalies, and actions or follow-up items for the next phase, e.g. acquiring reliable data.
- Obtain an approval from all the stakeholders on the analysis.

11.2 Phase II, Design and Implementation

Phase II of our 3-3 Approach embraces the sustainable design for design and migration to Green Supply Chains. This phase focuses on meeting the demands via minimizing resource consumption and maximizing profitability as the processes are re-engineered to optimize remanufacturing, reuse, and recycling of waste material. Finally in this phase, the tools for sustainable procurement, logistics, packaging, and so on are designed and implemented (see Figure 11.5).

The first step in Phase II is the total involvement from all parties:

- Liaise and coordinate via means of workshops or other preferred modes of communication to notify supply chain partners, internal and external, of your new Green requirements for the supply chain entity.
- Jointly develop plans/proposals for changes required to the supply chain partner process to achieve your Green objectives.
- Keep the partners abreast of your timeline and encourage them to update you on their progress periodically as agreed.
- Supply chain partners should get approval from all key stakeholders in your organization and their own organization on their Green plan and design process.
- Agree upon methods as to how the suppliers need to report on greenhouse reductions and emissions. It should be in a format that can interface seamlessly with your reporting system.
- Apply for any relevant Green certification available for your industry.
- Form core design and core implementation teams; these teams will carry out the Green changes through to implementation.

SUPPLY CHAIN PARTNER COORDINATION & INTEGRATION	DESIGNING A GREEN SUPPLY CHAIN ENTITY	ESTABLISHING IMPROVEMENT PROCEDURES
• Coordinate with equipment manufacturer and raw material suppliers to increase use of recyclable and reusable materials	• Based on gap analysis of Phase I and approved analysis, reconfigure and redesign the supply chain element to be greened	• Configure strategies to improve product and process designs for better outputs
• Engage with vendors (SCP, transportation management, third party logistics, strategic network design) or IT organizations to determine if optimization is being applied to the level of granularity needed to model environmental factors	• Prioritize and develop alternatives to address environmental requirements of a supply chain and identify best overall option	• Analyse baseline design and design concepts to develop performance measurement systems
	• Define and design supply chain systems metrics to measure baseline environmental impact of each process to be greened and then measure and evaluate the impact on a periodic basis	
	• Practices of waste minimization and source reduction should be followed across all processes and these practices should be translated to all the supply chain partners	

Figure 11.5: *Phase II framework for migration strategy*

The second step in Phase II is the design phase:

- Based on the gap analysis performed in Phase I, reconfigure and redesign the supply chain entity to remove the gaps. This should involve engaging all the relevant stakeholders and utilize their expertise and get their input.
- All the options for greening the entity should be considered for cost effectiveness or time consumption with pros and cons for each of these options listed and documented. These should include cost, timeframe to implement, requirements met/unmet, side effects, and scope for further enhancement in future. Once all the options are on the table and everyone is aware of these options, then the option that fully meets the

environmental needs in a cost effective manner should be chosen. This will need a mindset that no option should be discarded because it is too costly or time consuming. Any option that appears to be such may actually prove to be beneficial in the future and hence a thorough understanding of the options and their impact analysis is mandatory.

- The resultant so-called sustainable or eco design should focus on greening the entity internally, within the supply chain community, or holistically encompassing the society, which will entirely depend on whether a piecemeal approach is embraced for just changing the process within the organization, or a unison approach is adopted where other supply chain partners are also involved. Again, the chosen design will depend upon the readiness and speediness of the supply chain partners.
- The design opted for may also adopt and advocate the concepts discussed earlier, such as supply loops, Six Sigma, and others.
- This is the time when the internal benchmark metrics for measuring Greenness before and after the change to the entity are defined and designed. These should be communicated to key stakeholders and supply chain partners so that any changes to the associated systems, whether in terms of configuration, design, or reporting, can be made in a timely manner. The following items may be of interest when designing such a performance system:
  - Amount of recycled or virgin material used
  - Usage of hazardous components
  - Water and renewable energy usage
  - Packaging use and reuse
  - Increase or decrease in processing time
  - Emissions levels and control
  - Carbon contribution
  - Asset use
  - Equipment use
  - Inventory levels
  - Amount and type of waste generated and type of waste management.
- Obtain an approval on the agreed design and move on to the next step.

In the following step we will need to look at improving the design of the supply chain entity being greened and the corresponding Green performance measurement and reporting systems. The following is involved here:

- Develop and test prototype for both the entity and the performance system.
- Refine the prototype until the desired Green outcomes are achieved.
- Document the changes to the system and make these available internally and externally, as appropriate.
- Develop any new procedures that may arise due to greening of the entity
- Communicate and train the relevant parties.
- Change over to the new Green system.

11.3 Phase III, Organizational Change Management

The objectives of change management and Green performance evaluation are to investigate any negative impacts on the environment that still exist after implementation of the new Green system, to continue to improve on the environmental impacts that are uncovered in the above step, and to seek feedback on the effectiveness of environmental management through internal and external surveys (see Figure 11.6 overleaf).

After any implementation, there is the prime importance of having proper communication by keeping everyone aware of the progress, actions, and anomalies, and also keeping track of the performance. The first step in Phase III is therefore all about change management and Green performance measurement:

- For the proper management of the Green element post implementation, a supply chain wide environment management system should be installed. All key personnel internally and externally should be provided appropriate access to this system and any progress towards, or regress from, Green objectives should visible to them.
- Continuously scan for new Green regulations and check the conformity of the Green entity to these regulations.
- Perform regular internal and external audits of the Green entities to ensure adherence to the Green principles and regulations.

CHANGE AND MEASURE	SHARE SUCCESS	IMPROVE CONTINUOUSLY

- Implement Environment Management Systems (EMS) across the entire supply chain for the elements greened

- Regular internal and external audits for Green performance evaluation

- Greater visibility of carbon contributions and management, emission levels, asset and equipment use, inventory availability, and any aspect of the supply chain that affects its Green performance

- Develop tools (e.g. evaluate bills of material for waste or returned items) to determine the overall impact on the environment of individual supply chain entities separately

- Periodic information session with stakeholders and top management to keep them abreast of key Green activities and achievements owing to implementing Green Supply Chains

- Challenge the management with the environmental supply chain indicators and collaborate to make further improvements

- Develop a road map and engage with supply chain partners for Green supply chain multi-enterprise planning, execution, and coordination so that joint supply chain decisions about resource consumption, waste management etc. can be built across trading partner boundaries

- Develop process of continuous improvement as a part of corporate culture of the organization

Figure 11.6: *Phase III framework for migration strategy*

- Identify any anomalies in the Green element, raise the issue with the top management and Green committee, get an approval for the remedy and fix the problem.
- Monitor Green performance of supply chain partners. A regular import of Green performance data from supply chain partners will be input to the periodic reports.
- Generate daily, weekly, monthly, or quarterly Green reports or journals and distribute them as appropriate.

Sharing success and recognition of efforts are vital to longevity of any progression and so they are here, for example:

- Organize information sessions and team building events to share success of Green implementations.
- Recognize individual or team efforts involved in achieving the Green success.
- Provide incentives and a platform for people to promote innovation in sustainability subject matter.
- Confront decision makers on sustainability-related supply chain concerns and Green performance indicators. Collaborate to achieve further Green improvements.
- Develop a roadmap of Green Supply Chain activities to be jointly carried out by all supply chain partners. This is a stepping stone for the next wave of Green changes.
- Test the effectiveness of the Green Process by obtaining feedback from supply chain partners and internal key stakeholders.

Finally, develop a culture of continuous Green improvement within your organization. Build and develop corporate activities where your organization genuinely takes part to improve the environment and wellbeing of society.

Performance measurement and continual improvement are two extremely important elements of the migration strategy and the overall change management programme. For this reason we will discuss them in a lot more detail in Chapters 12 and 13 in Part 7 of this book.

PART 7

Continuous Improvement and Performance Evaluation

GREEN SUPPLY CHAINS			
GREEN SUPPLY CHAIN PLANNING	**GREEN PROCUREMENT**	**GREEN SUPPLY CHAIN EXECUTION**	**CARBON MANAGEMENT**

1. Life Cycle Engineering
2. S&OP
• Demand Planning
• Supply Planning
   ○ Production Planning
   ○ Inventory Planning
	• Collaboration
	• Incentive Alignment
	• Supplier Development
	• Energy-Efficient Procurement
	• Sustainable Sourcing
		• Green Production
		• Green Logistics
		• Green Packaging
		• Green Marketing
		• Supply Loops
			• Carbon Footprint Minimization

Green Supply Migration Strategy

Green Supply Chain Continuous Improvement

Green Supply Chain Performance Evaluation

12

Green Supply Chain Continuous Improvement

As the name implies, continuous improvement is all about making sure that the organization continues its efforts on Green Supply Chains long after the migration strategy is fully implemented. This means that the process of thinking, generating ideas or hypotheses for improvement, testing and confirming these hypotheses, formulating action plans based on these ideas, and putting them into practice should continue well into the future and after the initial major Green Supply Chain programme has bedded down.

In our experience, the concept of Green Supply Chains is so new, and the information is still so disjointed, that a big bang approach to Green Supply Chains is impossible. Recognizing the inherent difficulties with an all encompassing big bang approach, most organizations are in a quandary, and often become paralysed into inaction, despite their best intentions. The problem is further exacerbated by the ever increasing mix of misinformation and disinformation.

We believe such catch 22 circles must be broken, even if the short-term results are going to be suboptimal. After all, every journey starts with a single step and for this reason we recommend the three-wave migration programme (in Chapter 11) which is then followed up by the continuous improvement strategy. In this chapter therefore, we will discuss continuous improvement, a strategy which is an integral part of the result-oriented action plan towards Green Supply Chains.

12.1 Benefits of Continuous Improvement in Green Supply Chains

Major breakthroughs over time

Continuous improvement is important because many small steps taken one at a time over a period of time can lead to major movements, providing there is reasonable coordination between them.

Easier on the budget

The use of a continual improvement practice ensures that, for the major projects, the costs, investments, and outlays are managed within budgets. A big bang approach, in contrast, would entail a huge amount of expenditure at the very outset with the hope that all the analysis and strategies would pay off one day. By using phased migration followed by continual improvement, the organizations manage their investments in a much more responsible manner.

Less disruption to the business

In comparison to the big bang approach, a three-wave approach followed by continuous improvement is far less disruptive. Because of gradual change, the business objectives are always being kept at the forefront while simultaneously making sure that the imperative for Green Supply Chains is making gradual progress.

Risk management

Continuous improvement is an excellent method of sound risk management in the face of organizational change in a volatile business environment. As part of continuous improvement, any impact from previous steps can be taken into account as they become apparent and accessed, before taking the next steps. This leads to a very robust risk management strategy.

Builds learning supply chains

The whole philosophy of continuous improvement relies on surfacing the knowledge deeply embedded throughout the length and breadth of the entire supply chain in order to create a Green Supply Chain. In this way organizations will build a learning supply chain that is capable over time of moving towards an environmentally responsive Green Supply Chain.

12.2 Prerequisites of Continuous Improvement

Continuous improvement in an organization is only possible when it is deeply rooted within an organization's corporate philosophy. For example, many Japanese organizations say everyone has two jobs; their first job is to do the job as per the job description, their second job is to improve it.

There are a number of other prerequisites as well, as the process of continuous improvement requires the following:

- Recognition of the importance of continuous improvement.
- Commitment from top management.
- Well defined teams and responsibilities.
- Links with migration strategies, teams, and information.
- A culture of a number of small improvements over time leading to major breakthroughs.
- Regular performance evaluation, reporting, and usage to redefine goals and strategies.

12.3 Methodology of Continuous Improvement

To be successful, all continuous improvement programmes must be:

- designed as a comprehensive programme so that everyone in the organization participates vigorously;
- tailored to the organization;
- tied to the overall corporate strategy;
- linked to the strategy through data and metrics.

A Green Supply Chain continuous improvement programme is no exception to these requirements. There are many recognized methodologies for continuous improvement and we have adapted elements of these to formulate the following methodology for Green Supply Chain Continual Improvement.

12.3.1 Green Supply Chain Continual Improvement Cycle

To understand how continual improvement can be consistently used in Green Supply Chain Management, we have primarily adapted Deming's cycle into plan-do-study-act (PDSA) which incorporates our four main steps in the process of continual effort towards a "Greener" supply chain.

The first step is the *Plan* which consists of planning ahead for change, analysing, and predicting the results. In practice, this step is about generating ideas and hypotheses from all levels of the organizations in a systematic team-based manner. The ideas then have to be assessed and the benefits quantified before planning for their execution.

The second step is the *Do* which consists of executing the plan and taking small steps in controlled circumstances. While none of the ideas in itself would lead to massive change, a number of these executed in unison would create a big enough impact. At the same time, a multitude of ideas results in making sure that the system is always kept fine-tuned as the circumstances change, for example, the technology, suppliers, markets, products, customer demand, supply chain partners' capabilities, or priorities.

The third step is *Study* which consists of checking and analysing the results. This is to ensure that what they do is coherent with their sustainability and environmental commitments. The organization also has to make sure that the supply chain is responding to what they expected at the beginning.

The fourth step is the *Act* step which consists of taking actions to standardize or to improve the process. Organizations have to make sure that each of these actions has the potential to reduce the direct and indirect environmental impacts of an organization's supply chain footprint on the Earth.

The main thing to understand about continuous improvement is that it is never really completely over. Once a cycle is done, a new one starts all over again because either the circumstances have changed, or residual work from previous projects is still outstanding.

12.4 Green Supply Chain Benchmarking

Another element of continual improvement process is benchmarking. There are a number of good business books dealing with benchmarking in a great deal of detail. However, the practice of benchmarking has been so overused (and misused) over the last couple of decades that we notice a mild benchmarking fatigue in many organizations. However, if carried out with the right intent and rigour, benchmarking can reveal significant improvement opportunities.

The information explosion as a result of the internet has made it extremely easy to carry out benchmarking effectively. It is now much easier to find the world's best practice for most processes with the power of instantaneous communication and the information explosion. However, it still requires a great effort and a learning attitude to benefit from this knowledge and the key question to ask is *"Who has the world's best practice in this process and what can we learn from them to adapt and use in our company?"*

It will be seen here that the question is not *"Why are they different and why could we never do that?"* as obviously the answer to this question would be not a very useful one, unless we wanted to justify the status quo!

Clearly, Green Supply Chain Benchmarking will focus on each major element of the Green Supply Chain, for example:

1. Green Supply Chain Planning
2. Green Procurement
3. Green Supply Chain Execution
4. Carbon Management
5. Green Supply Chain Migration
6. Green Supply Chain Continuous Improvement.

The intention with benchmarking is to find organizations that either undertake a major element or one of the key subelements at a world's best practice level. While there is still some understandable nervousness about sharing confidential information, we find that with Green Supply Chain projects, most people will actually share information with a lot more readiness than is found with other benchmarking projects.

Once the right benchmarking partners are identified, it is essential to approach them with the right mindset and develop their confidence and trust. Generally the key questions that need to be answered are: *"What is in it for me?"* and *"Will this harm my company in any way?"* We find that the first question can be more easily answered by pointing out the opportunity to help the environment, the opportunity to help other non-competing supply chains, and the positive publicity. The second question can only be answered by the individuals making a careful consideration of their specific circumstances.

Finally, once the benchmarking exercise begins, the organization must approach with an open mind and with a learning attitude. It is indeed easy to dismiss the achievements of another organization and find reasons why none of those things will apply in your business. But the key here is to remember that you are not there to find things to copy, but rather to change your thinking and to generate ideas on how you could adapt some of their practices into your supply chain model. If after choosing a world's best practice supply chain to benchmark, and gaining their confidence to let you benchmark them, you find nothing of value to use within your business, it will mainly be because your team asked the wrong questions. However this possibility should be limited, because in that case you would rarely be able to gain their confidence to share this with you in the first place.

12.5 Pareto Analysis

Pareto analysis is very useful to determine the relative importance of various continual improvement projects based on their impact on the final outcomes. The Pareto principle or the 80/20 rule as a general rule states that 80% of one variable factor comes from 20% of another variable factor, for example 80% of problems come from 20% of the people, which means that a small portion of people cause the main problems.

A Pareto chart can therefore help to show the relative importance of different factors and will allow the team to focus on the most important problems, or on the most important causes of problems. As has been noted before, Pareto analysis directs you to concentrate on the important few and not the trivial many. Applying this rule to Green Supply Chain Continual Improvement, the teams can quickly isolate those problem areas where the action will lead to the maximum outcomes in terms of reduced environmental impact. For this purpose a number of other techniques, such as root cause analysis or fishbone diagrams, are very useful. A cause and effect diagram (or fishbone diagram) allows you to develop a map of the possible factors that may contribute to the problem. The analysis leads to a greater understanding of the problem and shows the possible factors that may contribute to the problem.

12.6 Example of Green Supply Chain Continuous Improvement

Let us now look at how one organization has carried out Green Supply Chain Continuous Improvement.

Wal-Mart, the world's biggest retailer and the tenth largest company in the world (Forbes.com), applied continuous improvement strategies in their Green Supply Chain. Driven by a sense of corporate social responsibility and by pressure from nonprofit organizations, they took some Green Supply Chain Continuous Improvement steps.

Over the past few years Wal-Mart launched a sweeping business sustainability strategy to dramatically reduce the company's impact on the global environment and thus become "the most competitive and innovative company in the world". We can observe that the *Plan* for them was to set big goals and with strategic intent: they in fact wanted to be supplied 100% by renewable energy, to create zero waste, and to sell products that sustain the company's resources and environment. Then, they went to the *Do* part and executed the plan. A number of programmes such as Global Greenhouse Strategy, alternative fuels, energy design, and construction to use renewable energy were initiated and executed. The *Study* part, which is about checking and analysing the initial results, was beneficial because they consistently reduced the impact on the environment through their Green Supply Chain programme. It created $75 million in annual savings and reduced 400 000 tons of CO_2 per year. Finally, in the *Act* part they standardized their processes and tried to improve them. To emphasize that this is a multi-iterative loop process, Wal-Mart did not stop just because of good results they achieved in the first pass. Rather, they started down the journey again with a new plan in which they promised that by 2011 they will only carry seafood certified as coming from oceans that are not overfished.

The reason for their continuous improvement drive is simple; there is no end to the improvement opportunities that add value to both the business and the Earth.

13

Green Supply Chain Performance Evaluation

All through this book we have alluded to measuring and managing progress towards Green Supply Chains. As has been said, what you cannot measure, you cannot manage. For the most part we would agree with this. Of course there are some intangible parts, such as team spirit or supply chain collaboration, which are more difficult to measure objectively and directly. Indirect or subjective measures can also quite quickly degenerate into a pure exercise of organizational bureaucratic nonsense. However, if the measurement methodology is developed, deployed, and used properly there is no reason that both objective and subjective measures will form a great building block of Green Supply Chains.

In this chapter we will therefore discuss how to create, deploy, use, present information, and use the output of a good Green Supply Chain Performance Evaluation methodology. Before we do that, let us briefly examine the benefits of such a methodology to understand in more detail why it is important.

13.1 Benefits of Performance Evaluation

A consensus view of the situation

While all the parties will have their own view on the current "Greenness" at any point of time and how the Green Supply Chain project is progressing, only a comprehensive performance evaluation methodology can achieve a consensus view of the situation prevailing at any point of time. There might be minor quibbles with the measurement methodology and timings, but in general, most parties will agree with most of the findings. This provides them with a common platform to build their further discussions on, whether they are for allocation of resources, for discontinuing some projects, reenforcing some others, or for incentives alignment. This common platform is extremely important to achieve in order to have an informed discussion within an organization, as well as with the supply chain partners outside the organization.

Gauge progress

By their very nature, all change programmes represent times of high turbulence; indeed, philosophically we can say that the future is always going to be one of stable turbulence. With change, therefore, it can be very difficult to measure progress without a comprehensive methodology. A well designed Green Supply Chain Performance Evaluation system should allow organizations to gauge their progress against peers, against their own goals, as well as against their performance at the beginning. This then provides a clear picture of how effective the efforts have been and highlights the areas where they have not been very effective.

Focus resources where they maximize impact

Aligned to the gauging progress is the ability to focus the resources on those areas where they can maximize the impact to achieve the overall goals of the organization. This type of periodic adjustment is necessary in order to optimize the use of resources and results from them.

Incentives management

Supply chain partners as well as the key team members must be completely on board through incentives alignment. In the absence of such a buy-in, the Green Supply Chain change programme risks not achieving their full potential. A robust performance evaluation methodology is necessary in order to agree on incentives and in order to distribute them in an objective manner.

External reporting and Green Marketing

It has now become a statutory requirement, or is now a recommendation in many jurisdictions, to report the progress on the environmental efforts of organizations. For obvious reasons these reports must be well documented, substantiated, and based on a robust measurement methodology. Reports without sufficient evidence to support any claims will attract charges of greenwashing or of giving misleading advertising. Additionally, false reporting carries heavy penalties in many jurisdictions. Clearly then, for both external reporting and for Green Marketing, it is fundamental that all reports, claims, advertising, and marketing messages are based on data measured through robust methodologies.

Objective audit trail

Finally, all change management programmes need an objective trail of data which is clearly auditable in order to justify the actions and responses taken at any point in time. A robust performance evaluation system should be able to provide such an auditable information repository for post-hoc use.

13.2 Performance Evaluation Methodology

Each Green Supply Chain programme is unique, just as each supply chain is unique. While there will be a number of common elements across a multitude of supply chains, the differences will make it necessary to create and adopt a purpose built performance evaluation methodology for each Green Supply Chain programme. To do this, the three key questions of what, how, and who need to be answered in order.

13.2.1 What to Measure?

Most people equate Green Supply Chain Measurement with carbon emissions measurement. While this is a big part of the overall Green Supply Chain drive, there are other, equally important, issues that form the complete picture. As discussed throughout this book, transition towards a Green Supply Chain involves movement along several core elements:

- Green Supply Chain Planning
- Green Procurement
- Green Supply Chain Execution
- Carbon Management
- Green Supply Chain Migration
- Green Supply Chain Continuous Improvement.

In each one of these core elements of Green Supply Chains there will be multiple subelements that need to be measured. These subelements will change over time as the programme progresses towards conclusion.

The first job of the measurement team will be to establish the key subelements which will be measured as part of the performance evaluation programme. This is done by studying the key processes that form each element and establishing parameters for measurement of these processes. For example, as Green Procurement involves collaboration, then one measurement of collaboration is the percentage of Green Supply teams which comprise members from two or more organizations across the entire supply chain. Another measure of collaboration is the time spent codeveloping ideas for the sustainable sourcing programme.

The task here is to create a set of meaningful measurements that are relevant, mutually exclusive, and collectively exhaustive; at the same time they must be unambiguous, objective, and easy enough to measure and report.

Another thing we must point out at this stage is that some measurements are input-oriented; for example, the two measurements given above are both input-oriented, while others, such as carbon dioxide produced in the entire supply chain of the product (in kg), are clearly output-oriented. Both are essential for the efficient management of Green Supply Chain programmes. Input-oriented measurements denote whether we are doing the right things in the right order, while output-oriented measurements denote whether we are getting the right results. Analogously, input-oriented measurements denote whether we are using the right ingredients as per the recipe, while output-oriented measurements denote whether the final produced dish has met expectations.

Finally, it should be noted that a robust measurement programme should be able to stand up to scrutiny at any point in time. It takes time, effort, and imagination to create a custom tailored measurement programme. Short cuts will only lead to frustrated teams who are directed to run a marathon and are then being measured in 100 m time slots. For this reason, we are not big supporters of commercially available prepackaged measurement programmes; whilst in theory they could be adapted to do the job, we find that, in reality, it is far easier to start from scratch and create an imaginative and robust measurement programme that will additionally, and importantly, have the full ownership of its designers.

13.2.2 How to Measure?

Our advice here is to start slowly, be sure of what you are measuring, use the information for a couple of cycles for decision making, fine-tune the measurement programme, and then try and automate it as much as possible.

We find the alternative approach, touted mainly by software vendors and by prepackaged measurement companies, starts with a big bang and produces, in an instant, reams of data. This however rarely stands up to scrutiny when looked at closely. It then becomes incredibly hard to adapt the system later after all of the shortcomings have become clear. In fact, many shortcomings will only become clear after a substantial time has elapsed and only if a government body, an NGO, or similar institution is looking closely at the reports, especially following incidents. The organization also remains very open to charges of having misleading advertisements or false reports, without ever suspecting that the possibility existed.

The performance measurement and evaluation programme will of course need to be fine-tuned and updated on a regular basis to make sure it still meets the need of the Green Supply Chain programme.

13.2.3 Who Will Measure?

While any of the involved partners may be in a position to do the job, generally it falls on the dominant supply chain partner to provide this service while taking on the mantle of leadership. Process integrity will of course dictate separation between the Green Supply Chain change management teams and the performance evaluation team. A fairly robust case can also be made for an external third party performance measurement group to provide this service in an objective and transparent manner that will also be credible to all of the internal and external stakeholders.

13.3 Presenting Finding of Performance Evaluation

While presenting the information derived from the measurement programme for performance evaluation, care must be taken to make sure that it is presented in a useful, objective, and relevant manner. All information which is non-relevant for the purpose at hand must either be deleted, or kept in a separate appendix. Charts must have uniform axes and clear titles and labels. The user should have the ability to drill down and reach a point where they can trace the cause and effect of individual events on the overall measurement.

Finally, many are drowning in far too much information. Our mantras when presenting information are "keeping it short and simple" (KISS) and "where less is more".

Following are some examples from disguised case studies.

Figure 13.1 below shows a radar diagram of an overall Green Supply Chain programme and as we can see, Green Procurement, which is one of its elements, rates 6.7 on a 10-point scale. Other noteworthy points in this diagram are that carbon management and Green Procurement are the most advanced of the six elements, while Green Supply Chain Continuous

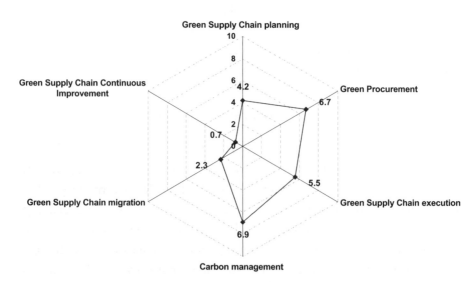

Figure 13.1: *Example of a Green Supply Chain performance evaluation*

Improvement has not yet started in earnest. This was to be expected as the migration was still underway and the core Green Supply Chain Planning and Execution was only halfway through. It should be noted that the scale of 10 is the aspiration scale based on the targets set by this organization, and they are measuring all progress against this scale for the entire programme.

Figure 13.2 takes one element, "Green Procurement", out of Figure 13.1 and drills down further along this element on the same scale.

As seen in Figure 13.2 the six subelements of Green Procurement range from a low of 3.2 to a high of 8.8 on the scale of 10. Collaboration, one of the subelements which we explore in further detail in Figure 13.3, rates 6.2 on this scale.

Figure 13.3 overleaf measures various parameters of collaboration on the same scale and finds that while top management commitment and cross-organizational teams are in place, codevelopment time and joint raw material trial programmes are the main culprits for an average rating of 6.2 for collaboration.

While there is a considerable amount of detail behind each of these parameters, it is clear that presentation of the information in a clear and succinct format will better facilitate action.

Next we look at using this information for decision making as all of the hard work so far is for a central core purpose.

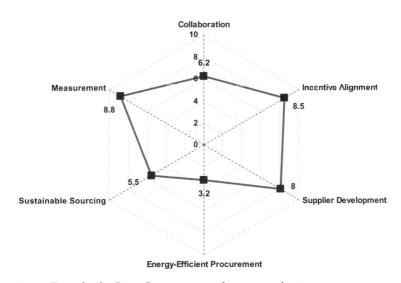

Figure 13.2: *Example of a Green Procurement performance evaluation*

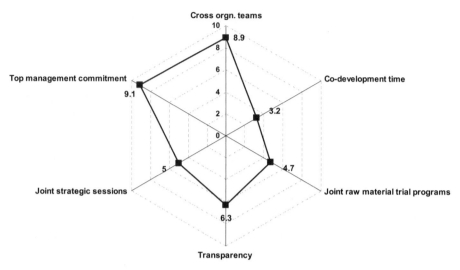

Figure 13.3: *Example of a Green Collaboration Performance Evaluation*

13.4 Using Information from Performance Evaluation for Making Decisions

So now we have radar diagrams and supporting data and information on Green Supply Chain Performance. It is a formidable information set and most executives should have no problems deciphering the information and making appropriate decisions based on it. However, a few guidelines will be helpful to make the best use of information.

Be aware of the data accuracy and reliability

While this is an obvious point, sometimes neat radar diagrams make people lose sight of how robust or reliable the underlying data sets are. No matter how good the presentation, the decisions are only as good as the data that support it.

Use information at the right level of aggregation for each decision

This is a frequent error where the information being looked at is either too detailed or at too high a level for the decision being made. For strategic, high-level decisions a more aggregated picture would be needed. Of necessity, it will have to ignore some details which are not relevant to the decision being made, even though these details might be very relevant in another context. On the other hand, for an execution decision, then a great deal of detail is required. Decisions made on assumptions or partial information are suboptimal, especially when more information could easily be procured.

Make decision at the right time; avoid "paralysis by analysis" or "jumping to conclusions"

Some people are uncomfortable making decisions till they have 100% information at a very high level of accuracy, while others jump to decisions without much information. For each decision, the happy medium is somewhere in the middle, though it is likely to vary, depending on the full implications of the decision. More strategic decisions require better information while tactical and operational decisions need easily obtainable data.

Don't lose sight of the end goal

It is possible to lose sight of the end goal when all the data become available. It is important to keep in mind that the end goal is emissions reduction and waste reduction to make the supply chains "Green".

13.5 Measurement Toolkit

Global Supply Chain Group (GSCG) has developed a measurement toolkit that gives a broad understanding of the status of Greenness across specific supply chains. Respondents are asked to select five alternatives for each question; this will automatically rate the status on Greenness.

In broad terms, then, the following areas are covered by the toolkit:

1. Green Supply Chain Planning
2. Green Procurement
3. Green Supply Chain Execution
4. Carbon Management
5. Green Supply Chain Migration
6. Green Supply Chain Continuous Improvement.

Each of these areas is subdivided and is then followed by a further division which asks the detailed questions, for example on Green Procurement:

1.1 Awareness of Green Procurement
    1.1.1 How is Green Procurement defined in your end-to-end supply chain?
    1.1.2 How much importance is given to Green Procurement?
    1.1.3 How are competitors on Green Procurement?
    1.1.4 What is the market for recycled materials?
1.2 Supplier Collaboration
1.3 Supplier Incentive Alignment
1.4 Supplier Selection

Respondents pick from five alternative answers for each question; for example with 1.1.4 above:

1. There is a huge market for recycled materials and true potential of this market is yet to be exploited.
2. There is a big market for recycled products. Some firms have recognized the potential and are rapidly expanding in this space.
3. There is a need to recycle products but organizational structure, suppliers' monopoly, and top management reluctance have kept this market growth restricted.
4. Consumers don't want to use recycled products.
5. There is no market for recycled products.

When all questions are answered, the overall scores will provide a clear indication on the current Green status. Importantly it will also indicate the areas for development and will very clearly broadly indicate what needs to be done in each development area.

Further details on this toolkit are available from Vivek Sood.

PART 8

Appendix – Case Studies

In this section we have placed a series of articles and case studies that amplify, in their own specific context, what we said in the book. These also serve to demonstrate that not only is the concept of the Green Supply Chain good social and environmentally friendly practice, it is also good business practice.

Case Study 1: Making an End-to-end Supply Chain Green: the GFTN/WWF Initiative

The supply chain, whilst it is an embracive and total concept, is really a philosophical approach. This means therefore that any supply chain approach on, for example, creating a Green Supply Chain, can mean different things to different people.

Supply Chain Management (SCM) has been defined as the planning, organizing, directing, and controlling of all of the individual supply chain processes by integrating/coordinating and controlling both the internal company and the external suppliers/customers to deliver value to the customer.

SCM therefore involves managing, cross-functionally, a series of processes that extend both internally, and also reach externally, to both suppliers and customers. Visually the supply chain embraces all of the following:

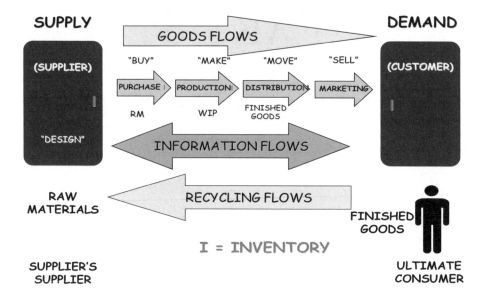

The term "Supply Chain" therefore primarily covers:

- everything in and between supply and demand;
- the movement of materials/inventory/information;
- from suppliers to company to customers;
- and doing this in a timely manner to meet the customers' demand requirements.

There is usually going to be more than one supply chain in any one organization and the supply chain processes and activities will represent between 30 and 70% of the organization's business cost.

The supply chain will also reach locally, regionally, and globally; meanwhile, every supply chain will be driven by demand as, if there is no demand, then there is no supply.

Every product supply chain will ultimately involve every one of the following standard economic sectors:

- Primary sector: Raw materials from farming/fishing (food, beverages, and forestry), quarrying/mining (minerals, coals, metals) or drilling (oil, gas, water).
- Secondary sector: Conversion of these raw materials into products by milling, smelting, extracting, refining into oils/chemicals/products and

then maybe machining, fabricating, moulding, assembly, mixing, processing, constructing into components, subassemblies, building construction/structures and furniture/electronic/food/paper/metal/ chemicals and plastic products.

- Service or tertiary sector: Business, personal, and entertainment services, which involve the channels of distribution from suppliers to customers, via direct, wholesale, or retail channels. Services include packaging, physical distribution, hotels, catering, banking, insurance, finance, education, public sector, post, telecoms, retail, repairs, etc.

These sectors are all located globally, as no one country has a single total ownership of every one of these sectors; indeed, as popularized by the former US President, Ronald Reagan, "We live in a global village" (this term being actually coined in 1962 by Canadian media theorist Marshall McLuhan).

The supply chain philosophy and approach therefore aim to integrate, locally to globally, all of the flows of information, physical goods, and product/services flows, the money flows, and any returning or recycling or reverse flows.

The supply chain can be labelled as involving all of the "ground to ground" flow processes, where the successful integration will provide a competitive edge in the market place, for those organizations who apply the philosophy. In so doing, SCM will add value and remove waste. The use of the word "ground" represents the literal origin and source of raw materials and also the eventual return to the ground of the ultimate and final product disposal to landfill (which is directly a Green issue).

Managing the supply chain however does not actually start with supply as the supply chain is always triggered and started by demand; it is ultimately the end consumer demand that drives everything. This end demand is then adjusted and changed and passed on through all of the appropriate supply sides of the services and secondary sectors to the other end, the supply from the primary sector.

There are very few examples of the management of the "end-to-end" or "start to finish" supply chains that will take such a total global managed view from the initial triggering end of the consumer demand, right through to the other end of the primary sector supply; one reason for so few examples is that to do this, and do it on a global basis, is an enormous challenge.

Such a challenge has however been successfully taken on by the Global Forest & Trade Network (GFTN), an initiative of the global conservation organization WWF to eliminate the supply of illegal wood and transform the global demand market place, for timber and paper products, into a force for saving the world's valuable and threatened forests.

The GFTN does this by facilitating trade links between companies that are committed to achieving and supporting responsible forestry. The GFTN then creates market conditions that help to conserve the world's forests, while providing economic and social benefits for the businesses and people that depend on them.

The GFTN uses independent, multi-stakeholder-based forest certification as a vital tool to apply the principles of responsible forest management and trade practices throughout the supply chain. The success of the GFTN can be seen as follows (as of April 2009):

- Scope: represents 16% of all forest products traded internationally every year, with combined annual sales of $62 billion.
- Represents: 187 trading deals with other GFTN participants.
- Covers: with forests over 21.5 million ha of certified forests and 12.2 million ha in progress to certification and with trade covering 16% of the volume of internationally traded timber and fibre.
- Employs: over 2.4 million people globally and supports 670 local families through community operations.

Whilst, theoretically, there is enough wood in the world's forests to supply global wood requirements, an analysis carried out by WWF and the World Bank in 2001 indicated that by sustainably managing 60% of the world's forests, at different levels of intensity and for different purposes, the remaining 40% could be protected.

WWF therefore believes that by engaging organizations in challenging and innovative partnerships, companies can not only contribute to the sustainability of the planet, but to their own business viability and success. Through the GFTN, WWF works with the forest products industry to help it change the way it does business. The GFTN encourages trade links between companies committed to achieving responsible forestry and trade, and works to create those market conditions that support forest conservation, while providing economic and social benefits for the businesses and people that depend on them.

The GFTN provides a framework for companies, a proven "stepwise approach" which allows companies to develop forest management plans by outlining the various steps needed to achieve credible certification within an agreed timeframe. The GFTN also helps companies phase out products from unwanted timber sources and increase those from certified sources via this stepwise approach. WWF staff therefore provide local, on the ground support to ensure participating companies continuously improve their business practices. The GFTN has offices in 34 countries and engages with companies committed to responsible forest management and trade all around the world.

The following case studies clearly detail the GFTN Green approach and the connections from demand to supply, a classic Green Supply Chain; therefore we will draw some lessons at the end of these case studies.

Case Study: GFTN in Ghana

Where are the trees? The ride from Accra, Ghana's capital, to Samreboi, a sawmill town in the southwestern part of the country, reveals the impact of 50 years of indiscriminate logging and clear-cutting at the expense of the once-extensive forests of this West African nation. Likewise, very little forest can be seen on the five-hour drive northwest from Accra to Kumasi, Ghana's second-largest city. Rainforests once covered more than one third of Ghana, but today less than 10% of the original forest survives as a result of deforestation and poor forest management. This loss of forest is not only threatening Ghana's fragile economy, but the livelihoods of people who depend on forests.

Ghana's forests are part of the Guinean Moist Forest Ecosystem, identified by WWF as one of West Africa's and the world's most biologically important and diverse areas. Home to chimpanzees and pygmy hippos, these species and many others are being threatened by shrinking habitats.

"It would be hard to overstate the threat because when it's gone, it's gone," said George White, responsible purchasing coordinator for the Global Forest and Trade Network (GFTN).

The GFTN is WWF's initiative to eliminate illegal logging and improve the management of valuable and threatened forests. By facilitating trade links between companies committed to achieving and supporting responsible forestry, the GFTN creates market conditions that help conserve the world's forests while providing economic and social benefits for the businesses and people that depend on them. The GFTN seeks to form forest and trade networks (FTNs) in markets and production areas where they can have the greatest beneficial impact on valuable and threatened forests.

Joining the network

Since 2003, WWF and Friends of the Earth-Ghana (FOE) have been working with logging companies in Ghana to help improve their forestry practices, and by extension, to conserve more forests and their wildlife.

A breakthrough for forest conservation in West Africa came in December 2004 when Samartex Timber and Plywood Co. Ltd, one of Ghana's leading producers of forest products, signed an agreement with WWF and FOE to work towards independent certification of environmentally-sound forest management practices on 159,000 ha under its management. The agreement made Samartex the first participant in the Ghana Forest & Trade Network (Ghana FTN). Since then, eight other companies in Ghana have applied to join the network, six of which have undergone baseline audits of their operations.

Samartex took this important step with the encouragement of two of its major buyers: Timbmet Silverman, a UK timber importer, and Travis Perkins, a UK building materials supplier, both members of the UK Forest & Trade Network (UK FTN). The two buyers also pledged to increase the amount of timber they buy from legal and sustainable sources.

"The Samartex story represents an achievement we envisioned when the GFTN was formed," said Darius Sarshar, GFTN's responsible forestry coordinator.

"With a push from environmental groups, demand for wood from legal and well-managed forests has been increasing. But rising market demand alone is not enough. What we have added through our new partnerships with logging *companies like Samartex is much needed help on the supply-side of the equation."*

Building demand

The demand chain affecting forests in Ghana begins with Travis Perkins, a publicly traded company that is a main supplier to the building and construction market and one of the largest companies in the UK. In recent years, the company has been criticized for the sources of wood used in some major government building projects, including renovations to cabinet offices in Westminster, the British parliament.

"We came under pressure from some of our shareholders such as the large pension fund holders who made a point of investing in companies that are seen as environmentally and ethically run," said Steve Ford, Travis Perkins' environmental manager.

About 15% of the company's clients are builders involved in contracts with the central government, which now requires the use of timber from legal and sustainable sources. Its other clients are large home builders that also have shareholders who are disturbed when their company's image is tarnished.

One of Travis Perkins' major suppliers is Timbmet Silverman, a family-owned company that is the largest importer of hardwood in the UK, with 40 per cent of its supply coming from the tropics, including Ghana.

"Timbmet was bombarded by its customers asking questions about its sources and wanting certified timber," George White said.

Mike Packer, Timbmet's director of responsible solutions, said that the company is committed to minimizing its environmental footprint and welcomes the demand for responsibly-harvested timber.

"Without market demand, no amount of goodwill or desire to save the world's forests will have much of an impact," he said. *"Our difficulty is a lack of supply of certified wood, especially hardwoods from the tropics where many of the world's most valuable and threatened forests are located."*

Creating supply

Timbmet has long had a commercial relationship with Samartex Timber and Plywood Co., a Samreboi-based company with long-term logging concessions on government-owned timber reserves in western Ghana. Samartex's sawmill, employing over 2,000 people, is the largest in the country.

Hundreds of species of flora and fauna inhabit the Guinean moist forests like the ones where Samartex extracts timber, including chimpanzees, forest elephants, and rare red colobus monkeys. Several forest blocks in the Samartex concession contain forest that has never been logged, and some have been withdrawn from production and set aside by the government as "globally significant biodiversity areas".

The company's commercially-valuable timber species, however, include iroko, African mahogany, utile, and sapele. In an effort to increase its supply of sustainably-produced wood, Timbmet encouraged Samartex to join the newly established Ghana FTN.

"It's a good network, providing a stepwise framework and technical assistance to help companies like Samartex move towards certification by the Forest Stewardship Council (FSC)," Packer said.

"We wanted independent checks and verification so there would be no question when we sell to Travis Perkins where the timber comes from."

The Ghana FTN was launched in 2003, based on the need of Timbmet and other buying members of the GFTN's international network. Abraham Baffoe, a Ghanaian forester who worked for FOE, became its coordinator and began trying to recruit timber companies and explaining how FSC certification worked.

"The level of awareness and understanding of certification was very low," said Baffoe. "Company operators did not understand what forest certification meant and how to get there."

"The breakthrough with Samartex and the other Ghanaian companies that have applied to join the network came through the encouragement of its major buyer. If one of their key buyers comes in and says that they want certification, then local forest companies will get interested."

For Samartex, Timbmet is one of its biggest customers and its request for certified productions was taken to heart.

"Right from the beginning we said that there is an increased cost factor and if we get our forests certified we should receive a cost benefit," explained Gilmour Dickson, Samartex's forest coordinator.

Timbmet pays a premium for Samartex wood and is favouring them with additional business.

Improving practices

The GFTN provided technical assistance and paid some of the costs of the experts and audits required in the certification process, using funds provided by the US Agency of International Development and the UK's Department for International Development.

"To be honest, if you went off on your own seeking FSC certification, there are so many consultants offering services that there is the danger that it would be a long and expensive process," Dickson said. *"Thanks to the GFTN, we were able to accomplish this process efficiently."*

Since it joined the GFTN, Samartex has received about US$2 million in new business enquiries from buyers in the network.

"There is a big demand for FSC certified tropical hardwood and not many companies are in a position to supply it," Dickson added.

In joining the Ghana FTN, Samartex declared a moratorium on logging in 20,000 ha of its primary forests, developed benefit-sharing plans with local communities within Samartex-managed concessions, and put together a comprehensive road map for achieving FSC certification by 2007.

"A serious problem in Ghanaian forestry is the collateral damage done by poor felling and hauling practices," Baffoe said. *"For every tree taken, four or five often go down with it."*

Since Samartex joined the FTN, this problem has been dramatically reduced in the company's forests. Samartex has also improved its roads and replaced outmoded hauling machines.

As another part of its commitment to the GFTN, Samartex signed social responsibility agreements with communities on the fringe of its forests. It set up a committee, consisting of Samartex managers and village leaders, to determine what the communities needed, school buildings, water systems, a community centre, and what the company would provide. The company, which employs thousands of people in its forestry operations and mills, is also helping develop alternative sources of income for people living in the area.

Some 300 households adjacent to one of the company's concessions are now involved in an agro forestry project that includes planting fast-growing timber species for future sale; cultivating a native plant species from which they extract a natural, low-calorie sweetener; beekeeping; and fish and snail farming. The company also trains and employs 30 professional wood carvers who make bowls and animals out of leftover wood that are sold at international craft fairs and on the internet (www. ecocraft.org).

"Obviously, to be successful we have to find other forms of income generation," Dickson said.

Since Samartex became the first member of the Ghana FTN, eight other companies have followed its lead and applied for membership. Two of them have prepared action plans to achieve FSC certification based on the baseline audits of their forests totaling over 85,000 ha.

In January 2006, Baffoe and an auditor from SmartWood, an FSC-accredited certification body, conducted the baseline audits of the operations of three additional Ghanaian timber companies that are seeking certification and membership in the FTN. A fourth also has had an audit of its forest holdings.

"There are just a handful of big Ghanaian timber exporting companies, and most of them are now either members or applicants," said GFTN's Darius Sarshar, adding that the GFTN will now focus on enlisting the country's numerous small- and medium-sized companies. Because Samartex has large-scale timber harvesting concessions, its membership in the GFTN puts more than 22% of Ghana's production forests on the path to responsible management. When the other companies complete their audits and action plans for certification, that figure will reach nearly 60%.

"These percentages demonstrate the significant contribution the GFTN is making to retain the rich biodiversity of Ghana's remaining production forests and ensure that they generate economic value for the country for years to come," said Sarshar.

Source: Making markets work for forests and people in Ghana, 26 May 2006,
Julia Cass on www.panda.org/gftn

Case Study: GFTN in Russia

Russia has the world's largest remaining tracts of old growth forests. But continuous logging, dating back to the days of Peter the Great, to the extensive clear cutting and illegal logging of today have gradually reduced the extent and ecological significance of these forests.

When the post-Soviet Russian government began privatizing its timber industry in the early 1990s, WWF, the global conservation organization, jumped on the opportunity to help shape the emerging free market Russian forestry sector into a more environmentally responsible model. Through its Global Forest & Trade Network (GFTN), WWF started working with the new Russia forestry companies and their buyers, primarily in Europe, to eliminate illegally logged and traded forest products, and to improve the overall quality of forest management.

Guided by its philosophy of using market mechanisms to drive improvements in forestry, the GFTN has helped organize the growing demand in Europe for "green wood" by establishing groups of companies committed to buying wood products certified as being responsibly produced.

"We want to eliminate illegal logging and improve the management of valuable and threatened forests in Russia," said Duncan Pollard, Director of WWF's Global Forests Programme.

"By facilitating trade links between companies committed to achieving and supporting responsible forestry, the GFTN creates market conditions that help conserve the forests while providing economic and social benefits for the businesses and people that depend on them."

The results have so far been impressive. Forest areas certified under the Forest Stewardship Council (FSC), an independent group that sets standards for sustainable forestry, jumped exponentially from 350,000 hectares in 2003 to 7.36 million hectares by the end of 2005, including 1.6 million hectares in Siberia. By November 2006, the certified area had grown to 12.8 million hectares. It is estimated that by the end of 2007, 25 million hectares will be certified to FSC standards in Russia.

Stimulating European demand ...

Responding to growing public concern that imported lumber was being sourced from old growth forests and responsible for habitat destruction, many European wood retailers, importers and distributors took action by joining newly formed national forest & trade networks (FTNs).

To be part of the network, purchasing-oriented participants agree to analyse their wood sources and increase the amount they buy from legal and certified suppliers, while production-oriented participants agree to manage forests and production facilities legally and eventually attain certification.

"We've managed to get the important actors in the key sectors talking about certification," said George White, GFTN's coordinator for responsible purchasing.

"We have achieved critical mass throughout Europe, especially in the do-it-yourself markets and their supply chains. Selling FSC is becoming the normal way to do business."

Today, European FTN members include some of the largest companies, such as the Swedish international retail furniture giant, IKEA, and British suppliers St Gobain and Travis Perkins. Membership in Germany includes major do-it-yourself chains Hornbach & Bahr Baumarkt.

... and Russian Supply

By the late 1990s, European demand for certified lumber reached Russia, but most of the newly privatized companies there were not yet in a position to supply it.

"No one really understood what certified lumber or FSC was," explained Elena Kulikova, WWF Russia's Forestry Programme Coordinator.

To help companies understand, WWF Russia founded the Russian Forest & Trade Network in 1999 to promote sustainable forest management and voluntary forest certification. Companies that join the network make a public commitment to responsible forestry and credible forest certification. By doing so, they exclude the use of wood from unknown, illegal and uncontrolled sources, while phasing in the use of wood from known reliable sources. WWF certification centres have also been set up in several Russian cities, providing FTN member companies with consulting services and forest auditing training to achieve their goals. Another initiative to assist members is a model FSC certified forest, located south of St Petersburg.

According to Kulikova, Russian loggers traditionally clear-cut forests employing inefficient harvesting methods and pay little attention to reforestation. The model forest, on the other hand, uses Scandinavian methods that are more cost-effective and sustainable, taking steps to conserve biodiversity, preserve standing deadwood as nests for birds and identify "high conservation value" areas that require special protection.

"The model forest is a fantastic showcase on how to do FSC certified forestry in Russia," said Darius Sarshar, GFTN's Responsible Forestry Coordinator. *"We are trying to demonstrate that modern, sustainable practices work better than traditional ones."*

Impressed by a visit to the model forest in 2004, the manager of Cherepovetsles, one of the largest timber companies in north-west Russia, joined the Russian FTN. Since then the company has been actively introducing modern forestry methods on its 580,000 ha of forest concessions, all of which are now FSC certified.

"FSC certification is important for us because it is recognized by our business partners in Sweden and the Netherlands," said Anastasia Djakovskaya, the company's spokeswoman.

Russian suppliers for IKEA are also coming on board. Furniture factory Swedwood Tikhvin, for example, joined the Russia FTN in 2004, with 51,000 ha of its forest concessions now certified. Three additional IKEA suppliers also are members.

"North-west Russia and Siberia are very important sources of pine and birch for the Swedish company," said Alexey Naumov, a forestry manager for IKEA Russia. *"Our long term goal is to source all wood from well-managed forests, and at the moment this means FSC certified. Being in the WWF group means our suppliers can get support in preparing for FSC certification."*

Looking east

The GFTN is now focusing its attention on the Russian Far East and the mixed coniferous-deciduous forests of the Amur-Heilong river basin, identified by WWF as one of the world's most biologically important forests and the heartland of the endangered Siberian tiger and Amur leopard. These wild cats face serious threats from illegal and unsustainable logging, which is destroying their once pristine habitat.

"*Illegal and unsustainable logging is a real problem here,*" said Dr Darron Collins, Director of WWF's Amur-Heilong programme. "*There is huge pressure to harvest these forests.*"

An estimated 70% of the timber trade heads to neighbouring China, where demand is high. In fact, several large Chinese factories using substantial quantities of wood are located just across the border with Russia in the Amur-Heilong region.

"*At present, timber companies in this region have little market incentive to harvest wood in an environmentally sensitive manner,*" added GFTN's George White. "*The Chinese are so hungry for wood they're not asking questions. They, as well as most of the Japanese and Korean companies that trade in the Russian Far East, are not interested in certification. Few put any premium on it at all.*"

The GFTN is taking hold in Russia's Far East in much the same way as it did in Europe and north-west Russia ten years ago by working with timber companies to understand and ultimately achieve FSC certification, and by developing demand for responsibly harvested wood in Japan and China.

The GFTN recently established buyer-oriented FTNs in Japan and China in an effort to improve consumer awareness in Asia.

"*Most of the Chinese members are locked into export markets in Europe and North America where there are strong signals for legal wood and good demand for FSC,*" White said. "*The Japanese market is a consumer market in itself, and there are signs of an increase in demand for legal and certified products.*"

One company at a time

In 2002, Terneyles, the leading timber exporter in the Russian Far East, came under attack by international environmental organizations for logging a virgin forest that is home to endangered tigers.

Sensitive to the NGO attacks and pressure from its Japanese trading partner, Sumitomo, which wanted environmentally sourced wood, Terneyles turned to WWF for help. As part of its commitment to FSC certification, the company altered its logging practices to minimize impact in tiger areas. It also agreed to a moratorium on harvesting trees in areas of high conservation value, and made an agreement with the local Udege people to respect their hunting and fishing areas.

Today, Terneyles is a member of the Russia FTN, with millions of hectares of its concessions now FSC certified. With Terneyles on board and an active campaign to get others to join the process, many are optimistic about seeing a tipping point in responsible forestry in the Russian Far East.

"The Russian Far East is a big challenge," said WWF's Duncan Pollard. *"But we expect to make serious inroads in the coming years, just as we did when we began in north-west Russia a decade ago."*

Source: Russia's sustainable forestry revolution, 19 February 2007
Julia Cass on www.panda.org/gftn.

Case Study: GFTN and Sustainable Forests

More than ten years ago, Derek Young, a senior manager with UK retailer Homebase Ltd, realized the company would have to find an environmentally responsible source for half a million cubic metres of plywood, hardwood, softwood, doors, and furniture; in total several thousand products. Campaigning non-government organizations (NGOs) were already demonstrating outside competitors' stores, blaming them for the destruction of rainforests in Kalimantan, Indonesia, and other places.

"We were horrified and knew we would be next," says Young. *"We had a longstanding policy of environmental responsibility, but didn't know how to find timber from well-managed forests."* That is when Homebase joined the WWF-UK Forest and Trade Network and became part of the WWF Global Forest and Trade Network (GFTN).

Campaigning NGOs have a good reason to protest against European and North American companies' buying policies. Asia's forests, which supply a substantial share of tropical hardwood to the western market, are in crisis.

The Philippines' forests are gone. China has imposed stringent bans on logging in the wake of the Yangtze River floods. Indonesia's tropical rainforests, some of the richest in the world, are being cut down at an alarming rate of over 3.5 million hectares per year, the equivalent of 500 soccer fields per hour. As such, furniture manufacturers have started to talk about finding timber suppliers in Indochina when Indonesia can no longer meet their demands.

Supply & demand

While the world's most important forests deteriorate, global trade in forest products continues to grow at a rapid pace. Each year the world consumes approximately 1.6 billion cubic meters of industrial round wood, and consumption is projected to grow to between 2 and 3 billion cubic metres per year by 2050.

Yet the quality of management of production forests around the world is highly variable. In Asia, home to some of the world's most valuable and threatened forests, just 2.79% of forests have attained credible, independent, certification as being well-managed.

Meeting this demand comes at a high price to Asia. Not only may businesses find Asian timber a much more expensive and scarce commodity in the future as a result of overlogging, but they may also lose services vital to the well-being of the planet that Asia's forests provide. Forests reduce soil erosion and landslides, act as a buffer against global warming, and even filter the water and air we breathe.

Millions in China and Indonesia now face more flooding, mudslides, and wildfires as a result of denuded forests. Protecting forests can also help to provide high quality drinking water, and city authorities throughout the world need cleaner, cheaper and more secure water supplies. Today, half the world's population is urban and one-third of these people live without clean water. These 1 billion have-nots are unevenly distributed, and almost 700 million city dwellers without access to clean water live in Asia.

Demand in Asia as well as in Europe and North America contributes heavily to the logging frenzy in countries like Indonesia. In North America and Europe, some markets already favour environmentally friendly forest products, and major retailers, including Homebase, IKEA, The Home Depot, Lowe's, and Carrefour, have announced policies to exclude illegally cut timber from their supplies.

With their global sourcing, these companies are bringing green buying policies to Asia. Smaller companies manufacturing furniture and other wood products in Asia are also seeking third-party verification of responsible practices to gain preferential access to high-value markets in North America and Europe.

The Asian wood consuming countries, primarily China and Japan, may be poised on the brink of a paradigm shift. According to Lily Lee, Coordinator of EcoWood Asia, the Architectural Services Department of Hong Kong has recently rewritten its general specification for building with, remarkably, the objective of sustainable forestry in mind. Beginning January of this year, contractors may only use wood certified by the Forest Stewardship Council or other approved authority.

WWF's GFTN intends to leverage this demand for responsibly produced wood into concrete changes in forest management and conservation, while helping businesses meet the demand for sustainable forest products. The GFTN consists of demand oriented FTNs, called buyer group and producer group. The buyer group includes retailers, distributors and specifiers, like Hong Kong's Architectural Services Department. The producer group includes forest owners or managers and forest product processors and manufacturers.

GFTN works to improve the management of valuable and threatened forests through trade links between companies committed to responsible forestry. GFTN helps responsible buyers and sellers to locate one another and provides technical assistance that aids in realizing the market push towards environmentally sustainable wood products.

"With the right market conditions," says Dr Justin W Stead, senior advisor, and former executive director of GFTN, *"we can conserve the world's forests while providing economic and social benefits for the businesses and people that depend on them."*

Certification programme

At its inception, the GFTN focused primarily on buyer group members purchasing wood that received independent certification. The United Nations reported in 2001 that more than half of the demand for certified forest products in the 1990s was generated by members of GFTN.

Today, certification is recognized as a useful tool in the achievement of responsible forest management, and the use of certified forests is expanding rapidly. Credible certification is the most effective way to guarantee that wood comes from legal and non-controversial sources, but credibly certified wood is difficult to find, particularly in valuable and threatened areas such as the tropics.

Accordingly, WWF's GFTN has endorsed another process for obtaining "good wood". Known as the "stepwise approach", it is designed to improve the environmental status of forests and supply chains. It is a pragmatic approach to sourcing responsibly.

Supply chains do not change overnight and neither does forest management. Buyers start on a path that leads to 100% sourcing of certified wood. It begins with identifying the source of wood products, rejecting those identified as illegal, progressing to working with sources that are on the road to certification, and finally, purchasing only certified wood.

To assist buyers looking to improve their supply chains, the GFTN has recently published a guide called *Responsible Purchasing of Forest Products*, which strongly encourages buyers to work with WWF producer groups to help buyers and sellers achieve their goals. In many countries, these producer groups are likely the only means of effecting forest certification, with producer group members also engaging in a step by step process that ends with credible certification.

Value for business

One new producer group member, Inspiration Furniture, hopes to play a leading role in the push for responsible forestry in Malaysia, and by doing so, to increase its business opportunities. Inspiration Furniture Sdn Bhd became the first member of Malaysia's producer group, Kumpulan Khazanah Hijau, on 10 May 2004.

Established only four years ago, Inspiration has already become one of Malaysia's top manufacturers and exporters of garden furniture. Between November 2002 and February 2003, Inspiration exported more than 4,000 units of furniture a month to European buyers. Its product lines include garden chairs, tables, and benches of various designs. Inspiration is committed to supporting sustainable forest management, through increasing the percentage of its source materials purchased from forests moving towards certification.

Many companies have used similar approaches over the past decade with significant success, organizations that could otherwise risk their reputations and potentially even legal action as a result of knowing nothing about the origin of their wood. This can move to a position of greater security, which will increase with time.

"After ten years working with WWF we know that there are benefits all round," says Homebase's Young. *"When it comes to trying to keep our supply chain moving in the right direction, we know we are working with the right people. We are now achieving the results our business needs."*

Source: Sustainable forest, sustainable future, 01 October 2004, Kate Fuller on www.panda.org/gftn, first published in www,FDMasia

Key insights

The success of the GFTN is now being applied to other products like fish, palm oil, and soya.

Meanwhile what lessons for a Green Supply Chain are shown in the above case studies?

We have summarized our view on these lessons below.

General comments

- Need to change the way business is done.
- Modern sustainable Green practices work better than the previously used traditional ones.

- Success comes from the sustainability contributions plus the business viability and success, for example, the benefits to reputations by having full knowledge on the sourcing of products.
- Supply chains do not change overnight.

Approach used

- Facilitator for trade linking.
- Challenging and innovative partnerships.
- A proven stepwise approach with local on the ground support
- Independent multi-stakeholder-based certification, this being seen as a vital and efficient tool to apply the Green principles.

Demand side needs

- The right demand market conditions.
- Encouragement of major buyers who, in turn, are pushed by environmental groups, public concern, and pressure from shareholders who require up and running environmental and ethical companies to invest in.

Supply side aspects

- Start with the leading producers.
- Provide suppliers and others that depend on the supplier with the economic and social benefits.
- Increased costs of supply must be paid for by increased selling prices, though there are often cost savings from simplifying supply chains.

Case Study 2: Collaboration in Supply Chains

The above WWF/GFTN case study clearly illustrates the need to work with others in the supply chain process. What follows are extracts from a paper delivered by Stuart Emmett at SAPICS 2007 in Sun City RSA.

The supply chain is a process and a process is defined as:

"A sequence of dependent events, involving time, which has a valued result for the eventual end user."

Clearly there are direct parallels here to supply chain management, which can be seen clearly from the three key aspects of all processes:

Dependence

- Sequential and related, "knock on effects".
- Receives inputs and changes them to outputs.
- What happens "here" causes events "there".
- "A" needs to be finished before "B" can start.
- In any process, it is only as efficient as its most inefficient part.
- "A chain is as strong as its weakest link".
- The most important factor is, therefore, the most limiting one.

Variability

- Normal statistical influences apply (e.g. normal distribution curve); the "fixed, known, and expected" can become "variable, unknown and unexpected".
- Causes changes from a state of "certainty" to "uncertainty".
- Each part with variability causes knock on effects, with sometimes catastrophic results.

Interfaces

- The potential friction points between processes.
- Often ignored, as our minds concentrate on "the box" and what happens there.
- Real dependencies also exist in/at the interface.

A Proposition

"Managing a dependent process in isolation and managing it independently is plain folly. Managing the supply chain without the collaboration of the other players is a fruitless strategy."

(Source: Emmett and Crocker, 2006)

Supply chain management is therefore fundamentally about how we are able to "integrate, coordinate and control the supply chain". However this integration and coordination is also needed "in the hearts and minds of people" and not just by using technical tools/systems/techniques.

This importance of "people" has been noted by the master management guru Peter Drucker who has noted:

"Because the object of management is a human community held together by the work bond for a common purpose, management always deals with the nature of man."

Lessons from experience emphasize this critical aspect:

"The most critical and important business opportunities are:

- *Understanding customers' needs and requirements*
- *Customer service excellence*
- *Collaboration amongst supply chain partners."*

What is collaboration?

Collaboration can be seen as:

- Selective dialogue between the "right" people.
- Intense and focused with investments of time/resources, of the whole organization.
- Taking the long-term and strategic view.
- To improve the performance of the whole supply chain.

Collaboration however is not:

- an SRM software package
- "I will take all the benefits"
- a quick fix
- easy
- for everyone
- a "one size fits all" approach.

The eminent UK Supply Chain academic, Professor Martin Christopher, noted in the early 1990s that:

"The future is one not of competing companies but of competing supply chains."

Therefore success in the future comes from how we manage our supply chains; however to do this we will need to have a "collaborative advantage". Managing a supply chain effectively has well known benefits such as:

Increased

- return on assets
- profit
- customer service levels
- performance.

Reduced

- stock/ inventory levels
- cost.

However, "there may be trouble ahead" as the UK's Professor Alan Waller has noted:

"The supply chain lies no longer with an individual company; we have global networks cutting across countries and organizations. The only way forward is to get players working to a common agenda, the collaboration agenda. We have been taught to compete: nobody has taught us to work together. The need and awareness is there but still nobody has taught us how to do it."

Misunderstandings between supply chain players can still rule, for example:

"The Mail on Sunday alleges the Retailer was asking 700 of its suppliers for a contribution from their contracts and the company was to lengthen its payments terms from 60 to 90 days.

"The Company is locked in a bitter dispute battle with its suppliers over attempts to extract cost savings from its supply chain … One supplier claimed the company were arrogantly out of touch."

Ways forward on better relationships

The comments or lessons from experience are useful (if challenging to do):

- *"We have to be interested in being criticized"* (when talking with other supply chain players).
- *"Business is increasingly interdependent, where action takes place between and not within."*
- *"Trying to get through years of accumulated baggage is tough."*
- *"Personal relationships that bridge former gaps in communications between vendor and retailer are what can really spell success."*

As with any relationship, trust is the key principle. If there is no trust, then there is no relationship. Trust involves the following additional lessons from experience:

- *"It changes the paradigm. It's definitely a different type of relationship with your customer. It's based on mutual trust and it's got to be there to succeed."*
- *"On paper, the process seems simple to implement, but in the real world of personalities and professional relationships, there are many obstacles to climb. Trust is very important for success."*
- *"You can define any relationship by the degree of trust. No trust then no relationship. This applies both in business and also in personal life."*
- *"The biggest thing my boss could do for me is to trust me."*

Trust is therefore critical, and three levels of trust have been usefully identified:

- Trust Level one, Contractual and "Service": Boundary time bound trust for standard performance. Exchanged data for transactions.
- Trust Level two, Competence and "Satisfaction": Reliable trust for satisfactory performance, with some information sharing and cooperation.

- Trust Level three, Commitment and "Success": Goodwill open-ended trust giving beyond expectations success with cognitive connected decision making.

(Source: After Dr. Mari Sako)

Deeper trust is the crucial ingredient of collaborative supply chain success. Building it, maintaining it, and restoring it if damaged, must be at the top of every chief executive's agenda. The following are keys:

- Understand each other.
- Agree fundamental objectives such as "reductions", "improvements".
- Share information.
- The "how" is not easy.

Rules for relationships have been identified:

- Mutual goodwill and being in this together.
- Compromise is the key and sorting out problems together.
- Don't try and prove who is right.
- Don't stonewall but keep talking.
- Understand each other.
- Talk about what is valued in each other.
- Don't break commitments and promises.
- Separation is painful and expensive.

However, relationships between suppliers and buyers may also involve an uneven distribution of power, especially in the buying process.

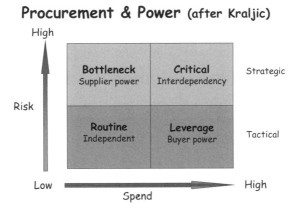

Procurement & Power (after Kraljic)

Whilst this is not the place to fully explore the above (but is in Emmett and Crocker, *Excellence in Procurement* (2008)), it readily illustrates the imbalance of power that can be found, simply:

- Leverage buying is where there are many suppliers with a buyer buying large quantities and the buyer is therefore able to leverage on price.
- Bottleneck items are where there are few suppliers but the buyer has to have their highly priced products; for example, OEM spares and inkjet printer cartridges.

We therefore do have variations in relationships, and six types may be identified below, ranging from tactical leverage buying to strategic alliance relationships, as for example found with Toyota car assembly in the UK where key suppliers actually sit on the Toyota management board.

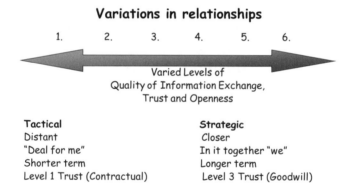

Variations in relationships

1.   2.   3.   4.   5.   6.

Varied Levels of
Quality of Information Exchange,
Trust and Openness

Tactical	**Strategic**
Distant	Closer
"Deal for me"	In it together "we"
Shorter term	Longer term
Level 1 Trust (Contractual)	Level 3 Trust (Goodwill)

This continuum can be seen as follows.

More tactical

- Trust is based on what the contract says.
- Suppliers must do what the contract says.
- Strong use of negotiation ploys.
- Emphasis on price reduction.
- Short-term.
- Measure supplier's performance by non-compliance.

More strategic

- Goodwill trust and cooperation.
- Suppliers will do whatever is needed.
- Mutual gains and goals "rule".
- Joint cost reduction (for example, Total Cost of Ownership, Cost to Serve, and Best Value orientations).
- Long-term.
- Both measure and jointly agree remedial actions.

To move to be more strategic or to change the way we manage relationships, then there is a need to change the thinking. Some important points on our thinking are as follows:

- Our thinking comes from our mental maps.
- These are like computer programs that give predetermined actions.
- For example, the attitudes/beliefs/values that give us our "reality".
- With computer programs we will check and re-calibrate the parameters when needed, for example, with independent/random demand.
- But, how often do we challenge our own mental map parameters?
- Changing our thinking means acquiring different perspectives, but such change may be uncomfortable and may be rejected, for example: *"Trust is the emotional glue that involves commitment to others"* versus *"Emotions have no part to play in business"*.

How do we think?

The simplified view is as follows:

- Logical left brain: Rational "facts"-based reasoning that converges.
- Creative right brain: Emotional "feelings" synthesis that diverges.
- "Rounded people" can use both sides.

Our thinking works through into company thinking and how we manage the supply chain. Simply, we do need to use both brain sides so that we can become more holistic.

Relationships are central to business success

"Supply-chain management is technically simple, but it is usually managerially difficult."

What must be fundamental is how the relationships are handled, with all of the internal and external supply chain players. Improving relationships is one of the main keys to enable SCM success. Relationship management must be a company strategy and become a core capability, as shown below.

"Benefits of our Collaboration programme include:

- *Improved service levels.*
- *Faster flow of product through the supply chain.*
- *Rational use of resources and more effective promotion planning.*
- *Synchronization of production to better match supply with demand.*
- *Shared responsibility and mutual trust."*

"A real focus on joint and collaborative planning has been critical. It's all very well putting in great capability and structurally changing our supply chain but at the end of the day you can't make it happen unless you work together."

"Key suppliers work collaboratively, ensuring efficient processing and best practices, driving out competitive edge"

Conversely there are costs associated with poor business relationships, for example:

- High administration costs.
- Time spend price wrangling.
- Time spent resolving problems.
- Too many meetings with too many people.
- Unwilling to consider simple solutions to problems.
- An atmosphere that discourages innovation.

Collaborative supply chains: conclusion

So the questions we need to ask ourselves are as follows:

1. How will we get these benefits?
   - By "partner-squeeze" or by "partnership"?
   - By competing or by collaborating?

2. What is there left to "squeeze"?

"We just can't continue with the mindless search for the lowest price, in the belief that, somehow, this will give us the best quality and the best performance."

3. The perennial question is:
   What benefits can be found from having better relationships?

Case Study 3: Green Reverse Supply Chain Waste and Kodak

It all started with the small disposable film cameras that Kodak produced in the mid-eighties. The product was great, the pricing was great, and the public liked the convenience. But there was this nagging feeling that somehow this was not an appropriate step, that this would mean more garbage, more dumping, and more environmental impact.

The company was a responsible corporate citizen. It did not like being associated with overflowing garbage dumps. The company also was in a position to do something about this. Most cameras were returned for processing of films to the camera shops. While collecting used cameras from these shops and taking them all the way back was an additional expense, the company decided to do this. Some of the parts in the cameras could then be reused and the rest of the material could be properly recycled.

Structuring the supply chain in the reverse direction had its usual challenges. Initially, most processing shops were not deeply engaged in the collection effort. After all they were photo shops and independently owned commercial businesses in most cases. It was not their role to be garbage recyclers. The company had to reconfigure its facilities to handle the incoming used cameras. Logistics costs were looming large. Reverse logistics was not a well honed concept at that time. However, gradually the supply loop was created.

After several successful months, a supply chain analysis revealed two key things:

1. More and more parts could be actually reused. This led to expansion of the programme.
2. As the programme expanded it resulted in cost savings. The company could afford to pay collection locations for their services. This led to renewed vigour in the programme.

As a result, more collection locations were enrolled, and the relationships were formalized. The cost reduction from the resultant "Green Supply Chain" was calculated and reported regularly, and the programme was truly underway.

The next step in the Green Supply Chain Evolution in Kodak came in product redesign. All the parts and the product itself were redesigned in order to maximize the reuse of parts, and minimize the waste. The material and specifications of the parts were changed in order to assure a minimum number of cycles. As a result of this application of production life cycle engineering concept to the product, additional savings were achieved.

The company continues to continuously improve their "Green Supply Chain" for this product family with alignment, balance and monitoring of the key supply chain parameters.

Case Study 4: Green Packaging and Reverse Logistics – The Free Pack Net SRL Case Study

Background

The use of disposable packaging is a non-core business for producers of domestic white goods; therefore based on an innovative business model, Free Pack Net decided to develop a business that rents out high protection packaging and arranges for the return of the packaging from the market via a network of reverse logistics.

The mission of Free Pack Net is therefore to serve its customers through improving the value chain, a reduction of costs, and by using sustainable economic development that integrates reusable packaging rental, with an advanced logistics management service.

Product and logistics system innovation

The packaging designed by Free Pack Net followed research and analysis of the most suitable materials and the technical, economic, and practical feasibility of such packaging.

At present (2009), Free Pack Net is the only business in the world to have created structural clampable packaging that satisfies the technical requirements of the distribution chain for domestic white goods.

After many improvements and redesigns to optimize costs and to maximize the technical characteristics of the product, Free Pack Net succeeded in creating a structural and modular packaging that is able to resist lateral and vertical loads up to 1.2 tonnes.

In addition, since the packaging is made up of modular elements, it can be collapsed when returned, such a volume reduction enabling reverse logistics costs to be controlled and contained.

The operating sector for domestic white goods is characterized by few producers, who operate worldwide, producing domestic white goods that have standard dimensions (60 × 60 cm). For example, washing machines produced by Whirlpool have the same dimensions as those produced by other producers such as Indesit, by Electrolux etc.

However in the last 30 years the sector has had no packaging innovation at all.

In Europe the cost/volume ratio for the transport of white goods is reasonable; the transport cost of a washing machine weighing 85 kg on average varies from €15 to €18. The European distribution network for white goods (and therefore also that in return) also has nodes that are distributed uniformly and therefore to return the packaging of a washing machine, clean it, recondition it, and resupply it to the factory does not cost more than €3.50 per piece.

Research and development

Free Pack Net's research and development activity consists of the creation of a preliminary advanced project of the structural packaging. During this activity, it is necessary to design the finished product considering the following:

- the type of material that one wants to use;
- the weight that it must support;
- the volume and dimensions.

The objective here is not only to define the technical parameters required to guarantee the physical characteristics and performance criteria of the structural packaging, but is also to design the packaging considering the costs. Every additional gram in weight or every cubic centimetre in volume will have significant incremental costs when creating the mould/moulding the packaging due to an increase in raw material, but above all, in the reverse logistics circuit, where transportation costs increase with volume.

The strategic importance of R&D/advanced project is considerable, as an error in the design of the product can be fatal, both for failing to meet the technical performance that the packaging must guarantee, and for the exponential increase in costs; accordingly this activity in undertaken in house.

Prototyping and testing

Prototyping is closely linked to the above preliminary project, but it differs since it consists of adopting the guidelines defined in the project phase and transferring them to the production methods of the moulds and the packaging. Prototyping therefore belongs to the production process and in particular to the development of production technologies that are ever more highly performing and efficient and whose characteristics will ensure that the product complies with the technical specifications described in the preliminary project. Tests are then made to verify that the product passes the technical trials for which it is guaranteed.

The strategic importance of this activity is comparable to that of R&D/planning, since both activities are profoundly intertwined, continuously affecting each other. Prototyping/testing is carried out externally from Free Pack Net by those companies who, in a later phase, create the mould and the packaging. Due to the intertwining of R&D/advanced project and prototyping/testing, this involves a collaborative method of working.

Manufacturing 1

This activity can be split into two subcategories:

- Creation of the mould.
- Creation of the structural packaging.

The mould, intended as the production asset that enables production of the package, is made using as a guiding reference the preliminary project and the results of R&D. The production of the mould's components is carried out by both the same companies that go on to make the packaging (using the mould) and by those third party companies who are specialized in the production of moulds. The production of the moulds takes place in many businesses, each one creating a component. The finished mould comes from the aggregation of all the components, ready to be used in the moulding of the packages.

Production of the structural packaging is carried out by Free Pack Net exclusively through outsourcing agreements.

Logistics

Logistics in Free Pack Net can be divided into three subactivities:

1. Tracking (using IT) and the planning of the reverse logistics network involves monitoring the journey made by each piece and also provides the preliminary detailed planning for the eventual reverse logistics network operations. This activity is of high strategic importance since it needs correct preventive programming of the transportation networks and tracking methods for every product, and is carried out using an elaborate information technology system which ensures the package journeys are monitored smoothly and ensures the support of the operating structure. Tracking and programming is carried out internally using an IT system.

2. Delivery: the factories making the packaging deliver them to Free Pack Net's sorting centres (effectively these are logistic centres for preparation and reconditioning), that are located throughout Europe. Here they prepare the kits according to Free Pack Net's production plan (and thus according to the delivery plan to the domestic white goods factories) and next send them to the producers of domestic white goods. The domestic white goods manufacturers pack the electrical appliances and inform Free Pack Net, via the IT system, of the location and sales outlet to which they have been sent. In this way it is possible to track each product in the market. When the product arrives at the final consumer's house, the person installing the appliance (usually an employee of the sales outlet) recovers the packaging, closing it into a small suitcase and takes it back to the sales outlet. If, however, the consumer buys and installs the appliance themselves, the packaging must be returned to the sales outlet where in the future, the introduction of a guarantee deposit of €10/15

per packaging is foreseen; the adoption of such a small guarantee deposit is possible due to the limited industrial cost of the packaging.

3. Collection and reconditioning: once the packaging is brought back to the sales point, Free Pack Net intervenes using external companies specialized in the supply of logistic services to take the suitcase back to collection centres and then on to the sorting centres. Within these organizations, the logistics partners will clean and recondition the packaging, and reassemble the kit to send back to the domestic white goods producers according to instructions received through Free Pack Net's IT system.

The above takes place for the first 20 uses of the packaging. On the 21st cycle, the packaging has finished its useful life, and is sent by the sorting centres back to the factories that made the packaging. We then move on to "Manufacturing 2".

Manufacturing 2: packaging regeneration

This is the activity of regeneration/reproduction of packaging after 20 uses. The end-of-life packaging follows a variation in the logistics circuit: after arriving at the sorting centres, the shells are sent back to the businesses that produced them, where they are ground up and the packaging is regenerated with additional new material. Later, the regenerated packaging is sent back to the sorting centres which prepare the kits and then send them to the domestic white goods producers, restarting the circular flow.

Benefits

Free Pack Net's packaging has a number of advantages for all the players operating in the domestic white goods sector; it also has environmental benefits.

In market testing, the total rental costs of the reusable packaging are less than the purchase and disposal costs of disposable packaging.

Business customers also benefit from a considerable reduction in damages caused during the transportation and handling operations as the damage have been typically reduced from 5% to 0.4%. The packaging withstands loads from storage and handling of up to 1200 kg, therefore the metal structures of the product could be considerably lightened, thereby saving raw materials and industrial costs and providing the opportunity to obtain even more efficient product energy categories. *"The dishwasher must be designed to wash plates and not to withstand loads of 1200 kg"* (Massimo De Santis, President and Managing Director of Free Pack Net).

Lastly, it is also appropriate to consider the benefit for the image of the businesses that adopt the system. The environmental issue is used more and more by businesses to satisfy the needs of its customers, who nowadays show a greater sensitivity and awareness towards environmental issues. If traditional packaging materials such as polystyrene, stretchable plastic film, and cardboard are not being used, the volumes of waste created by the disposal of these materials is totally eliminated; for example it has been calculated that in the Lombardy region of Italy alone, every year 1600 tonnes of expanded polystyrene is disposed of from packaging of domestic white goods.

In 2006, Free Pack Net commissioned an Institute to quantify the environmental benefits when the current disposable packaging was compared to reusable packaging and against various environmental indicators.

For each indicator, reusable packaging in polypropylene had advantages that ranged between 70% and 95%.

The energy consumed in the life cycle of reusable packaging for a washing machine (e.g. production–used 20 times–final recycling) was 85% lower than that consumed in the life cycle of 20 different types of similar traditional packaging.

This represents a saving of approximately 39 barrels of petroleum for every 1800 washing machines produced. This becomes around 1 million barrels a year for the entire annual European production of domestic white goods and around 4 million barrels a year for 60% of the world market for domestic white goods.

The final consumer could also benefit from the purchase of more efficient domestic white goods (after a product redesign) that consume less energy and therefore offer a reduction in domestic energy utility costs for consumers and for society as a whole.

Case Study 5: Chicago Climate Exchange

The Chicago Climate Exchange (CCX), a US corporation, is a voluntary greenhouse gas (GHG) reduction and trading system involving emission sources and emission offset projects worldwide. It started trading operations in 2003 and in 2005 launched the European Climate Exchange (ECX), an exchange operating in the European Union Emissions Trading Scheme.

CCX works on the basis of a cap and trade programme where the member organizations agree to reduce their emissions by a certain level each year.

The regulatory bodies first set a cap or limit on the amount of the pollution or environmental degradation allowed in a region.

Then the member companies that reduce their emissions below their set limit receive emission allowances/permits which they can bank or trade/sell to companies that have not been able to meet their targets at a market price.

So by setting up this emission trading market, the member organizations have commitment to reduce their emission levels and also receive incentives to develop programmes that aim to reduce emissions. Companies also have flexibility as to how they bring about the reduction in emission levels.

Categories of membership

Chicago Climate Exchange has six categories of membership:

1. Member: emits significant amount of greenhouse gases and agrees to an emission reduction commitment.
2. Associate Member: office-based businesses that have almost no direct emissions. Such members commit to offset 100% of all indirect greenhouse gas emissions associated with energy purchases and business travel through 2010.
3. Offset Provider: owner of qualifying offset projects that destroy or displace greenhouse gas emissions. They register and sell their offsets directly on the exchange.
4. Offset Aggregator: acts as administrative representative for sale of offset from multiple offset projects or offset project owners. Projects that offset less than 10 000 metric tonnes of CO_2 equivalent per year should be registered and sold using Offset Aggregator.
5. Liquidity Provider: trades on CCX for purposes other than reducing emissions such as market makers, trading groups, and hedge funds.
6. Exchange Participant: purchases CFI contracts to offset the emissions associated for special events or activities and does not adopt emission reduction commitments.

The CCX members can trade allowances for the following six GHG gases:

- carbon dioxide (CO_2)
- methane (CH_4)
- nitrous oxide (N_2O)
- hydrofluorocarbons (HFCs)
- perfluorocarbons (PFCs)
- sulphur hexafluoride (SF_6)

Non-CO_2 GHG emissions are converted to metric tonnes CO_2 using the one-hundred-year Global Warming Potential (GWP) values established by the Intergovernmental Panel on Climate Change.

CFI (Carbon Financial Instrument) contracts are the CCX tradable commodity and one CFI contract represents 100 metric tonnes of CO_2 equivalent (CO_2e).

CFI contracts comprise Exchange Allowances and Exchange Offsets:

- Exchange Allowances are issued to member organizations that are responsible for emitting GHG. These allowances are based on their emission baseline and the CCX Emission Reduction Schedule.
- Emission Offsets are issued to owners or aggregators that own offset projects that destroy or displace GHG. Emission offsets are issued once the eligible offset projects have been verified by a third party to assess the quantity of GHG reductions and the verification results have been presented to the CCX.

Individuals and organizations in the forestry, waste management, agricultural, and renewable energy segments can participate in CCX by registering their offsets. CCX has developed rules for the following types of offset projects and issues CFI contracts accordingly:

- Agricultural methane
- Coal mine methane
- Landfill methane
- Agricultural soil carbon
- Rangeland soil carbon management

- Forestry
- Renewable energy
- Ozone depleting substance destruction
- Energy efficiency and fuel switching
- Clean Development Mechanism (CDM) eligible projects.

Case Study 6: Green Grocery Stores in the Retail Sector

Sustainable supply chain practices are growing in number and we will see more and more responsiveness among users and end users as the time passes by. Food Lion, one of largest food chains in the United States, is building a green grocery store in northeast Columbia, South Carolina. Food Lion was founded in 1957 as Food Town in Salisbury, North Carolina. Today it is one of the largest supermarket chains in the United States. It is operating 1300 supermarkets directly under its name or under the names of its affiliated entities such as Bloom, Bottom Dollar, Harvey's, and Reid's.

For many years Food Lion has been working on energy conservation programmes. It has earned its eighth consecutive ENERGYSTAR award in 2009, these being the US Environmental Protection Agency's highest energy conservation honour.

The new stores that Food Lion are building will be Leadership in Energy and Environmental Design (LEED) certified and will feature a number of environmentally friendly construction and energy-efficient attributes. It is estimated that these eco-friendly attributes will reduce energy costs by more than 20% compared to a typical supermarket and in addition conserve 44% more water than other Food Lion stores.

The new eco-friendly features of the new stores will include:

- Use of skylights for natural lighting, and high efficiency lighting which can dim lights based on natural sunlight in the store, or when areas such as offices and restrooms are not in use.
- Preferred parking for low emitting vehicles and bike racks.
- LED lighting that consumes lower energy, has a longer lifetime, and is smaller in size will be used in the frozen food cases.
- Sensor activated and low flow fixtures in restrooms.

- Native plant species that minimize irrigation requirements.
- Use of low toxicity materials to improve air quality and the safety of staff and customers.
- Installation of environmental education kiosks in the store to educate people in sustainability practices.
- Reduced air pollution and fuel consumption by purchasing a significant amount of building materials manufactured within 500 miles of each location. This will also assist local economies.
- Recycling of construction waste via appropriate waste management plans.
- Onsite recycling centre for customers and staff.

Case Study 7: Product Design and Recycling and Sony

Sony has made good progress in reducing the environmental impact of its products. It has taken steps right from design phase to recycling to combat environmental issues. It is recycling and using recycled material for either exterior packaging or internal components of its products. This way it has been able to reduce the use of new natural resources and use recycled plastics for its products. Sony Group uses more than 10 000 tonnes of recycled plastic each year in a wide variety of products such as televisions, recording media, audio equipment, computers, and digital camcorders.

An internal group promotes the reuse of products or recycled material in products. A resource recovery technology for plastic also helps to reduce carbon emissions. Below are some of the examples of progress that Sony has made to minimize environmental impacts.

Recycling of CD waste

Sony had developed a proprietary method that successfully recycles the CD scrap produced during the manufacturing of optical discs and other products. The recovered material is used in product components. In the recycling process the polycarbonate CD waste gets converted into recycled polycarbonate using this proprietary method. The quality of recycled polycarbonates is equivalent to new materials. The recovered material is then used in product casing, top covers, cradles, etc.

Green mindset using design phase

Sony has taken initiatives to keep recycling in mind during the design phase of it products. It is now producing televisions that use recycled plastic from its own supply loops. It is using polystyrene foam used for packaging and plastic parts from other models for producing recycled plastic that is used in manufacturing televisions. In 2008 nine out of 11 models of Sony's Bravia brand LCD televisions used recycled plastics. This not only reduces the amount of new material used but also reduces carbon emissions

Case Study 8: Renewable Energy and Geothermal Power Usage

Icelandic transformation

Geothermal energy has been instrumental in transforming Iceland from relying on fossil fuels for basic necessities to become a global leader in the use of geothermal power. In Iceland the geothermal power is used to generate electricity, provide heating for towns and cities, provide hot water for daily needs, and produce electricity for manufacturing plants such as an aluminium smelter. The savings are huge, for example when producing aluminium using hydropower energy instead of coal, as it reduces the CO_2 emissions per ton by 90%.

Geothermal heat is considered sustainable as the total heat extracted is small compared to the total heat content of Earth.

Vital statistics for Iceland

- Iceland has among the highest per capita energy consumption in the world. In 2005 the primary energy consumption was 500 GJ. A proportion of this energy comes from renewable resources.
- Nearly 29% of primary energy is imported and the rest is domestic, renewable energy.
- Geothermal energy is the primary source of energy.
- In 2005, 54.9% of the total national primary energy consumed was geothermal energy. The remaining distribution: hydropower 16.3%, petroleum 25.9%, and coal 3%.

- In 2006 26.5% of total electricity generated was using geothermal energy, up from 19.1% in 2005.
- More than 85% of the housing and building heating needs are met by geothermal energy.
- 90% of houses are heated using geothermal water.
- Huge financial savings have been achieved by Iceland with its use of geothermal power which otherwise would have been used in importing the fossil fuels to Iceland. The financial savings were around US$3000 million for the period 1944–1995 as compared to the cost of heating using oil.
- Iceland is now becoming self-sufficient rather than relying on the outside world for its energy needs.
- It is believed that in future Iceland may not use any fossil fuels.

Comments

The Earth's core is very hot and the temperatures may reach 4000–7000 °C. Geothermal heat is the heat from the core of the Earth. Many countries and continents have these heat supplies underneath. The geothermal heat comes to the surface of the Earth through cracks, fissures, and permeable rocks. Energy from natural steam, hot water, and hot rocks is harnessed in the form of geothermal energy for generating electricity and heating. Electricity generation requires high temperature resource that are only available at great depths.

In addition to very hot temperatures down deep in the Earth's crust, the top few metres of the ground warm up during summers and cool down during winters. This shallow ground heat is easily accessible and evenly distributed and can be extracted using a geothermal power pump anywhere in the world for heating homes.

Geothermal sites can provide heat for many decades. The production from a geothermal well can reduce or even dry up after a few years. However, these wells can be rejuvenated and brought to full potential, in theory, after reinjecting water.

References and Bibliography

Emmett, Stuart (2005) *Excellence in Warehouse Management: How to Minimise Costs and Maximise Value*, John Wiley & Sons, Ltd.

Emmett, Stuart (2008) *Excellence in Supply Chain Management: How to Understand and Improve Supply Chains*, Liverpool Academic Press.

Emmett, Stuart (2009) *Excellence in Freight Transport: How to Better Manage Domestic and International Logistics Transport*, Cambridge Academic.

Emmett, Stuart and Crocker, Barry (2006) *The Relationship Driven Supply Chain: Creating a Culture of Collaboration Throughout the Chain*, Ashgate Publishing Limited.

Emmett, Stuart and Crocker, Barry (2008) *Excellence in Procurement: How to Optimise Costs and Add Value*, Liverpool Academic Press.

Emmett, Stuart and Crocker, Barry (2009) *Excellence in Supplier Management: Suppliers and Add Value*, Cambridge Academic.

Emmett Stuart, and Granville, David (2007) *Excellence in Inventory Management: How to Minimise Costs and Maximise Service*, Cambridge Academic.

PricewaterhouseCoopers (2008) Achieving Superior Global Financial Performance in a Challenging Economy.

Sood, Vivek (2008) Resource boom highlights acute need for supply chain revolution down under, *Supply Chain Asia Magazine*, Nov/Dec.

Sood, Vivek and Fedorowicz, Tony (2008) Demand is from Mars, Supply is from Venus and S&OP is from Pluto, *Supply Chain Asia Magazine*, May/Jun.

Sood, Vivek and Fedorowicz, Tony (2008) How green is your supply chain, *Supply Chain Asia Magazine*, Mar/Apr.

The Environmental Association for Universities and Colleges (EAUC).

World Business Council for Sustainable Development Report (2007).

www.panda.org/gftn
  Making markets work for forests and people in Ghana, 26 May 2006
  Russia's sustainable forestry revolution, 19 February 2007.
  Sustainable forest, sustainable future, 1 October 2004.

Index

80/20 rule *see* Pareto analysis

accidents 66, 95–6
accountabilities
  see also responsibilities
  concepts 109–12, 203–13
  product-stewardship parameter to the
    production framework 109–10,
    153–4
accuracy/reliability factors, information
  232
acidic waste water 156
acquisition costs, procurement framework
  60, 70–91
action plans 87–8, 132–7, 145–50,
  179–80, 192–7, 201–13,
  217–23
  see also continuous improvements
advocacy groups, procurement challenges
  69
Africa 239–44
aggregation levels of information, decision
  makers 232–3
agri-business 166–7, 271–2
alternative fuels 19–26, 64–7, 90, 125,
  134–5, 204–13, 274–5
Amur-Heilong programme 248
analytical methodology, cost-benefit
  analysis 25–6, 48–52
asset recovery drives, supply loops 178,
  263–9
audits 88, 89, 204–13, 227, 244
automobile industry 19–21, 72, 113–15,
  124–5, 131–2

Baffoe, Abraham 242–4
barriers to trade 70
The Benchmark Foundation (Tutu) 10–11
benchmarking
  see also best practices
  concepts 210–13, 221–2, 226, 234
  continuous improvements 221–2, 226
  definition 221
best practices
  see also benchmarking
  concepts 81–4, 221–2
  supplier-development 81–4
big bang approaches 217, 218, 229
bill of materials (BOM) 130, 212
biodegradable products 90, 158
biodiesel 65, 90, 134–5
blame cultures 40, 41, 74–5
boards of directors 3–4, 5, 23, 107, 145
  see also leadership ...
  GSCM opportunities 3–4, 5, 23, 145
bottleneck items, spend/cost and criticality/
  risk procurement evaluations 61–3,
  259–60
bottom line impacts of green supply chains
  17–26, 30–1, 89–91, 113–21
brand-image benefits of green supply chains
  7, 8, 19–26, 31, 63, 67, 98, 107, 121,
  126, 145, 151–64, 176–7, 253–4
budgets, continuous improvements 218–19
buildings 132, 135–7, 195, 272–3
buying *see* procurement framework
by-products 13–15, 19–27, 36, 142,
  165–80
  see also supply loops

carbon credits 19–26, 106–7, 185, 195–7,
    270–2
carbon footprints 5, 9, 13–15, 19–26, 27,
    43, 47–8, 54–6, 57, 63–91, 95–6,
    101–2, 103, 106–7, 129–30, 134–5,
    178, 181–97, 201, 270–2
  concepts 13–15, 19–27, 181–97, 270–2
  minimization efforts 181–97, 201,
    270–2
carbon life cycle analysis (CLCA),
    concepts 193
carbon measurement
  concepts 185–92, 196, 208–13, 219–23,
    225–34, 270–2
  definition 185–6
  methodologies 187, 188–92
  orange juice example 187
  organizational boundaries 187–8
  responsibilities 188
carbon monitoring
  concepts 185–6, 193, 196
  definition 196
carbon offsetting
  concepts 185, 192, 195–6, 270–2
  definition 195
carbon reporting
  see also greenwashing
  concepts 185–6, 193, 196–7, 208–13,
    219–23, 227, 270–2
  definition 196
  legislation 197, 270–2
carbon sequestration (storage), concepts
    192–3
carbon tracking, concepts 103, 106–7
carbon trading
  concepts 185, 195–6, 269–72
  definition 195
carbon-management framework 13–15,
    19–26, 27, 43, 57, 63–91, 95–6,
    101–2, 103, 106–7, 129–30, 134–5,
    181–97, 221, 228–34, 270–2
  action plans 192–7
  carbon-reduction potential results 193–5
  concepts 13–15, 19–26, 181–97, 221,
    228–34, 270–2
  cycle of steps 185–97
  definition 183–5
  regulations 19–26, 106–7, 183–97, 227,
    270–2
  traditional/green-supply-chain
    approaches 193–4
cars 19–21, 72, 113–15, 124–5, 131–2
case studies 235–75
Cass, Julia 244, 249
CDs 273

centre-point perspective, customers 48,
    69–70, 88–91, 101–2
CEOs
  see also leadership ...
  GSCM opportunities 3–4, 5, 23, 144–5
certification schemes 239–54
CFOs
  see also leadership ...
  packaging costs 144
change management 20–6, 33–4, 102, 144,
    145–50, 201, 205, 211–13, 217–23,
    226–34
  see also continuous improvements;
    migration-strategy ...
  big bang approaches 217, 218, 229
  concepts 211–13, 217–23, 226–34
  organizational change management phase
    III of the migration-strategy
    framework 211–13
  turbulence factors 226
channels
  channels-and-sales-force elements of
    green marketing 159–60, 161–2
  supply loops 177
chemicals industry 19, 22, 115, 166–7
Cherepovetsles 247
Chicago Climate Exchange (CCX) 269–72
China 23, 101–2, 115–16, 248–51
Christopher, Professor Martin 257
circular supply chains, concepts 169–71
civil actions, legal frameworks 99, 107, 126
CLCA see carbon life cycle analysis
Clean Air-Cool Planet 194
climate change 5, 8–10, 19–26, 30–1, 33,
    35, 66, 82–3, 88, 95–7, 103, 106–7,
    112, 117, 124–37, 155–64, 183–97,
    204–13, 269–72
coal 124, 271, 274
Coca-Cola 154, 156, 158
collaborating partners 11, 13, 27, 30–1,
    34–5, 39–41, 43–5, 46–7, 60–8, 73–91,
    100–2, 103–5, 136–7, 144–5, 147–50,
    201–13, 225–6, 228–9, 231–2, 234,
    254–63
  see also trust
  concepts 254–63
  definition 256–7
  EGL model 104–6, 201–13
  feedback 75–7, 79–80, 254–63
  information 75–87, 147–8
  migration-strategy framework 13–15, 27,
    57, 199, 201–13
  opportunities 68, 73–91
  strategic collaborative alignments 73–7,
    259–63

Collins, Dr Darron 248
communications 40, 41–2, 52, 88, 105,
    109–10, 114–17, 145–50, 156, 159–64,
    204–13
    see also marketing
    pricing-and-communications elements of
        green marketing 159, 162–3
    production framework 103, 109–10,
        114–17, 204–13
    S&OP 40, 41–2, 52
community groups, green supply chain
    drivers 12–13, 68, 124–5, 192–3,
    240–9, 273
competitive-advantage benefits of green
    supply chains, concepts 7, 8, 13, 30,
    66, 79–82, 89, 98–9, 121, 148, 153–5,
    175–6, 180
conformance concepts 84–5
congestion problems on roads 130–1
consensus views, performance evaluations
    225–6
construction industry, bottom line impacts
    19–20
consumer goods 19–26, 33, 127–30, 166–8,
    265–9
    see also FMCG industry
    explosive growth 33, 127–30
consumer organizations 13
consumers
    see also customers
    emotional resonance 12–13
    green supply chain drivers 12–13, 25,
        44–5, 67–8, 88–91, 97–9, 124–5,
        128, 152–7, 192–5, 202–13, 241–54
    marketing framework 159–64
    segmentation 47–52, 159–60, 163–4
    traditional/green supply chains 9–10,
        39–47, 104–5, 193–5
contingency planning 52
continuous improvements
    see also migration-strategy framework
    benchmarking 221–2, 226
    benefits 218–19
    concepts 10, 13–15, 20–1, 27, 57,
        118–20, 150, 168, 180, 204–13,
        215–23, 225–34
    definition 217
    examples 223
    methodologies 219–20
    Pareto analysis 222–3
    PDSA 220, 223
    prerequisites 219
    strategies 219–23
    supply loops 180
    Wal-Mart 223

contracts
    see also incentives ...
    suppliers 77–8, 81–2, 88, 204–13
cooking oils 65
corporate social responsibility (CSR)
    concepts 3–4, 10–11, 89, 126, 154,
        176–7, 195–6, 223
    definition 10–11, 176
    drivers 176
    supply loops 176–7
cost-benefit analysis 19–26, 30–1, 48–52,
    64–7, 89–91, 113–21
    see also profits
    analytical methodology 25–6, 48–52
    bottom line impacts 19–26, 30–1,
        89–91, 113–21
    industry examples 19–26
costs 5, 6, 8, 19–26, 30–1, 32, 34–6, 38,
    48–52, 53–6, 60–91, 95–121, 126–7,
    140–1, 143–50, 155–64, 178, 192–3,
    259–60
    acquisition costs 60, 70–91
    externalities 127, 184–5
    inventories 55–6, 71, 135–7
    LCC 38, 71–2, 82–7, 90–1, 95–6,
        146–50, 194–7, 204–13
    'only cost' mindset 70–2
    packaging 140–1, 143–4, 145, 146–50
    poor relationships 262–3
    procurement framework 60–91
    spend/cost and criticality/risk
        procurement evaluations 61–3,
        259–60
    sunk costs in outdated technologies 100
    supply loops 178
    TACs 60, 70–91
    TCO 38, 71–2, 90–1, 261–3
    types 38, 53–4, 70–2
    WLCs 71–2
costs/efficiency benefits of green supply
    chains 5, 6, 8, 19–26, 30–1, 32, 34–6,
    48–52, 61–91, 95–121, 126, 134–7,
    143–50, 155–64, 178, 192–7, 204–13,
    231–2
credit crunch see global economic crisis
    from 2007
critical items, spend/cost and criticality/risk
    procurement evaluations 61–3,
    259–60
Critical To Quality (CTQs) 120
CSR see corporate social responsibility
customer-centric issues
    demand planning 50–2, 101–2, 104–5
    marketing 159–64
    production framework 101–2, 104–5

customers
  see also consumers
  centre-point perspective 48, 69–70,
      88–91, 101–2
  collaborating partners 75–7, 81–2
  educational issues 101, 106, 128, 192–4,
      204–13, 273
  lean production 114–17
  requirements 4–13, 44–5, 47–52, 68–70,
      76–7, 81–2, 88–91, 101–2, 104–5,
      118–21, 124–5, 127–30, 140–1, 145,
      152–7, 160–4, 176–7, 180, 192–3,
      196–7, 236–57
  returns management 169, 171–80
  segmentation 47–52, 159–60, 163–4

De Santis, Massimo 269
decentralized organizations, procurement
    challenges 69–70
decision makers 3–4, 5, 23, 31–4, 38,
    46–7, 48–52, 54–6, 68, 80–2, 83–7,
    125, 144–5, 152–3, 193, 204–13,
    231–3
  GSCM pressures 3–4, 5, 23, 68, 125,
      144–5, 152–3
  information 232–3
  'jumping to conclusions' dangers 233
  LCM 31–4, 38, 193
  modelling framework for quick decisions
      48–9, 54, 232–3
  'paralysis analysis' dangers 233
  performance evaluations information
      232–3
defective products 49, 165–80
demand planning
  see also planning ... ; sales ...
  concepts 13, 27, 30, 43–4, 47–52, 61–3,
      184, 236–75
  definition 47–8
  processes 50–2
  variability data 50, 51, 55
  what-if analysis 51–2
Deming, W. Edwards 113–14, 220
demographics
  green marketing 163–4
  GSCM enabler 4
design & implementation phase II of the
    migration-strategy framework 208–11
Design of Experiments (DOE) 119
detailed-analysis phase I of the migration-
    strategy framework 205–8
developing world, sustainable
    developmental models 23
Dickson, Gilmour 242–4
diesel 65, 90, 127

disassembly approach to product designs
  concepts 121, 169–80
  definition 170, 175
disposals 4–10, 19–26, 32, 33–7, 38, 60–3,
    64–7, 71, 88, 89–90, 95–121, 126,
    137, 140–50, 154–64, 165–80, 194–7,
    204–13
  see also downstream ...
distribution 35, 37, 48, 56, 59–62, 71,
    75–7, 104–5, 123–37, 167–80, 193–5,
    236–54, 267–9
  see also logistics
  carbon-reduction potential results
      193–5
  definition 123–4
  LCE 35, 37, 75–7, 194–7
DMADV, concepts 118–20
DMAIC, concepts 118–20
downstream aspects of green supply chains
  see also disposals; end-of-life ... ; recovery;
      recycling
  concepts 4–5, 13–15, 63–4, 73, 89,
      121
Drucker, Peter 256
durable products, concepts 32–7, 113–21
dynamic balancing tools 40, 42

e-commerce 130
economic benefits of green supply chains
    4–5, 6, 7, 8, 11, 19–26, 31–2, 33–7,
    82–7, 98–9, 126, 251–4, 257–63
  see also cost ... ; profits
ECR *see* efficient customer response
    methodology
EDI *see* electronic data interchange
efficiency benefits of green supply chains,
    concepts 5, 6, 8, 19–26, 30–1, 32,
    61–91, 95–121, 134–7, 143–50,
    155–64, 178, 192–7, 204–13, 231–2
efficient customer response methodology
    (ECR), concepts 104
efficient green leadership (EGL), concepts
    103, 104–6, 201–13
effluents 155, 184
EGL *see* efficient green leadership
Einstein, Albert 45
electricity 82–7, 271, 274–5
electronics industry, bottom line impacts
    19–22
emotions 12–13, 261–3
employee satisfaction 19–26, 32, 34–5, 67,
    74–7, 89, 98–9, 107, 126
  see also workplace ...
EMS *see* environmental management
    systems

end-of-life management
  see also downstream ...
  concepts 4–5, 19–26, 32, 35–8, 60–3,
    108–9, 121, 158, 167–80, 193–5,
    203–13
  LCE 35, 37, 38, 194–7
end-to-end supply chains, concepts 4–5,
  41, 76–7, 86–7, 151–2, 234, 235–54
energy efficiencies 11, 13, 19–26, 32–7,
  57, 64–5, 82–91, 96–121, 134–7,
  192–7, 204–13, 231–2, 269, 272,
  274–5
ENERGYSTAR award 272
environment experts 76–7, 179–80, 229
environmental champions 87–8
environmental concerns 3–15, 33–7,
  60–91, 123–6, 140–50, 235–75
environmental management systems
  (EMS), concepts 60, 211–13
'environmentally preferable', definition
  problems 69
ethics, concept 3–4, 7, 89
European Climate Exchange (ECX) 270
execution framework
  see also logistic ... ; marketing; packaging;
    production ... ; supply loops
  concepts 13–15, 27, 30, 57, 93–180,
    221, 228–34
experts 76–7, 179–80, 229
external help, S&OP 45, 46–7
externalities, concepts 127, 184–5

facilitation services to 'go Green' 157,
  254
faulty products 112, 118–21, 165–80
feedback, collaborating partners 75–7,
  79–80, 254–63
financial performance benefits of green
  supply chains 6, 7, 8, 17–26, 63–91,
  126, 257–63
  see also profits
fines 6, 31, 99, 125, 227, 229
  see also regulations
fishbone diagrams 223
fleet management, logistics 132, 134–5
FMCG industry 19–22, 89, 166–8,
  265–9
  see also consumer goods
food and drinks industry 89, 272–3
Food Lion stores 272–3
Ford, Henry 40–1
forest and trade networks (FTNs) 240–4,
  246–53
Forestry Stewardship Council (FSC) 68,
  88, 242–9, 251

forests 68, 88, 152, 155–6, 195, 238–54,
  271–2
  case studies 238–54
  protective effects 250–1
Forum for the Future 194
forward logistics, supply loops 166–80
framework overview, green supply chains
  13–15
Free Pack Net 264–9
free-market solutions, externalities 184–5
Friends of the Earth (FoE) 240
fuel-efficient vehicles 19–26, 64–7, 82–7,
  124–7, 132–5, 204–13
fulfillment processes
  see also logistics
  concepts 5, 30
Fuller, Kate 253
future ideal state, migration-strategy
  framework 206–8

gap analysis, migration-strategy framework
  206–13
gasoline 127, 195, 274
'gate keeping', concepts 171–3
General Motors 5
geothermal energy 274–5
GFTN/WWF initiative 151, 235, 238–54
Ghana 239–44
global economic crisis from 2007 23–5,
  142–3, 144, 184
Global Forest & Trade Network (GFTN)
  151, 235, 238–54
Global Supply Chain Group (GSCG)
  233–4
global warming 5, 8, 33, 66, 82–3, 124,
  250, 271–2
globalization effects, lean production
  115–16
government support
  green marketing 154–8
  product-stewardship parameter to the
    production framework 109–10
Gray, John 38–9
green grocery stores case study 272–3
green reverse supply chain waste
  see also reverse logistics
  Kodak 263–4
green supply chain management (GSCM)
  benefits 4–5, 6–8, 10, 63–7, 96–8,
    257–63
  collaborating partners 11, 30–1, 41,
    43–5, 46–7, 60–8, 73–91, 100–2,
    103–5, 144–5, 147–50, 201–13,
    225–6, 228–9, 231–2
  concepts 3–15

definition 3–5, 11
enablers 3–4, 12–13, 23, 63–7, 89–91
historical background 3–4
green supply chains
    see also downstream ... ; logistics;
        production ... ; upstream ... ; within-
        the-organization ...
    action plans 87–8, 132–7, 145–50,
        179–80, 192–7, 201–13, 217–23
    benchmarking 221–2, 226, 234
    benefits 4–5, 6–8, 10, 17–26, 63–7,
        82–7, 96–8, 126, 141–50, 178,
        257–75
    bottom line impacts 17–26, 30–1,
        89–91, 113–21
    carbon-reduction potential results 193–5
    case studies 235–75
    concepts 3–15, 17–26, 65–8, 123–4,
        215–23, 225–34, 235–75
    continuous improvements 10, 13–15,
        20–1, 27, 57, 118–20, 150, 168,
        180, 204–13, 215–23
    CSR 10–11, 89, 154, 176–7, 195–6, 223
    definition 123–4
    drivers 3–5, 12–15, 17–26, 65–8, 83–7,
        88–91, 97–9, 102, 107, 109–10,
        124–5, 128, 141, 142–5, 152–7,
        175–8, 192–3, 197, 205–8, 211–13,
        241–54, 270–2
    framework overview 13–15
    integrated systems 174–5, 208–13,
        255–63
    overview 9–10
    performance evaluations 4–5, 13–15, 27,
        57, 78–82, 115–21, 148, 199,
        201–13, 215–23, 225–34
    profits 4–5, 6, 12–13, 17–26, 43–5, 53–6,
        89–91, 129–30, 155–6, 208–13,
        257–63
    roadmap 14–15, 212–13
greenhouse gas emissions (GHG) 9–10,
    19–26, 30–1, 33, 35, 88, 95–7, 103,
    106–7, 112, 117, 124–37, 155–64,
    183–97, 204–13, 269–72
    see also carbon ...
    types 271–2
greenwashing
    see also carbon reporting
    concepts 101, 109–10, 151–4, 159–60,
        191–2, 196–7
    definition 151
    examples 152
Grove, Andy 43
GSCM see green supply chain management
Guinean Moist Forest Ecosystem 239–44

Hanna Andersson 176–7
hazardous substances 6, 8, 11, 19,
    21–6, 32–7, 60–91, 99, 155, 204–13,
    273
health and safety issues 66, 86–7, 90–1,
    98–9, 107, 126, 204–13
holistic systems thinking 30–1, 35–7,
    91, 133–4, 146–50, 187–8, 193,
    261–3
Homebase Ltd 249–53

Iceland 274–5
IKEA 246–7, 251
impact assessments, LCE 34–5
implementation
    design & implementation phase II of the
        migration-strategy framework
        208–11
    EGL model 104–6, 201–13
    green packaging 145–50
    incentives alignment 110, 203–13
incentives alignment
    concepts 13, 19, 27, 57, 77–8, 81,
        89–91, 103, 110, 125, 146–50,
        203–13, 226, 231, 234
    definition 77–8
    implementation 110, 203–13
    logistics 125
Indonesia 249–51
industry examples, cost-benefit analysis
    19–26
information 4, 50–2, 63–4, 72, 75–87,
    100–1, 139–41, 153–4, 157–8, 174,
    180, 196–7, 208–13, 217–23, 227,
    230–4, 236–54, 270–2
    accuracy/reliability factors 232
    aggregation levels 232–3
    carbon reporting 196–7, 208–13, 227,
        270–2
    collaborating partners 75–87, 147–8
    decision makers 232–3
    GSCM enabler 4, 63–4
    'keeping it short and simple' (KISS) 230
    packaging 139–41, 157–8
    presentations 230–2
    requirements 72, 75–7, 100–1, 153–5,
        157–8, 196–7, 221–2, 230–4
    'where less is more' presentation
        guidelines 230–1
information systems, reverse logistics
    174–5
initiatives, increasing trends 68
innovations 7–8, 23, 31–2, 34–5, 67–9,
    82–7, 104–5, 121, 145–50, 156–7, 177,
    202–13

input/output-oriented measurements, performance evaluations 228–9
Inspiration Furniture 252–3
integrated systems, green supply chains 174–5, 208–13, 255–63
Intel 43
intellectual property (IP), excess product movements 129–30
Internet 62–3, 88, 130, 221
inventories
  see also supply planning; warehousing
  concepts 44–5, 48–56, 71, 112–17, 127–8, 132, 135–7, 210–13, 236–54
  costs 55–6, 71, 135–7
  JIT 5, 89, 117, 127–8
  lean production 5, 89, 103, 113–21, 127–8
  minimization campaigns 55, 112–21, 135–7
  planning 52–3, 55–6, 136–7
investments, concepts 7, 8, 65–6, 68, 80–2, 195–6
investors 68
IP see intellectual property
ISO 14064 189–90

Japan 113–15, 219, 248, 251
JIT see just-in-time processes
Jones, Daniel T. 115
'jumping to conclusions' dangers 233
just-in-time processes (JIT)
  see also logistics
  concepts 5, 89, 117, 127–8
  definition 117

kanban 103, 117
'keeping it short and simple' (KISS) 230
knowledge-dissemination benefits of green supply chains 7, 8, 10, 48–52, 75–82, 180, 196–7, 203–13, 221–2, 254–63
Kodak 263–4
KPIs 128–9
Kulikova, Elena 246–7

labels, concepts 68, 70
labour standards 8, 11, 19–26, 32, 89–91, 107
  see also workplace ...
landfill sites 65–7, 88, 140–1, 173, 177, 271–2
lateral thinking 43–4, 168
LCC see life cycle costing
LCE see life cycle engineering

LCM see life cycle management
lead times 48–52, 137
leadership commitments
  concepts 3–4, 5, 23–6, 40, 42, 43–7, 80–2, 87–8, 103, 104–6, 109–10, 201–13, 219, 231–2
  EGL model 104–6, 201–13
lean production
  see also process designs
  concepts 5, 89, 103, 113–17, 127–8
  definition 113–15
  globalization effects 115–16
  JIT 5, 89, 117, 127–8
learning from failures 40–1, 180
learning supply chains, concepts 219–22
Lee Cooper jeans 129–30
Lee, Lily 251
legal frameworks
  civil actions 99, 107, 126
  CSR 3–4
legislation
  see also regulations
  carbon reporting 197, 227, 270–2
  green supply chain drivers 12–13, 65–6, 88–91, 97–9, 102, 107, 124–5, 154–5, 177–8, 183–5, 192–3, 197, 205–8, 227, 251, 270–2
  supply loops 177
leverage items, spend/cost and criticality/risk procurement evaluations 61–3, 259–60
life cycle costing (LCC), concepts 38, 71–2, 82–7, 90–1, 95–6, 99, 146–50, 204–13, 264
life cycle engineering (LCE)
  see also planning ...
  concepts 13, 27–38, 52–6, 64, 71–2, 75–7, 95–121, 146–50, 193, 194–7, 204–13, 264
  reuse/reduce/recycle paradigm 33–7, 88, 95–121, 141–4, 145–50, 194–7, 204–13, 264–9
life cycle management (LCM)
  see also planning ... ; product-stewardship ...
  concepts 27–38, 64, 71–2, 75–6, 82–7, 95–121, 146–50, 193, 194–7, 204–13, 264
  cost reductions 30–1
  definition 30
  goals 32
load planning, logistics 19, 20–1, 129–30, 132–7, 204–13
locations of raw materials 63–4, 99, 101–2

logistics 4–5, 9–10, 13–15, 19–27, 35–43,
    48, 49–52, 56, 59–62, 75–7, 93, 97,
    103–6, 112, 117, 123–37, 161, 166–80,
    193–7, 202–13, 263–9
    see also execution ... ; fulfillment ... ; just-
        in-time ... ; lot size ... ; quality ...
    action plans 132–7
    benefits 125–6, 263–9
    carbon-reduction potential results 193–5
    challenges 126–32
    concepts 123–37, 161, 166–80, 193–7,
        202–13, 263–9
    customization demands 129–30
    definition 123–4
    drivers 124–5
    e-commerce 130
    excess product movements 128, 129–30
    externalities 127, 184–5
    fleet management 132, 134–5
    forward logistics 166–80
    government incentives 125
    incentives programmes 125
    information systems 174–5
    IP protection problems 129–30
    LCE 35, 37, 75–7, 194–7
    load planning 19, 20–1, 129–30, 132–7,
        204–13
    'on time in full' KPI 128–9
    optimization issues 19, 20–1, 129–30,
        132–7, 168–80, 204–13
    packaging 140–1, 146–7, 264–9
    reliability objectives 128–9
    response times 19, 127–8
    reverse logistics 125, 166–80, 263–9
    road congestion problems 130–1
    supply loops 166–80, 204–13, 263–9
    taxation benefits 125, 129–30
    technological developments 124, 130–7,
        174–5, 179–80, 195, 267–9
    traditional/green supply chains 9–10,
        39–47, 104–5, 193–4
    transportation & logistics realignment
        parameter 103, 106, 112, 117
    trips 19–26, 127–37
    utilization-maximization aims 132–5
    vehicle maintenance 19, 125–7, 132–7
    wheel of green logistics 132
logistics industry, bottom line impacts
    19–21
lot size management
    see also logistics
    concepts 5

The Machine that Changed the World
    (Womack, Jones, and Roos) 114

maintenance costs 19–26, 38, 71–2, 126
Malaysia 252–3
management systems
    EMS 60, 211–13
    procurement challenges 69–70, 75–7
manufacturing 4–5, 9–10, 12–13, 22–6, 27,
    34–7, 57, 61–3, 75–8, 95–121, 125,
    146–50, 166–80, 202–13, 236–54,
    263–9
    see also production ...
    carbon-reduction potential results 193–5
    collaborating partners 75–7, 100–2,
        228–9, 254–63
    incentives alignment 13, 27, 57, 77–8,
        110, 125, 146–50, 203–13, 226,
        231
    supply loops 166–80, 204–13, 263–9
    traditional/green supply chains 9–10,
        39–47, 104–5, 193–4
Marine Stewardship Council 68
market research 50–2
market shares 19–26, 151–64
marketing 7, 8, 12, 13–15, 19–26, 47–52,
    93, 97, 101, 104–5, 109–10, 140–50,
    151–64, 202–13, 227, 236–54
    see also communications; execution ...
    benefits of green supply chains 7, 8,
        140–1
    challenges 157–8
    channels-and-sales-force elements
        159–60, 161–2
    concepts 13–15, 19–26, 140–1, 146–7,
        151–64, 202–13, 227, 236–54
    consumers 159–64
    customer-centric issues 159–64
    definition 152–3, 158–9
    drivers 152–7, 227
    elements of green marketing 158–64
    greenwashing 101, 109–10, 151–4,
        159–60, 191–2, 196–7
    importance 152–3, 227
    media 162–3
    packaging 140–1, 146–7, 153, 157, 161
    pricing-and-communications elements
        159, 162–3
    processes-and-products elements 159–60,
        161
    profits 155–6
    purposes 152–3, 158–9, 227
    segmentation-and-physical-evidence
        elements 159–60, 163–4
material preparation, LCE 35, 36, 75–7,
    194–7
media 12–13, 67, 89–90, 99, 109–10,
    162–3

migration-strategy framework
 see also change ... ; continuous
   improvements
 action plans 201–13
 concepts 13–15, 27, 57, 199, 201–13,
   215–23, 227–9, 233–4
 design & implementation phase II
   208–11
 detailed-analysis phase I 205–8
 EGL model 104–6, 201–13
 future ideal state 206–8
 gap analysis 206–13
 organizational change management phase
   III 211–13
 phases 203–13, 217–19, 227–8
 shared successes 212–13
 teamwork 201–13, 219–23
 time factors 203–4, 217–19

network remapping production parameter
   103, 106
new business opportunities/markets 31,
   67–9, 79–82, 156–7
NGOs 13, 51, 63–5, 99, 125, 157, 229, 249
noise pollution 126–7, 184

obsolescence problems 32–7, 71, 100, 112,
   113–21, 137, 177
OEM spare parts 62, 260–1
oil 109, 156–7, 192–3
'on time in full' KPI (OTIF), concepts
   128–9
'only cost' mindset, procurement challenges
   70–2
operational changes 34, 38, 48, 65–7,
   194–7
opportunity costs 71–2
optimized routes, logistics industry 19,
   20–1, 129–30, 132–7
optimized truckloads, logistics industry 19,
   20–1, 129–30, 132–7, 204–13
orange juice example, carbon measurement
   187
organic products 155–6
organizational change management phase
   III of the migration-strategy framework
   211–13
organizational learning 7–8, 75–7, 180
organizational parameters, production
   framework 103, 107–10
organizational stakeholders, green supply
   chain drivers 12–13, 67–8, 97–9, 102,
   107, 124–5, 128, 152–7, 192–3, 241–4
outdated technologies 32–7, 71, 100, 112,
   177

output-oriented measurements, performance
   evaluations 228–9
outsourcing issues 101–2, 145–6, 151,
   183–4, 187, 194, 267–9
ownership issues 38, 48–52, 71–2, 90–1,
   261–3

packaging
 see also execution ... ; within-the-
   organization ...
 action plans 145–50
 benefits of green packaging 141–50,
   264–9
 change management 144, 145–50,
   211–13
 concepts 4–5, 13–15, 19–26, 33–4, 103,
   111–12, 121, 139–50, 153, 157,
   173–80, 203–13, 264–9
 costs 140–1, 143–4, 145, 146–50
 definition 139–41
 differentiators 141, 142–50
 drivers 141, 142–5
 hierarchy of functions 139–41
 information dissemination 139–41,
   157–8, 203–13
 LCE 33–4, 194–7
 logistics 140–1, 146–7, 264–9
 McDonald's 153, 157
 marketing 140–1, 146–7, 153, 157, 161
 production framework 103, 111–12, 121,
   139–50
 purposes 139–41
 realignment issues 146, 148–50
 redesigned packaging 142, 143, 144,
   145–50, 209–13, 264–9
 reengineered packaging 142, 143, 144,
   146, 147–50, 208–13
 reformed packaging 141, 142–50
 requirements' analysis 145–50
 returns management 173–80, 264–9
 reuse/reduce/recycle paradigm 141–4,
   145–50, 204–13, 264–9
 suppliers 144–50
 teamwork 147–50
 time factors 147
 waste 140–50
Packer, Mike 241–4
paint industry 163–4
paper 65–7, 142, 153, 187, 238–54
'paralysis analysis' dangers 233
Pareto analysis (80/20 rule), concepts
   222–3
partners 9–10, 11, 12–13, 27, 30–1, 33–7,
   39–47, 60–8, 73–91, 100–2, 144–5,
   201–13, 225–6, 254–63

see also collaborating ... ; trust
product designs 10, 12–13, 31–2, 76–7,
  104–5, 107–9, 121, 142–5, 201–13
traditional/green supply chains 9–10,
  39–47, 60–3, 104–5, 193–4
PDSA *see* plan-do-study-act
performance evaluations
  see also carbon measurement; carbon
    reporting; upstream ...
  audits 88, 89, 204–13, 227, 244
  benefits 225–7
  concepts 4–5, 13–15, 27, 57, 78–82,
    115–21, 148, 199, 201–13, 215–23,
    225–34, 257–63
  consensus views 225–6
  decision makers 232–3
  focused resources 226
  gauging-progress benefits 226
  input/output-oriented measurements
    228–9
  KPIs 128–9
  measurement toolkit 233–4
  methodologies 219–20, 225, 227–9
  presentations 230–2
  radar diagrams 230–2
  Six Sigma 103, 113, 117–20, 175, 210
  software tools 229–30
  supplier-development aim of
    procurement framework 19–20, 57,
    78–84, 88, 89–91, 231–2
  what/how/who measurement questions
    227–9
philanthropy 176–7
  see also corporate social responsibility
plan-do-study-act (PDSA), concepts 220,
  223
planning framework
  see also demand ... ; life cycle ... ; sales
    and operations ... ; supply ...
  concepts 4, 5–6, 13–15, 27–56, 57,
    136–7, 194–7, 220, 221, 228–32,
    233–4
  overview 13, 27–30
  PDSA 220, 223
political commitments 23, 109–10,
  125–31, 192–3
Pollard, Duncan 245–9
pollution 4–8, 9–10, 11, 19, 21–6, 32–7,
  60–91, 97–8, 106, 124–37, 152,
  154–64, 183–97, 271–3
positioning, concepts 163–4
PR 151–2, 195, 205
presentations, performance evaluations
  230–2
PricewaterhouseCoopers 89

pricing 52, 61–3, 86–7, 155–6, 159, 162–3,
  254
primary economic sector, concepts 59–63,
  236–54
proactive approaches 40, 41, 45, 46–7,
  75–7, 102–3, 126, 153
process charts 40, 42
process designs
  see also production ...
  concepts 11, 14, 19–26, 95–120, 127–8,
    129–30, 156, 159–60, 161, 204–13,
    254–63
  DMADV 118–20
  DMAIC 118–20
  JIT 5, 89, 117, 127–8
  lean production 5, 89, 103, 113–17,
    127–8
  production framework parameters 103,
    112–20
  Six Sigma 103, 113, 117–20, 175, 210
  supply loops 166–8, 210–13, 263–9
processes-and-products elements of green
  marketing 159–60, 161
procurement framework 4, 8, 13–15,
  19–26, 27, 30, 35–6, 38, 49–52, 56,
  57–91, 97, 104–5, 108, 123–4, 144–50,
  166–8, 193–5, 202–13, 221, 228–34,
  235–63
  see also sourcing; upstream ...
  action plans 87–8
  affecting factors 73–87
  benefits 63–7
  carbon-reduction potential results
    193–5
  challenges 69–72
  collaborating partners 57, 68, 73–91,
    144–5, 147–50, 228–9, 231–2, 234,
    254–63
  concepts 13–15, 19–26, 35–6, 38, 49–52,
    57–91, 123–4
  costs 60–91
  definitions 59–63, 69, 123–4
  drivers 65–8, 83–7, 88–91, 241–54
  energy efficiencies 11, 13, 19–26, 32–7,
    57, 64–5, 82–91, 204–13, 231–2,
    269, 272, 274–5
  five-rights definition 59–60, 123–4
  goals 59–63
  incentives alignment 13, 19, 27, 57,
    77–8, 81, 89–91, 103, 110, 125,
    146–50, 203–13, 226, 231, 234
  isolated functions 86–7
  LCE 35–6, 38, 75–7, 194–7
  packaging 144–50
  performance evaluations 228–34

power distribution 62–3, 259–63
processes 60–3
scope 59–63
specifications 72, 74–5, 81–2, 84–7, 88,
    146, 148
spend/cost and criticality/risk evaluations
    61–3, 259–60
strategies 61–3, 259–63
supplier development 19–20, 57, 78–82,
    88, 89–91, 231–2
sustainable sourcing 84–7, 231–2
'sweatshops' 89
traditional procurement processes 60–3,
    73–7, 104–5, 193–4
transactional approaches 73–7
trust levels 73–5, 147–50, 203–13
product designs
    see also production ... ; upstream ... ;
        within-the-organization ...
    benefits of green supply chains 7, 8,
        12–13, 19–26, 31–2, 67–8, 76–7,
        107–9, 121, 142–5, 273–4
    concepts 4, 7, 8, 10, 12–13, 19–26,
        31–2, 47–52, 67–8, 71–2, 75–7,
        90–1, 95–121, 125, 142–5, 156–7,
        159–60, 161, 166–80, 201–13,
        273–4
    disassembly approach 121, 169–80
    durable products 32–7, 113–21
    partners 10, 12–13, 31–2, 76–7, 104–5,
        107–9, 121, 142–5, 201–13
    processes-and-products elements of green
        marketing 159–60, 161
    production framework parameters 103,
        121
    recycling 274
product-centric issues, demand planning
    50–2
product-differentiation benefits of green
    supply chains, concepts 7, 8
product-safety benefits of green supply
    chains 7, 8, 98–9, 107
product-stewardship production parameter
    103, 107–10, 153–4
production framework
    see also efficiency ... ; execution ... ;
        manufacturing; process designs;
        product designs; supply planning
    benefits 96–8
    carbon-reduction potential results 193–5
    challenges 99–102
    change management issues 102, 145–50,
        211–13
    communications 103, 109–10, 114–17,
        204–13

concepts 4–6, 13–15, 19–26, 27,
    33–5, 36–7, 49–56, 75–7, 93,
    95–121, 145–50, 156, 159–60,
    161, 166–8, 173–5, 193–7, 202–13,
    236–54
customer-centric issues 101–2, 104–5
definition 95–6
drivers 97–9, 102, 107, 109–10
goals 95–6
JIT 5, 89, 117, 127–8
key components 102–21
LCE 35, 36–7, 52–6, 75–7, 194–7
lean production 5, 89, 103, 113–17,
    127–8
organizational parameters 103, 107–10
outdated technologies 100, 177
outsourcing issues 101–2, 145–6, 151,
    183–4, 187, 194, 267–9
packaging 103, 111–12, 121, 139–50
parameters to the framework 103–21
planning 53–6, 194–7
processes-and-products elements of green
    marketing 159–60, 161
product-stewardship parameter 103,
    107–10, 153–4
regulations 97–9, 177–8, 183–5, 205–8,
    211–13, 227, 270–2
Six Sigma 103, 113, 117–20, 175, 210
supply chain parameters 103
supply loops 166–80, 204–13, 263–9
zone of optimality 54–6
production postponements, concepts 53–6
productivity improvements, lean production
    115
profits
    see also financial performance ...
    bottom line impacts of green supply
        chains 17–26, 89–91, 113–21,
        129–30
    concepts 4–5, 6, 12–13, 17–26, 43–5,
        53–6, 89–91, 129–30, 155–6,
        208–13, 257–63
    cost-benefit analysis 19–26, 48–52,
        64–7
    key contributors 17–26, 44–5, 155–6
    marketing programmes 155–6
prototypes 211–13, 266–9
public activism, GSCM enabler 4–5,
    12–13, 25, 63–5, 97–9, 141, 145,
    152–5, 176–7, 249–54
pull/push supply planning options, concepts
    53–6
purchasing
    see also procurement ...
    concepts 5–6, 57–91, 235–54

quality management
 see also logistics
 benefits of green supply chains 7, 8,
  49–52, 111–12
 concepts 5, 7, 8, 19–26, 49–52, 60–91,
  111–12, 113–21
 Six Sigma 103, 113, 117–20, 175, 210

R&D 21, 104–5, 111, 202–13, 265–6
raw materials 4, 8, 13–15, 19–26, 27, 30,
 35–6, 38, 49–52, 56, 57–91, 95–121,
 137, 166–80, 193–7, 204–13, 231–2,
 236–54
 see also procurement ...
reactive/proactive S&OP orientations 40,
 41, 45, 46–7
reclaimed parts 167–80
reconditioned products, concepts 170–80,
 267–9
recovery
 see also downstream ...
 concepts 4–5, 6
recycling
 see also downstream ... ; supply loops
 concepts 4–5, 11, 14–15, 19–26, 32–7,
  63–91, 96–121, 135–7, 141–50, 153,
  154–5, 165–80, 194–7, 204–13, 234,
  236–54, 263–4, 273–4
 definition 170–1
 product designs 274
redesigned packaging 142, 143, 144,
 145–50, 209–13, 264–9
reduce paradigm, concepts 34–7, 95–121,
 141–4, 145–50
reengineered design processes
 see also process ... ; production ...
 concepts 11, 14, 95–121, 142, 143, 144,
  146, 147–50, 208–13
references and bibliography 277
reforestation methods 247–54
reformed packaging, concepts 141, 142–50
refrigerated storage systems 136
refunds, returns management 169, 171–80
refurbishments 114–17, 170–80
regulations
 see also legislation
 benefits of green supply chains 7, 8,
  11, 65–7, 83–7, 97–9, 126, 177–8,
  197
 carbon credits 19–26, 106–7, 185,
  195–7, 270–2
 carbon reporting 197, 227, 270–2
 carbon-management framework 19–26,
  106–7, 183–97, 227, 270–2
 fines 6, 31, 99, 125, 227, 229
 future prospects 184–5

green supply chain drivers 12–13, 65–7,
 83–7, 88–91, 97–9, 102, 107, 124–5,
 126–7, 154–5, 157–8, 177–8, 183–5,
 192–3, 197, 205–8, 211–13, 227,
 251, 270–2
 production framework 97–9, 177–8,
  183–5, 205–8, 227, 270–2
relationships
 costs 262–3
 trust 40–1, 73–91, 147–50, 203–13,
  254–63
reliability objectives, logistics 128–9
remanufactured products, concepts 170–80
renewable energy, concepts 11, 32–7,
 95–121, 135–7, 210–11, 231–2, 271–2,
 274–5
repairs, concepts 170–80
reprocessing, concepts 19, 170–80, 204–13
reputational benefits of green supply chains
 7, 8, 19–26, 31, 63, 67, 98, 103, 107,
 121, 126, 145, 151–64, 176–7, 253–4
requirements' analysis 145–50, 196–7, 219
resource-sustainability benefits of green
 supply chains, concepts 6, 8, 19–26,
 31–7, 49–52, 60–91
response times, logistics 19, 127–8
responsibilities 3–4, 10–11, 24–5, 34–7, 89,
 103, 107–10, 126, 152–64, 176–7, 188,
 219–23
 see also accountabilities
 carbon measurement 188
 CSR 3–4, 10–11, 89, 126, 154, 176–7,
  195–6, 223
 product-stewardship production
  parameter 103, 107–10, 153–4
retailers 9–10, 39–47, 67–80, 89–90, 101,
 108–10, 130, 143, 193–5, 272–3
 carbon-reduction potential results 193–5
 green grocery stores case study 272–3
 product-stewardship production
  parameter 108–10
 returns management 173–80
 traditional/green supply chains 9–10,
  39–47, 104–5, 193–4
retooling plants 21–2, 100
returns management
 competitive pressures 175–6, 180
 concepts 169, 171–80, 264–9
 retailer–producer conflicts 173–5
 types of returns 173–4
reuse paradigm
 see also supply loops
 concepts 4–5, 6, 11, 32–7, 88, 95–121,
  141–4, 145–50, 165–80, 194–7,
  204–13, 263–9
 definition 170–1

reverse logistics
   activities 171–3
   concepts 125, 166–80, 263–9
   definition 169, 171
   supply loops 166–80, 263–9
RFIs 84–5
RFPs 104
RFQs 84
risk-management benefits of green supply
      chains, concepts 7, 8, 22, 32, 63–91,
      98–9, 103, 107, 126, 218–19, 259–63
risks, spend/cost and criticality/risk
      procurement evaluations 61–3,
      259–60
roadmap, green supply chains 14–15,
      212–13
root cause analysis 222–3
routine items, spend/cost and criticality/risk
      procurement evaluations 61–3,
      259–60
Russia 245–9

S&OP see sales and operations planning
sales forecasts 39–40, 47–52, 53–6, 136–7
sales and operations planning (S&OP)
      13, 27, 30, 38–56, 104–5, 136–7,
      159–60, 161–2, 202–13
   see also demand ... ; planning ... ;
         supply ...
   attitudes 40–1
   communications 40, 41–2, 52
   concepts 38–56, 104–5, 136–7, 161–2
   definition 38–9
   external help 45, 46–7
   focus issues 40, 41
   goals 40, 43, 44–52
   key principles 45–7
   leadership issues 40, 42, 43–7, 103,
         104–6
   measures of success 40, 43
   reactive/proactive orientations 40, 41,
         45, 46–7
   teamwork 40, 41–2, 45–7
   tools 40, 42, 45, 46–7, 52
   traditional/green S&OP contrasts 39–47,
         104–5
sales-revenue benefits of green supply
      chains 7, 8
Samartex Timber and Plywood Co. Ltd
      240–4
scenario planning 32, 52, 76–7
SCM see supply chain management
secondary economic sector, concepts
      59–63, 236–7
segmentation, customers 47–52, 159–60,
      163–4

segmentation-and-physical-evidence
      elements of green marketing 159–60,
      163–4
service designs, concepts 31–2, 76–7,
      156–7
services (tertiary) economic sector,
      concepts 59–67, 236–7
shared successes, migration-strategy
      framework 212–13
Siberia 245–9
silo attitudes 40–7, 104–5
Six Sigma
   see also process designs
   concepts 103, 113, 117–20, 175, 210
   definition 113, 117–18
   DMADV 118–20
   DMAIC 118–20
SmartWood 244
social benefits of green supply chains 8, 11,
      33–7, 63–8, 82–7, 90–1, 126, 154–64,
      243–4, 251–4, 256–63
soft skills, concepts 75–82, 86–7, 254–63
software tools, performance evaluations
      229–30
solar panels 135–6
Sony 273–4
sourcing
   see also outsourcing ... ; procurement ...
   concepts 4, 9–10, 13–15, 27, 33–7,
         57–91, 143–4, 167–80
   sustainable sourcing 84–7, 231–2
space-wasting problems 111–21
specifications
   procurement framework 72, 74–5, 81–2,
         84–7, 88, 146, 148
   types 85–6
spend/cost and criticality/risk procurement
      evaluations 61–3, 259–60
stakeholders
   collaborating partners 11, 13, 27, 30–1,
         34–5, 39–41, 43–5, 46–7, 60–8,
         73–91, 100–2, 103–5, 136–7, 144–5,
         147–50, 201–13, 225–6, 231–2,
         235–63
   CSR definition 11
   green supply chain drivers 11–15, 48–52,
         67–8, 88–91, 97–9, 102, 107, 124–5,
         128, 152–7, 192–3, 241–4
   incentives alignment 13, 27, 57, 77–8,
         89–91, 103, 110, 125, 146–50,
         203–13, 226, 231, 234
   migration-strategy framework 13–15, 27,
         57, 199, 201–13, 227–8
   product-stewardship production
         parameter 103, 107–10, 153–4
Stead, Dr Justin 251–2

stock-outs 43, 44–5, 131
strategic changes, LCE 34, 53–6, 194–7
strategic collaborative alignments, concepts
    73–7, 259–63
strategies
    see also migration-strategy framework
    continuous improvements 219–23
    procurement framework 61–3, 66,
        259–63
Sumitomo 249
supplier-development aim of procurement
        framework
    concepts 19–20, 57, 78–84, 88, 89–91,
        231–2
    definition 78–9
suppliers 4, 7, 8, 9–10, 19, 39–47, 57,
    60–91, 100–2, 103–5, 136–7, 144–5,
    146–50, 180, 235–54
    see also procurement …
    carbon-reduction potential results 193–5
    categories 79–82
    collaborating partners 73–91, 100–2,
        103–5, 136–7, 144–5, 147–50,
        201–13, 228–9, 231–2, 234, 254–63
    contracts 77–8, 81–2, 88, 204–13
    educational issues 60–3, 78–82, 204–13
    green records 63–91
    incentives alignment 13, 19, 27, 57,
        77–8, 81, 89–91, 110, 125, 146–50,
        203–13, 226, 231, 234
    packaging 144–50
    sample products 88
    selections 4, 7, 8, 63–4, 79–91, 146–50,
        234
    specifications 72, 74–5, 81–2, 84–7, 88,
        146, 148
    traditional/green supply chains 9–10,
        39–47, 104–5, 193–4
supply chain management (SCM)
    concepts 3–4, 129–30, 235–54, 255–63
    definition 235–6, 255–6
    historical background 3–4
    IP protection problems 129–30
    overview 4–5
    traditional supply chains 9–10, 39–47,
        60–3, 104–5, 193–4
supply chain parameters, production
        framework 103
supply loops 13–15, 19–27, 36, 142,
    165–80, 204–13, 263–9, 274
    see also execution … ; recycling; reuse …
    action plans 179–80
    asset recovery drives 178, 263–9
    benefits 178, 263–9
    channel relationships 177

circular supply chains 169–71
    competitive pressures 175–6, 180
    concepts 13–15, 19–27, 165–80, 204–13,
        263–9, 274
    continuous improvements 180
    costs 178
    CSR 176–7
    definition 19, 165
    drivers 175–8
    elements 168–75
    examples 166–8, 263–9
    legislation 177
    logistics 166–80, 204–13, 263–9
    manufacturing examples 166–80,
        204–13, 263–9
    objectives 165, 178
    returns management 169, 171–80, 264–9
    technological developments 174–5,
        179–80, 267–9
supply planning
    see also inventories; planning … ;
        production … ; sales …
    concepts 13, 27, 30, 43–4, 52–6, 61–3,
        236–75
    definition 52–3
sustainability concepts 11, 23–6, 66–91,
    126–31
sustainable designs, concepts 11, 19–26,
    76–7
sustainable forests, GFTN 247–54
sustainable sourcing, concepts 84–7, 231–2
'sweatshops' 89
Swedwood Tikhvin 247
systems thinking 33–7, 91, 116–20, 133–4,
    146–50, 187–8, 193, 261–3

TACs *see* total acquisition costs
tactical planning
    see also demand … ; planning … ; sales
        and operations … ; supply …
    concepts 30, 34, 53–6, 259–63
TCO *see* total cost of ownership
teamwork 40, 41–2, 45–7, 80–2, 105,
    147–50, 201–13, 219–23, 225, 231–2
    migration-strategy framework 201–13,
        219–23
    packaging 147–50
    S&OP 40, 41–2, 45–7
technological benefits of green supply
        chains
    concepts 7, 8, 10, 19–26, 31, 95–121,
        124, 130–7, 174–5, 179–80, 195,
        209, 267–9
    logistics 124, 130–7, 174–5, 179–80,
        267–9

outdated technologies 32–7, 71, 100, 112, 177
supply loops 174–5, 179–80, 267–9
tendering 84–7
Terneyles 248–9
thinking processes, the brain 261–3
Timbmet Silverman 240–4
time factors
  migration-strategy framework 203–4, 217–19
  packaging 147
total acquisition costs (TACs), concepts 60, 70–91
total cost of ownership (TCO), concepts 38, 71–2, 90–1, 261–3
Toyota 114, 260
TQM initiatives, critique 24–5
traditional supply chains 9–10, 39–47, 60–3, 104–5, 193–4
training, concepts 5–6, 32, 41, 43–4, 66, 69–70, 204–13
transactional approaches, procurement framework 73–7
transparency issues
  concepts 7, 8, 83–7, 100–2, 109–10, 147, 153–4, 157–8, 161, 202, 231–2
  product-stewardship production parameter 109–10
transport 19–26, 64–7, 82–7, 90, 103, 106, 112, 117, 123–37, 204–13
  see also logistics
  concepts 103, 106, 112, 117, 123–37, 204–13
  methods 124–5, 128–9, 133–5, 204–13
  realignment production parameter 103, 106, 112, 117
  wheel of green logistics 132–5
Travis Perkins 240–1, 246
trips, green logistics 19–26, 127–37
trust
  see also collaborating partners
  concepts 40–1, 73–91, 147–50, 203–13, 254–63
  levels 73–5, 258–9
turbulence factors, change management 226
Tutu, Desmond, Archbishop 10–11

UK 24–5, 70, 124, 131–2, 240–4, 246, 257, 269–72
  coal power 124
  global economic crisis from 2007 24–5, 142–3, 144
  GMO foods 70

UK Forest & Trade Network (UK FTN) 240–4
United Nations 190, 252
upstream aspects of green supply chains
  see also performance evaluations … ; procurement … ; product designs
  concepts 4–5, 13–15, 63–91
USA 113–14, 158, 176–7, 187, 190–1, 269–73
utilization-maximization aims, logistics 132–5

value added services, concepts 77–8, 110, 114–17, 129–30
variability data, demand planning 50, 51, 55
variable costs 53–6, 71–2
variance analysis
  see also Six Sigma
  concepts 103, 113, 117–20
vehicle maintenance 19, 125–7, 132–7
viral marketing 8, 12
vision 66, 75

Wal-Mart 223
Waller, Professor Alan 257
Walt Disney World (WDW) 154, 158
warehousing 54–6, 71, 117, 123–37
  see also inventories; logistics
  green warehousing 132, 135–7
  wheel of green logistics 132, 135–7
waste 4–10, 19–26, 30–1, 33–7, 49–56, 60–3, 64–7, 71, 88, 89, 95–121, 126, 137, 140–50, 154–64, 165–80, 194–7, 204–13, 263–4
  disposals 4–10, 19–26, 32, 33–7, 38, 60–3, 64–7, 71, 88, 89–90, 95–121, 126, 137, 140–50, 154–64, 165–80, 194–7, 204–13, 263–4
  environmental impacts 111–12
  packaging 140–50
  recollections 19–26, 35, 36–7, 64–7, 103, 111–21, 126, 145, 154–64, 165–80, 263–4
  reduction methods 111–21, 137, 140–50, 154–6
  types 112, 116
water 64–7, 88, 106, 152, 156, 210–11, 250–1, 273, 275
what-if analysis, demand planning 51–2
wheel of green logistics 132
'where less is more' presentation guidelines 230–1
White, George 239, 246

whole life costs (WLCs), concepts 71–2
win/win situations 75–7
WIP *see* work-in-progress
within-the-organization aspects of green
    supply chains
  see also packaging; product designs;
      production ... ; sales and
      operations ...
  concepts 4–5, 12–15, 38–40, 48–52,
    95–121
WLCs *see* whole life costs
Womack, James P. 114
word-of-mouth benefits of green supply
    chains 8, 12–13
work-in-progress (WIP) 112, 114, 116–17,
    236–54
workplace benefits of green supply chains
    8, 19–26, 32, 34–5, 66–7, 74–7, 89,
    98–9, 107, 114–17, 204–13

see also labour ...
employee satisfaction 19–26, 32,
    34–5, 67, 74–7, 89, 98–9, 107,
    126
lean production 114–17
training issues 69–70
World Bank 238–54
World Business Council for Sustainable
    Development Report 2007 19
WRI/WBCSD Greenhouse Gas Protocol
    189–90
WWF 151, 235, 238–54

Young, Derek 249–53

zone of optimality, production planning
    54–6

Index compiled by Terry Halliday